The Political Economy of U.S. Policy Toward South Africa

Westview Special Studies

The concept of Westview Special Studies is a response to the continuing crisis in academic and informational publishing. Library budgets for books have been severely curtailed. Ever larger portions of general library budgets are being diverted from the purchase of books and used for data banks, computers, micromedia, and other methods of information retrieval. Interlibrary loan structures further reduce the edition sizes required to satisfy the needs of the scholarly community. Economic pressures on university presses and the few private scholarly publishing companies have greatly limited the capacity of the industry to properly serve the academic and research communities. As a result, many manuscripts dealing with important subjects, often representing the highest level of scholarship, are no longer economically viable publishing projects--or, if accepted for publication, are typically subject to lead times ranging from one to three years.

Westview Special Studies are our practical solution to the problem. As always, the selection criteria include the importance of the subject, the work's contribution to scholarship, and its insight, originality of thought, and excellence of exposition. We accept manuscripts in camera-ready form, typed, set, or word processed according to specifications laid out in our comprehensive manual, which contains straightforward instructions and sample pages. The responsibility for editing and proofreading lies with the author or sponsoring institution, but our editorial staff is always available to answer questions and provide guidance.

The result is a book printed on acid-free paper and bound in sturdy, library-quality soft covers. We manufacture these books ourselves using equipment that does not require a lengthy make-ready process and that allows us to publish first editions of 300 to 1000 copies and to reprint even smaller quantities as needed. Thus, we can produce Special Studies quickly and can keep even very specialized books in print as long as there is a demand for them.

About the Book and Author

By tracing U.S. involvement in South African political and economic development since the late 1800s, this
book analyzes U.S. corporate and government motives for
maintaining the political status quo in South Africa. In
recent decades, according to the author, U.S. policy
toward South Africa has grown more contradictory: En-
deavoring to protect the United States's reputation on
the question of race, government officials denounce apartheid, yet Washington remains the main force blocking an
international response to South African policies. As the
situation in South Africa continues to polarize, the U.S.
is increasingly isolated in its position of verbally condemning yet materially supporting South Africa's white
minority regime--a regime confronting the distinct possibility of civil war.

Dr. Kevin Danaher, formerly an associate fellow with
the Institute for Policy Studies, is currently employed
by the Institute for Food and Development Policy in San
Francisco. His publications include South Africa and the
United States: An Annotated Bibliography (1979) and South
Africa and the United States: The Progression of a Relationship (1984).

Dedicated to
Nelson Mandela

The Political Economy of U.S. Policy Toward South Africa

Kevin Danaher

Westview Press / Boulder and London

Westview Special Studies on Africa

Copyright © 1985 by Westview Press, Inc.

Published in 1985 in the United States of America by Westview Press, Inc.;
Frederick A. Praeger, Publisher; 5500 Central Avenue, Boulder, Colorado 80301

Library of Congress Cataloging in Publication Data
Danaher, Kevin.
    The political economy of U.S. policy toward South
Africa.
    (Westview special studies on Africa)
    Includes index.
    1. United States--Foreign economic relations--South
Africa. 2. South Africa--Foreign economic relations--
United States. 3. United States--Foreign relations--
South Africa. 4. South Africa--Foreign relations--
United States. 5. Corporation, American--South
Africa. I. Title. II. Title: Political economy of
US policy toward South Africa.
HF1456.5.S6D36 1985   337.73068   85-10682
ISBN 0-8133-0115-7 (soft)

Printed and bound in the United States of America

10 9 8 7 6 5 4 3 2 1

Contents

Tables

x

Preface

My pursuit of this research began as a personal response to the Soweto rebellion of 1976. Thousands of youths willing to confront police bullets, armed with little more than innocent courage, were a political phenomenon that riveted my attention. I and many other Americans were prompted to question the role of U.S. institutions in perpetuating apartheid. If this study makes a contribution to the eradication of that system, the many years of work embodied herein will have been well worth the effort.

Most books are the product of many people's labor. This work is no exception. I deeply appreciate the cooperation of the roughly one hundred scholars, journalists, businessmen, government officials, and activists who submitted to interviews in Washington, New York, London, Geneva, Harare, and Johannesburg. Institutions that proved helpful include the Institute for Policy Studies, the University of California library system, the Library of Congress, the National Archives, Howard University library, the United Nations Centre Against Apartheid, the Dag Hammarskjold Library, the London office of the British Anti-Apartheid Movement, and the World Council of Churches' Programme to Combat Racism. For timely financial assistance I thank the University of California and the International Organization for the Elimination of All Forms of Racial Discrimination.

The following people helped with various stages of the manuscript and have my deepest thanks: Nick Allen, Lynne Barbee, Medea Benjamin, G. William Domhoff, Christian Einfeldt, Steve Goldfield, Walter Goldfrank, Robert Lawrence, Stewart Lawrence, Bernard Magubane, Katherine Mitchell, Prexy Nesbitt, James O'Connor, Elizabeth Schmidt, Byron Schneider, and Bereket Selassie. Any mistakes or omissions are solely the responsibility of the author.

Kevin Danaher

1
Introduction

Conflict in South Africa continues to grow. Political activism by black youth and workers matures steadily as the state implements new repressive measures.[1] The guerrilla movement increases the size and sophistication of its operations, while the apartheid state carries out an unprecedented military buildup. The question is no longer whether or not a social upheaval will engulf the country; rather, it is a question of when that upheaval will occur and what form it will take.

The 1975-76 victories of guerrilla movements in neighboring Angola and Mozambique helped fuel mass protests by the black population of South Africa. Spearheaded by students and young workers, the sustained, nationwide rebellion raised the level of mass politicization to new heights. Since the 1976 Soweto rebellion, black student, church and worker organizations have intensified their political activity at an unprecedented rate.[2]

The South African state has reacted to mass radicalization with a dual program of reform and repression. The strategy is classic divide-and-rule: make life easier for the black middle class, especially those willing to accept class inequality, while cracking down on the students, workers, and peasants, especially those who are ideologically committed to structural change in the state and the economy.[3] Popular organizations have been outlawed, leaders arrested, and hundreds of activists have been shot down in the streets.[4] The resulting exodus of young refugees into neighboring countries has provided the liberation movements with thousands of new recruits. From 1977 onward, these young rebels have filtered back into South Africa, now armed with AK-47s and limpet mines instead of sticks and rocks.

The ruling National Party has responded to the growing strength of African nationalism in the region by intensifying its military buildup. Annual defense spending skyrocketed from R472 million in 1973 to more than R3 billion in 1982; the South African Defence Force

(SADF) grew from a total force of 269,000 members in 1974
to more than 400,000 in 1982.[5] In 1978, the National
Party chose Defence Minister P.W. Botha to replace John
Vorster as Prime Minister. Botha, nicknamed "Piet the
weapon" due to the phenomenal expansion of the military
under his leadership, began a program of concentrating
state power away from parliament toward the military and
the prime minister's office.[6]

The trajectories of African nationalism and the
apartheid state are on a direct collision course. Black
South Africans have demonstrated a willingness to
sacrifice life and limb in their struggle against
apartheid. Many white South Africans, particularly the
ruling Afrikaners, seem equally committed to defending
their privileges, and they are amply equipped to put up a
serious fight.

The U.S. government and U.S. corporations are deeply
involved in this cockpit of conflict. As chapter 2
reveals, American trade, investment, and personnel have
played a vital role in the development of capitalism in
South Africa. From the earliest days, the U.S. government
has facilitated growing ties between U.S. and South
African corporations. The U.S. banks and manufacturing
firms that are most deeply involved in South Africa are
among the most influential economic institutions in the
United States.

Another factor linking South Africa to the United
States is the military connection. The white minority
regime has received most of its hardware and expertise
from the NATO powers.[7] In return, Pretoria has been
cooperative with NATO strategy in the region. Thanks to
the NATO powers and Israel, South Africa possesses
delivery vehicles capable of handling nuclear weapons and
is probably capable of producing its own nuclear bombs.[8]
Obviously, the use of nuclear weapons by South Africa
would cause serious diplomatic problems for the western
powers.

In addition to these easily quantifiable ties, there
are other connections which deserve mention.
Afro-Americans have steadily increased their opposition
to the status quo in South Africa. They have been joined
by progressive whites in colleges, churches, and trade
unions in opposing U.S. governmental and corporate ties
to apartheid.[9] The movement for racial equality has
accumulated enough moral authority that most American
leaders feel obliged to at least verbally condemn
apartheid, even if they resist any action that would
materially weaken the white minority regime.

Another important factor is the ever closer
relationship between South Africa and the most dependent
ward of the U.S. state, Israel. Since the beginning of
its diplomatic isolation from Black Africa in 1973,
Israel has strengthened its military and economic ties to
Pretoria.[10] The two pariah states have given each other

considerable assistance. In the process, however, they
have reinforced their isolation from most African and
Arab states.
The special relationship between the United States
and Israel has implications for U.S. policy toward South
Africa with regard to two issues in particular:
mercenaries and international economic sanctions. African
leaders and progressive Americans have pressured the U.S.
government to do something about the hundreds of U.S.
mercenaries fighting on the side of white supremacy in
southern Africa. Although there are several federal
statutes outlawing this practice, the government has not
prosecuted anyone to date.[11] If the laws prohibiting
mercenary activity were enforced, it could set a negative
precedent for the many American Jews who perform military
duties while in Israel. On the second issue, if the U.S.
government acquiesced to pressure for international
economic sanctions against South Africa, Israel would be
the next country to be singled out in international
forums.[12]
Taken together, these various ties between South
Africa and the United States would be enough to justify a
detailed study of U.S. policy toward South Africa, but
there are other considerations. As Chapter Two argues,
apartheid is the South African form of capitalism. Any
serious attack on the basic structure of apartheid is
simultaneously an attack on the capitalist mode of
production in southern Africa as a whole.
The liberation movements, many of the black trade
unions, and even many churches are critical of capitalism
and sympathetic to socialism.[13] A socialist revolution in
South Africa would be the world's first revolution in a
society with so large an urban proletariat. With its
fantastic agricultural and mineral wealth, a South
African economy freed from the constraints of apartheid
could provide considerable support to revolutionary
movements in other parts of the globe.
Another important reason for studying U.S. policy
toward South Africa is that the United States has played,
and will continue to play, such a crucial role in the
political and economic development of southern Africa.
Britain has closer historical ties and a greater economic
stake in the region, but as the most powerful member of
the western alliance, the United States can make or break
international diplomatic initiatives. Any major shift in
U.S. policy, either toward greater support for Pretoria
or greater opposition, has a dramatic effect on the
local, regional and international politics of apartheid.
For all these reasons, a detailed critique of U.S.
policy toward South Africa is long overdue. By tracing
the historical development of U.S. relations with white
minority rule, this study shows how the current
contradictory policy--verbally denouncing apartheid while
materially supporting it--came to be.

NOTES

1. "Black" and "African" are often used interchangeably. Opponents of apartheid use Black to refer to non-whites generally, i.e., Africans, Coloureds, and Indians. "African" refers to those indigenous groups living in the region when Europeans first arrived in the 17th century: Zulu, Xhosa, Tswana, Swazi, Ndebele, Sotho, Venda, Shangaan/Tsonga, Khoi-Khoi, and San. "White" refers to people of European descent, particularly English and Afrikaner (of Dutch/Huguenot extraction). Throughout the text racial adjectives such as black and white are not capitalized.

2. The so-called Soweto rebellion was actually nationwide although it originated in the mass protests and police violence in Soweto on 16 June 1976. For details on the Soweto rebellion and the government's response see John Kane-Berman, The Method in the Madness (London: Pluto Press, 1979); Baruch Hirson, Year of Fire, Year of Ash (London: Zed Press, 1979); and Denis Herbstein, White Man, We Want To Talk To You (New York: Penguin, 1978). For background on black activism since the Soweto uprising see the following: "A fast rise for South Africa's black unions," Business Week, 19 October 1981; International Defence and Aid Fund, "Developments in South Africa Since the Uprising of 1976," United Nations General Assembly, document A/Conf.107/3, dated 20 April 1981; "Black unions pose the greatest threat," Financial Times, 26 May 1981; "South Africa: Labour muscle," Africa Confidential, 1 July 1981; Barry Streek, "Black Strategies Against Apartheid, Africa Report, July-August 1980; William Minter, "New Mood, New Factors in Struggle for South Africa," Christianity and Crisis, 18 August 1980.

3. For a detailed analysis of Pretoria's class-division strategy see John S. Saul and Stephen Gelb, "The Crisis in South Africa: Class Defense, Class Revolution," Monthly Review, July/August 1981; and Kevin Danaher, "Government-Initiated Reform in South Afria and Its Implications for U.S. Foreign Policy," Politics and Society, 13, 2, 1984. For a look at stratification within the black working class see the three-part New York Times series by Joseph Lelyveld: "South Africa Growth Lets a Few Blacks Aim Higher," 27 December 1981; "Transient Black Workers in South Africa Face a Maze of Tough Regulations," 28 December 1981; "For the Farmhands of South Africa, Employers' Feudal Attitudes Linger," 29 December 1981.

4. A generally useful source on state repression in South Africa is Focus, the news bulletin of the International Defence and Aid Fund, 104 Newgate Street, London. A representative sample of press accounts of government repression includes: Bernard Levin, "Count the

names and think: every one has died in the hands of South
Africa's police," The Times(UK) 9 November 1977;
"Political Prisoners: Numbers Rising," Southern Africa,
July-August 1979; "New Wave of Political Trials in South
Africa," Intercontinental Press, 31 July 1978; "South
Africa Arrests Clerics Protesting Colleague's Jailing,"
Washington Post, 27 May 1980; "14 Unionists Seized by
South Africans," New York Times, 28 November 1981.
   5. Richard Leonard, "Mobilizing for Total War,"
Southern   Africa,   January-February   1981,   p.13;
International Defence and Aid Fund, The Apartheid War
Machine (London: IDAF, 1980); Air Force Magazine,
December 1983, p.108. For background on the military
buildup see Robert S. Jaster, South Africa's Narrowing
Security Options (London: International Institute for
Strategic Studies, 1980); "Embargo Spurs S. Africa to
Build Weapons Industry," Washington Post, 7 July 1981;
Kenneth W. Grundy, The Rise of the South African Security
Establishment (Braamfontein: South African Institute of
International Affairs, 1983); and various issues of
Resister, Bulletin of the Committee on South African War
Resistance, B.M. Box 2190, London.
   NOTE ON THE VALUE OF THE RAND(R): The Rand was
officially linked to the British pound at a rate of R2=1
pound. Beginning in 1972 the Rand was tied to the
American dollar. With the floating of the dollar, the
value of the Rand varied between $1.40 and $1.50. In
September 1975 the Rand was devalued to $1.15. Values
since then have averaged as follows: 1977/$1.23,
1979/$1.33, 1981/$1.32, 1982/$.92, 1983/$.81, May
1984/$.86.
   6. Danaher, "Government-Initiated Reform..."; John
Fullerton, "South Africa: Day of the Generals," Now, 5-11
October 1979; South Africa's Generals in the Corridors of
Power," The Times U.K.) 1 September 1980; "South African
Military Exerts Greater Influence on Policy," Washington
Post, 30 May 1980.
   7. For details on arms transfers to South Africa
from the NATO countries see the following:
NARMIC/American Friends Service Committee, Automating
Apartheid: U.S. Computer Exports to South Africa and the
Arms Embargo (Philadelphia: AFSC, 1982); Patrick L.
Smith, "NATO Flirts with South Africa," The Nation, 24
September 1977; Sean Gervasi, The United States and the
Arms Embargo Against South Africa : Evidence, Denial, and
Refutation (Binghampton: State University of New York,
1978); Michael T. Klare, "South Africa's U.S. Weapons
Connection," The Nation, 28 July-4 August 1979; U.S.
Congress, House Subcommittee on Africa, Enforcement of
the United States Arms Embargo Against South Africa
(Washington, D.C.: Government Printing Office, 1982). For
official responses of NATO governments to charges that
they violated the U.N. arms embargo against South Africa,
see "Allegations of Violations of the Arms Embargo

Against South Africa: Replies of Governments," Objective Justice, vol.11, #3/4, Autumn/Winter 1979.

8. There is a large body of literature on South Africa's nuclear capability. Particularly useful are Barbara Rogers and Zdenek Cervenka, The Nuclear Axis (New York: Times Books, 1978); Richard K. Betts, "A Diplomatic Bomb for South Africa?" International Security, 4, 2, Fall 1979; U.S. Congress, House Subcommittee on Africa, United States-South African Relations: Nuclear Cooperation (Washington, D.C.: Government Printing Office, 1978); Robert Manning and Stephen Talbot, "American Cover-up on Israeli Bomb," The Middle East, June 1980; Dr. Frank Barnaby, Nuclear South Africa, U.N. General Assembly document A/Conf.107/2, 17 April 1981; United Nations Centre for Disarmament, South Africa's Plan and Capability in the Nuclear Field (New York: United Nations, 1981).

9. For current information on Afro-American opposition to apartheid, consult the newsletter of TransAfrica, an Afro-American lobbying organization focusing on U.S. policy toward Africa and the Caribbean. Also see "Interview with Randall Robinson, Executive Director of TransAfrica," Africa Report, January-February 1980; "From Selma to Soweto," Black Enterprise, April 1979; Richard J. Payne with Eddie Ganaway, "The Influence of Black Americans on US Policy Towards Southern Africa," African Affairs, 79, 317, October 1980.

For background on the antiapartheid movement in general see Alfred O. Hero, Jr. and John Barratt, eds., The American People and South Africa (Lexington, MA: Lexington Books, 1981); American Committee on Africa, "Summary of State and Municipal Legislative Action on South Africa," 1981. For regular information on the antiapartheid movement see ACOA Action News, American Committee on Africa; Anti-Apartheid News, British Anti-Apartheid Movement; Objective Justice, United Nations Office of Public Information; and ICSA Bulletin, International Committee Against Apartheid, Racism and Colonialism in Southern Africa.

10. See Richard P. Stevens and Abdelwahab M. Elmessiri, Israel and South Africa: The Progression of a Relationship (New York: New World Press, 1976); "Israel and South Africa: New Cooperation," Africa Confidential, vol.18, #12, 10 June 1977; Major Gerald J. Keller, "Israeli-South African Trade: An Analysis of Recent Developments," Naval War College Review, Spring 1978; "The Israeli Connection," The Economist, 5 November 1977; "South Africa Gains Arms and Trade as Israel Link Hardens," New York Times, 21 May 1977; "Israel joins SA nuclear sub project," 8 Days, 28 February 1981; "South Africa: The Israeli Connection," Africa Confidential, 4 August 1978; Africa Report (special issue on South Africa-Israel) November-December 1980; David Taylor, "Israel-South Africa Nuclear Link Exposed," The Middle

<u>East</u>, April 1981.

11. On the issue of mercenaries see Anti-Mercenary Coalition, <u>Guns for Hire</u> (San Francisco: AMC, 1978); Cynthia Enloe, "Mercenarization," in Western Massachusetts Association of Concerned Africa Scholars, eds., <u>U.S. Military Involvement in Southern Africa</u> (Boston: South End Press, 1978); Wilfred Burchett and Derek Roebuck, <u>The Whores of War: Mercenaries Today</u> (Middlesex, England: Penguin, 1977); Richard Lobban, "American Mercenaries in Rhodesia," <u>Journal of Southern African Studies</u>, 3, 3, July 1978; Michael Marchino and Robert K. Musil, "Guns of Bitterness: The American Mercenaries," <u>The Nation</u>, 10 April 1976; Malik Reaves, "In Zimbabwe 1,000 Mercenaries Fight Against African Liberation," <u>Southern Africa</u>, November 1978; Akbarali H. Thobhani, "The Mercenary Menace," <u>Africa Today</u>, vol. 23, #3, July-September 1976.

12. On the question of international economic sanctions against South Africa see the following: D. G. Clarke, <u>Policy Issues and Economic Sanctions Against South Africa</u> (Geneva: International University Exchange Fund, 1980); Dag Hammarskjold Library, <u>Sanctions Against South Africa: A selective bibliography</u> (New York: United Nations, 1981); Leo Katzen, "South Africa's vulnerability to economic sanctions," <u>Review of International Studies</u>, 8, 1982; Arndt Spandau, <u>Economic Boycott Against South Africa: Normative and Factual Issues</u> (Johannesburg: University of Witwatersrand Labor Research Program, 1978); Kevin Danaher, "Sanctions Against South Africa: Strategy for the Antiapartheid Movement in the 1980s," <u>UFAHAMU</u>, X, 1/2, Fall/Winter 1980-81; <u>South Africa and Sanctions: Genesis and Prospects</u>, papers and comments delivered at a symposium jointly organized by the South African Institute of Race Relations and the South African Institute of International Affairs, 24 February 1979, Johannesburg; Organization of African Unity, <u>Consideration of All Aspects of Sanctions Against South Africa</u>, report submitted to the International Conference on Sanctions Against South Africa, Paris, 20-27 May 1981, issued as U.N. General Assembly document A/Conf.107/4, 23 April 1981.

13. In a poll taken by the Johannesburg <u>Star</u> in late August 1981, the African National Congress of South Africa was chosen by a sizeable plurality of black South Africans as their favored political organization even though the ANC is outlawed (<u>Africa News</u>, 2 November 1981). For the official ideology of the ANC, consult its journal <u>Sechaba</u>, and the official organ of the South African Communist Party, <u>The African Communist</u>. For historical background on the anticapitalist content of the African nationalist movement in South Africa, see Edward Roux, <u>Time Longer Than Rope</u> (Madison: University of Wisconsin Press, 1948); Mary Benson, <u>South Africa: The Struggle for a Birthright</u> (Minerva Press, 1966); Gail M.

U.S. Policy toward South Africa

Gerhart, Black Power In South Africa: The Evolution of an Ideology (Berkeley: University of California Press, 1978).

2
The U.S. Role in
South African Development

The discovery of diamonds (1867) and gold (1886) in South Africa were without parallel for their impact on future developments in that country. The mining industry served as the motor force of capitalist industrialization. It was the sector that laid the foundations for subsequent race and labor policies. The gold mines provided an early opportunity for Americans to play a role in South African development. Also, South African gold elevated the country's international importance, eventually integrating the class interests of influential Americans, British and South Africans.

The wealth accumulated from the Kimberly diamond mines provided the indigenous seed capital needed to exploit the later discovery of gold on the Rand (the major gold-bearing area surrounding Johannesburg). "From the concentration of ownership of the diamond mines there emerged an autonomous colonial capitalism capable of both financing and securing state assistance for the forward movement of that frontier.[1]

The influx of capital into the gold mines created a booming market for local producers of food, clothing, construction materials, and basic services. The British-controlled provinces of the Cape and Natal built railways linking the Rand to the port cities of Durban, East London, and Port Elizabeth. By 1895 the fledgling city of Johannesburg had grown to a population of over one hundred thousand.[2] By 1910 gold comprised 80 percent of South African exports.[3]

The gold ore of South Africa is relatively low grade. It occurs mostly in small particles, firmly embedded in a matrix of other minerals. Tons of rock must be finely crushed and treated with several chemical processes in order to retrieve small amounts of the precious metal. "From its inception, mining development on the Rand was both labor and capital intensive. A large labor supply, elaborate machinery, and chemical works were required to profitably recover gold from the low-grade ore."[4]

The gold mines created a need for large numbers of European and African wage laborers.[5] The cost structure of other inputs, however, meant that African labor had to be available at a low price. The ore treatment processes were expensive, the engineers imported from Europe and America were expensive, and the Transvaal's tariff policies made supplies expensive. The mine owners realized there was one input whose price could be "artificially" (i.e., via political means) depressed: African labor. But gold mining is particularly dangerous and unpleasant work. The problem of recruiting sufficient labor at a low cost became the central problem of the South African gold mines.[6]

The key role of the mines in the early development of the South African economy bequeathed considerable political power on the mine owners. This leverage was used to press for state policies that would inhibit the full proletarianization of African labor. That is, the mine owners knew that a free labor market could not provide sufficiently cheap workers for their needs, and a system of coerced labor would be necessary. They did not want the workers to settle permanently with their families in urban concentrations, nor did they want the Africans to form proletarian political organizations. The only way this could be achieved was through direct involvement of the legislative and coercive agencies of the state.

South Africa is not unique with regard to the general outlines of this process. Seldom in the history of capitalist development have peasant farmers willingly, en masse, given up their poor but familiar agricultural life for the rigors and monetary rewards of industry. Peasant resistance to proletarianization typically leads the entrepreneur to the state in order to add coercive power to the dissolving effects of the market.

In 1889 the mine owners instituted the Chamber of Mines to secure their labor supply. By uniting all seven mining-finance houses and over 100 individual mines and collieries, the Chamber created a monopsony for the purchase of African mine labor. This was the Chamber's most important function: regulating the labor market so as to keep African wages as low as possible. The Chamber of Mines also consolidated the political power of mining capital relative to other class fractions.

From the early 1900s until the 1924 "Pact" government, the mine owners exercised greater influence on government policy than any other group in South African society.[7] This was not simply a manifestation of national bourgeois solidarity, it was a case of international bourgeois solidarity. By the latter stage of the 1887-1913 gold boom in South Africa, some 85 percent of gold mining shares were owned by foreigners.[8] The ownership and management of the gold mines were dominated by Europeans and North Americans.[9] The coercive

conditions imposed on African mine workers were not
necessarily devised in foreign boardrooms, but their
direct effect was to enrich bourgeois interests in the
United Kingdom, France, Germany, the United States, and
South Africa.[10]
The task of the mine owners was simplified by the
fact that the pre-existing white mode of production
(small-scale farming and herding) had laid institutional
and ideological foundations for a racially-based,
labor-repressive system. "The traditional attitude of a
farmer to his labour was similar to that of a man to his
slaves and in practice as remarkably medieval."[11]
Although never developing a full-blown slave system
of production like the plantation economy of the southern
United States, the Dutch Cape Colony was linked to the
slave trade of East Africa and Indonesia as early as
1658. By the end of the 18th century, "slavery had become
an integral part of Cape society," with slaves a
significant proportion of artisans and traders as well as
domestics and farm laborers.[12]
From its earliest years, white agricultural society
developed a dependency on African labor.

> One of the economic origins of the Great Trek
> lay in the shortage of labour. As they moved north
> settlers adopted several different methods to ensure
> an adequate supply of labour. In Natal there was the
> isibalo system whereby African chiefs were compelled
> to find men to be labourers on public works at
> relatively low wages. In the eastern Cape farmers
> relied on a thicket of pass and vagrancy laws to
> assist them in obtaining and controlling their
> labour. In the Transvaal there was "apprenticing" of
> children . . . the most important method of ensuring
> a supply of labour was the 'squatter' system,
> whereby the white conqueror allowed some of the
> native inhabitants to continue living on the land in
> return for some tangible benefit.[13]

White owners of the larger farms had developed a
system of pass laws and labor control well before the
growth of mines and cities.[14]
Alongside these early varieties of labor coercion
was the racist ideology that accompanied the increasing
incorporation of the Africans into the white production
system. The Afrikaners evolved an exceedingly
conservative Calvinism that legitimated their mastery of
the "kaffirs" as a God-given responsibility.[15] This
ideology was very convenient for the Afrikaners--mostly
small farmers until the mid-20th century--who extracted
land, cattle, and labor services from the rural
Africans.[16]

Because of their dependence on African labor, white farmers felt directly threatened by industrialization. "Realization of the nineteenth-century liberal ideal of a totally free labor market, with workers and employers equal under the law and liberated from noneconomic contraints, would in theory have made racial prejudice irrelevant to worldly success."[17]

The dominant agricultural classes had to ensure that the proletarianization and urbanization of young, male Africans did not proceed unchecked. This need gave impetus to a more militant white-supremacist ideology and practical steps to preserve a rural labor force. Although disagreeing over the details, white farmers agreed with the mining-finance capitalists that African labor should be tightly regulated by the state.[18]

The third group of class actors who had a need for state regulation of African labor was the white working class. The rapid expansion of the mines in the late 1800s, and the growth of related industries such as construction and the manufacture of explosives, had created a white proletariat composed of Afrikaners who had come into the cities from local farms, and immigrants from Europe and America. As we have seen, there was strong pressure on the mine owners to reduce their labor bill. If normal labor market structures were allowed to develop, mine owners would follow the dictates of profitability and replace higher paid whites with low-cost Africans. A Transvaal mine owner testified before a 1907 commission that "some of the Kaffirs are better machinemen than some of the white men...they can place the holes, fix up the machine and do everything that a white man can do."[19]

Since Africans were quite capable of learning the tasks originally performed by whites, it would only be through political barriers to black advancement that white workers could make their positions secure.[20] As Greenberg reveals in great detail, this structural pressure on the white workers to limit the proletarianization of Africans was acted on in different ways by different sectors of white labor.[21]

For the white artisan unions that developed in the late 19th and early 20th centuries, the key question was not whether there would be class restrictions based on race. For them the main consideration was who would oversee the restrictions, white unions or the state. "The unions therefore supported policies that permitted the development of African labor organization, as long as it took an 'evolutionary' form under the firm guidance of the registered trade unions."[22] With some exceptions, the artisan unions opposed increased state regulation of race lines in the labor market because "heightened state attention here directly threatened the artisan unions' own role in reserving work for dominant workers."[23]

The industrial unions, not protected by possession of craft skills, played a much more supportive role in the state's development of a racially stratified workforce. During the later decades of the 19th century and the early decades of the 20th century, the commercialization of South African agriculture gradually pushed more and more white farmers off the land into urban industrial settings where they were often poorly equipped to compete for jobs with Africans possessing years of proletarian experience.[24]

This growing body of white workers was replaceable within the division of labor but their numbers gave them political clout. They pushed for state policies that effectively gave supervisory positions to unskilled and semi-skilled whites. Contrary to some "open" industrial unions that argued for African inclusion in their ranks, the bulk of white workers opposed unionization of Africans: "African trade unionism almost certainly threatens the position of the European mailman, truckdriver, foundry worker, or miner whose position depends on organization at the work place and access to the state."[25]

The nature of South Africa's initial phase of capitalist industrialization, and the integration of this mode of production with the precapitalist agrarian system, produced three dominant classes that shaped the foundations of the South African state. Industrial capitalists, white farmers, and white workers all had a material interest in the state regulating the urbanization of Africans. Although these class actors differed over the details of specific policies, their positions in the system of production gave them an aversion to a free labor market and caused them to support state structures that would block the economic and political rights potentially accruing to a black proletarian majority.

Precapitalist South Africa possessed a complex apparatus for enforcing racial oppression, but "the existence of racially prejudiced attitudes alone on the part of European settlers from 1652 onwards did not by any means predetermine the structure of South African society."[26] It was the integration of South Africa into the world capitalist economy that created the antidemocratic state of modern South Africa.

> Capitalist development brought, along with wage labor, factories, and cities, the intensification of racial discrimination. The dominant class actors during early capitalist development inaugurated a period of intensification, a period where racial domination was given a "modern" form and where repressive features were elaborated and institutionalized.[27]

The labor-supply problem was at the heart of capitalist development in southern Africa. The essence of the problem was that relative to world prices for gold, the cost to mine owners for labor and technology was high. Though the mine owners needed the labor of Africans, they were unwilling to pay the level of wages that would cause African men to voluntarily abandon their farms. The preferred solution for the mine owners consisted of various forms of coercion designed to create and control an African proletariat. The de facto coalition of white settler classes formed the political base for this system of labor control.

Land policy was designed to reserve the most well-endowed areas for whites and to restrict the amount of land available to Africans, ensuring their dependence on wage employment. At the same time, it was not desirable from the capitalists' standpoint to have the Africans totally deprived of agricultural potential. Food grown on African farms lowered the reproduction costs of labor. By keeping African miners in all-male compounds, with their families farming subsistence plots in the native reserves, the mine owners could pay an individual wage rather than a family wage. The production in the African reserves amounted to a subsidy for the capitalists' wage bill.[28] This subsidization of capitalist development by African subsistence producers helped keep the wage bill of the mine owners very stable over the course of the century (Table 2.1).

Hut taxes, dog taxes, and other measures designed to increase the Africans' need for cash and consequent migration to the mines were not as successful in areas where African commercial farmers were effectively competing with white farmers and imported crops. Successful commercial farming by Africans threatened mine

Table 2.1
REAL MONTHLY WAGES OF AFRICAN MINERS, 1905-1969

Year	Wage (Rands)	Index
1905	54	-
1911	57	100
1921	66	69
1936	68	100
1946	87	92
1961	146	89
1969	199	99

Source: Darcy du Toit, Capital and Labour in South Africa: Class Struggles in the 1970s (London: Kegan Paul International, 1981), p. 75.

owners and other urban employers as well as white
farmers. If Africans could earn a living farming they
would have no need to work for white employers in the
cities. The urban employers, therefore, cooperated with
white farmers in pushing for state policies designed to
restrict the development of African farming.[29]
   Rural infrastructure development (e.g., railroads,
electricity, and irrigation), state subsidies, technical
inputs, and access to credit were directed away from
African farming toward white settler farms.[30] The
state-managed impoverishment of African farming ensured a
labor market for the industrialists, and a larger product
market for settler farmers and western food exporters.
"Legal land alienation transformed self-supporting
peasants into squatters, tenant farmers, or laborers on
settlers' farms or drove them into the mines and cities
in search of work."[31]
   Yet even the systematic impoverishment of African
agriculture was not capable of producing sufficient
numbers of African workers for the mines. The mining
industry, with assistance from the British government,
set up a regional 'recruiting' network to facilitate the
movement of young males from the hinterlands of southern
Africa to the mining centers of the Rand.

   The arms of this system reach far across the
   continent. Its fingers point into Northern Rhodesia,
   Nyasaland, far into Tanganyika, into all the High
   Commission territories; Bechuanaland, Basutoland,
   and Swaziland; and they point, in so doing, a
   dreadful accusation at the whole concept and career
   of British colonial policy.[32]

   Conditions in the mines have always been bad
relative to other economic pursuits open to Blacks in
South Africa, so bad that only half of the black miners
have come from South Africa itself (Table 2.2). The rest
were recruited throughout the region, primarily from
those areas where African cash-cropping was less
developed, making migrant labor the main way for Africans
to pay colonial taxes.[33]
   Treaties such as the Mozambique Convention (1909)
regulated the transfer of hundreds of thousands of young
African males in exchange for payments to the Portuguese
colonial administration. When cash inducements proved
insufficient to lure Africans to the mines, conscription
was utilized.[34] The migrant labor system became the basis
of structural integration and South African domination in
southern Africa. "In the interterritorial flow of labour,

Table 2.2
GEOGRAPHICAL SOURCES OF BLACK LABOR (PERCENT)
EMPLOYED BY THE SOUTH AFRICAN CHAMBER OF MINES

Region	1896-98	1936	1972
Transvaal	23.4	7.0	1.8
Natal and Zululand	1.0	4.9	1.2
Swaziland	-	2.2	1.4
Cape	-	39.2	17.7
Lesotho	11.0	14.5	18.5
Orange Free State	-	1.1	1.6
Botswana	3.9	2.3	5.2
Mozambique	60.2	27.8	21.4
North of Latitude 22 S.	0.5	1.1	32.2
Total	100	100	100
Total (thousands)	54	318	381

Source: Francis Wilson, Migrant Labour in South Africa
(Johannesburg: South   African   Council   of
Churches/SPRO-CAS, 1972), p. 4.

even more than trade in foodstuffs or agreements by
governments to connect their respective railway systems,
the economic interdependence of colonial Southern Africa
is most clearly demonstrated."[35]
     The labor migration system of southern Africa
provided the initial model for systems developed later in
various parts of sub-Saharan Africa.[36] But the migrant
labor system was contradictory. Although greatly
enriching the mine owners and financiers, migrant labor
also reflected "the desire of African wage-earners to
retain their links with kin and rights to land in rural
homelands which provided 'social security' against ill
health, unemployment and old age."[37]
     Migrant labor broke up families but it also brought
together men of many tribes and exposed them to new ideas
and technologies. While it undermined the independent
base of African agriculture, the introduction of the cash
nexus of capitalism also undermined the traditional
authority of the tribal chiefs. Some traditional leaders
were delegitimated by collaborating with the labor
recruiters.
     As Greenberg shows, all contemporary racial orders
originated in "the slave plantation economies of the New
World and the European settler societies that exploited
rather than eliminated their indigenous populations."[38]
The roots of modern institutional racism, in the United
States as well as in South Africa, are traceable to the
precapitalist countryside. It was not capitalism per se
nor the racial domination of the precapitalist mode of
production that produced the peculiar racial order of
South Africa. Rather, it was the mixing of the two, the

intrusion of capitalist relations of production on the
Rand and the gradual incorporation of South Africa into
the world capitalist system, that produced apartheid.

SOUTHERN AFRICA'S INTEGRATION INTO WORLD CAPITALISM

The reasons for gold assuming the role of the
universal money commodity are best explained by Marx in
Capital, volume I, chapter 1. The natural characteristics
of gold, its easy divisibility, resistance to decay,
etc., approximate the social content of all commodities,
i.e., abstract, undifferentiated human labor: "the money
form is but the reflex, thrown upon one single commodity,
of the value relations between all the rest."[39]
Gold mining, a specific form of labor creating
"specific use-value as a commodity (gold for instance,
serving to stop teeth, to form the raw material of
articles of luxury, etc.)" is simultaneously the human
activity that expresses its opposite: labor in the
abstract, the universal equivalent.[40] As the accepted
means of international exchange, gold became supreme
among all commodities. It is not forced to compete for
markets and can elude or smash barriers to its entry into
the circuit of capital. It is this unique quality of gold
that allowed South Africa to draw from the advanced
countries the capital and technology needed to
industrialize.
It was fortuitous for the economic development of
South Africa that the years of its mining boom fell
within the life span of the most stable international
gold standard (1870-1914).[41] The gold standard was
effectively managed by the Bank of England, with the
pound sterling, backed by gold, functioning as the world
currency. Britain's leading position was based on its
industrial and commercial superiority. London's use of
the gold standard as a disciplining mechanism on the
world economy helped reinforce Britain's hegemonic status
and sustained a ready market for South African gold.[42]
Not only South Africa, but "the whole of southern
Africa was drawn into the new mining boom which exceeded
anything yet experienced."[43] The capital accumulated from
the mines, and visions of similar discoveries to the
north, provided the wherewithal and impetus for people
like Cecil Rhodes to push into present-day Zimbabwe,
Zambia, and as far north as Zaire.[44] Although not finding
mineral wealth to match that of the Rand, the white
settlers expropriated the best farm land and made a
comfortable living selling sugar, tobacco, maize, and
livestock to the mining centers and the world market.

The British South Africa Company--"the largest and most persistent British chartered company in Africa"[45]--provided political and economic links to London for the settlers who pushed north from the Transvaal. However, "the venture was the outgrowth of colonial rather than metropolitan aspirations and initiatives."[46]

Other European powers utilized concessionary companies to penetrate and dominate sections of southern Africa. In the Belgian Congo, Portuguese Mozambique, and German Southwest Africa "the ruling power's grants of land to joint-stock companies...were the principal means by which economic change was imposed on local societies."[47] These charter companies, aiming to secure mineral rights but also to acquire land for European settlement, "were the cutting edge of a process by which metropolitan and colonial capital combined to extend into new locations the mining-settlement duality of the older Anglo-Afrikaner territories."[48]

South Africa provided a model for the transformation of the rest of the region, and its very size meant that "the performance and characteristics of the South African economy impacted directly upon the structural evolution of the newer colonial territories in the region, by way of a variety of commercial, financial, transport and cultural linkages."[49] This resulted in a "unique degree" of regional interdependence.[50]

Although the colonial charter companies were important conduits for European-imposed change in southern Africa, the main "bridge" linking the international economy to regional development was the mining industry of the Rand. By the early 20th century the regional infrastructure, trade, and migrant labor of southern Africa were inextricably linked to American and European capital, personnel, and technology.

At the same time, "South Africa had become an important part of the world capitalist economy, enmeshed in financial and diplomatic dependence."[51] Recovery from the depression afflicting the world economy during the last quarter of the 19th century was facilitated by huge amounts of gold from the Rand.[52] By 1913 yearly gold production reached 37 million pounds and accounted for 40 percent of total world output.[53] European manufacturers benefitted from purchases by the capital-intensive mines, and American wheat farmers were able to compete effectively in South African markets. Profits accumulated on the Rand were reinvested in Europe and America, as well as in southern Africa.

> Some of the superprofits its [the mining industry's] controllers made were[54] invested in European securities and real estate.

. . . Gold Fields American Development Company, had a capital of 2.5 million pounds. Gold Field's vendor interest, represented by a million one-pound shares, included holdings in alluvial gold fields and borax deposits in California, hydroelectric facilities on the Mississippi River, a power and coal company in Dawson City, and oil fields in Mexico. Other interests in the American hemisphere were held in an alluvial gold mining concern in western Canada and oil leases in Trinidad...a sizeable amount of British government stock completed Gold Field's investment portfolio.[55]

By 1911, the South African mining-finance group, the Corner House, held millions of dollars worth of investments in Alaska, California, Illinois, Utah, Mexico, Costa Rica, Chile, Colombia, England, France, Austria, Germany, Portugal, Russia, North Africa, West Africa, present-day Zambia, Malawi, Zimbabwe, Namibia, Swaziland, Mozambique, and 25 companies within South Africa.[56] The large concentrations of capital and technology, plus the important role of South African gold in the world economy, gave that country's big capitalists higher status and closer ties to the metropolitan ruling classes than those possessed by leaders of other export-enclave economies.

The relative autonomy of the white settlers was to play an important role in South Africa's development and deserves further comment. Much of the theoretical literature on imperialism is simplistic in that it portrays a two-sided confrontation between metropolitan powers and colonized indigenes. Robinson criticizes Eurocentric theories of imperialism and makes a strong argument for focusing on the nature of the "collaborating classes" that reside in the colony and provide the human bridge between exploited masses and imperialists: "...imperialism was as much a function of its victims' collaboration or non-collaboration--of their indigenous politics, as it was of European expansion."[57]

In the case of white settler colonialism it is particularly important to understand the role of this intermediary group vis-a-vis the imperialists and the natives. Indeed, as Emmanuel points out, the most difficult struggles for the imperialist powers were not with the natives but with their own settlers.[58] The cases of the United States, South Africa, Israel, and Northern Ireland show just how autonomous and troublesome settler populations can be.

In criticizing traditional views of imperialism Robinson makes an important contribution to a theory of international class alliances. He argues persuasively for

> an analysis of the most important mechanism of
> European management of the non-European world: the
> use of local collaborating groups--whether ruling
> elites or landlords or merchants--as mediators
> between Europe and the indigenous political and
> economic system. . . . It was the character of the
> collaborative mechanism which determined whether a
> country was allowed to remain independent or whether
> it was incorporated into the formal or informal
> empire of one of the major European powers.[59]

Despite the early dominance of foreign ownership in
South Africa's leading industry (gold), that country's
white settlers gained a level of independence early in
the 20th century that many third world nations have yet
to achieve. This was partly due to the fact that the
Afrikaners were willing to fight doggedly for their
independence (the First and Second Boer Wars). But more
important were the economic factors that strengthened
white settler rule:

> The abundance of gold and its ready
> marketability which induced a degree of competition
> among metropolitan investors; the long gestation
> period of mining investment which reduced the
> possibility of close control; and the long distances
> and poor communications between the capital markets
> of Europe and the gold fields.[60]

The single most important factor, however, was the
exploitation of African labor. The system of tight labor
control produced a surplus large enough to: 1) satisfy
metropolitan investors sufficiently to keep them
reinvesting; 2) foster a local bourgeoisie capable of
investing abroad as well as developing the local economy;
3) overpay the white managerial-working class; and 4)
fund the development of a large state apparatus.

There were serious political conflicts between the
settler classes and British colonial authorities, but by
the late 19th century there was general operational
agreement on the system of exploiting African labor. The
prosperity of the white classes was balanced on the backs
of Africans in both the industrial and subsistence
sectors. Although there have been numerous tactical
arguments over the years, the need for rigid control of
the black population has provided a basis for strategic
unity between metropolitan capital and the white settler
classes.

THE U.S. ROLE IN SOUTH AFRICAN INDUSTRIALIZATION

Americans . . . were destined to play a significant role; they brought with them a wealth of technological and practical experience that made their contribution to South African development disproportionate to their numbers."[61]

It was in the area of management and engineering skills that the United States played its most important role in South Africa's mining boom. Although the nature of gold deposits in the United States differed from those in South Africa, the California gold rush had given American mining engineers "much wider experience than was possessed by experts from other countries."[62] American engineers, managers, and businessmen played a key role in the late 19th century diggings on the Rand.[63]

Although Americans on the Rand totaled only about 1,500, they had influence out of proportion to their numbers. American engineers ran many of the mines on the Rand, and their countrymen supplied much of the expertise and material that allowed the continued tapping of the wealth of the Transvaal. Americans formed a managerial elite united by wealth, knowledge, and close ties with Rhodes and the British South African Company.[64]

As early as 1896 over half of South Africa's mines were run by U.S. engineers.[65] Cecil Rhodes praised the thoroughness of American managers and brought them in to run his DeBeers Diamond mines. A U.S. Army Major, Maurice Heaney, was a "trusted aide" of Rhodes and had secured mineral rights in Rhodesia as early as 1886.[66] Another American, Gardiner F. Williams, not only served as general manager of the Kimberly mines into the 20th century, but was also the American Consular Agent at Kimberly. Ethelbert Woodford "drew up the mining code that still undergirds much of the mining law of South Africa."[67] Hamilton Smith, fresh from a silver mine in Nevada, became a consultant to the Rothschild operations in South Africa.
Perhaps the most influential American during this period was John Hays Hammond. His position as Rhodes' personal engineering consultant, at a salary of $75,000 per year plus a share of the profits, helped Hammond become "the virtual czar of South African mining by 1894."[68]

A staunch Republican and a strong spokesman for American business expansion, Hammond constantly lobbied for a more active American policy towards South Africa. . . . Hammond was confident of the commercial potential of South Africa and actively

recruited American engineers and businessmen to come
to South Africa to work with England in the
development of the region. Because of his knowledge
of South Africa and the mining industry and his
contacts with Rhodes, as well as with American
businessmen and politicians, Hammond exerted great
influence on American policy.[69]

Largely due to the influence of Hammond and other
American personnel, the United States became the largest
supplier of equipment to the South African mines.[70]
"Hammond and others were most familiar with American
equipment and were also eager to increase American ties
with South Africa...they often directed contracts to
American firms, informed American companies of the
highest bids acceptable on equipment, and generally
promoted American involvement in the Transvaal."[71]
    The Transvaal government's tariff policy permitted
agricultural, railroad and mining equipment to enter duty
free. This, in addition to the general boom conditions
and the influence of American engineers, facilitated
early U.S. domination of heavy industry imports. American
exports to South Africa in 1890 were less than $2
million, but by 1895 they had surpassed $6 million, and
in the following year they jumped to $14 million.[72] In
comparison, of all Third World export markets, only Japan
and Brazil imported more U.S. goods.[73]
    The crucial role played by American technology and
technicians in the leading sectors of South African
industry was to establish a pattern that persists to this
day. The rise to world prominence of U.S. technology was
historically coterminous with the development of the
leading industrial sectors of the South African economy.
    South African gold greatly increased the reserves of
an international medium of exchange necessary for
economic expansion. Conversely, South African "prosperity
was inexorably linked and dependent upon American gold
requirements."[74] The prosperity of South Africa hinged on
the price of gold, which in turn depended on the policies
of the two largest purchasers: the British and American
governments. They arbitrarily pegged the gold price
considerably above production costs.

    The price of gold could not possibly have been
    maintained at the established level over this long
    period in the absence of strong and consistent
    government support--mainly by Great Britain and the
    United States, the two countries which acquired and
    converted into coin most of the world's gold
    production until 1933. If the policy of unlimited
    government purchases at a price well above
    production costs had not been adopted, gold after
    1850 would probably have behaved much like silver,
    with new production sources rather quickly dropping

the price to marginal production cost levels.[75]

The rapid development of the mining industry in the late 19th century began the process of structurally integrating the advanced economic sectors of South Africa and the United States. The owners and managers of these sectors (engineering, transport, electrical machinery, chemicals) have played a powerful role in both nations. Their economically based political alliance tells much of the story of U.S.-South African relations over the course of the 20th century.

EARLY U.S. GOVERNMENT POLICY

There were three groups of Americans who influenced late 19th and early 20th century relations with South Africa: mining engineers, businessmen, and missionaries. All were directly involved in the proletarianization and industrialization of South Africa. Engineers and businessmen derived their income from the exploitation of African labor. Missionaries also favored proletarianization because it brought the natives together into urban centers where they were more concentrated and easier to convert.[76] Opportunism and interfaith rivalry swayed American missionaries to support British domination of South Africa.

The growing notions of Anglo-Saxonism and the Anglo-Saxon world mission also influenced missionary thought. Britain was not only a progressive, capitalistic, and democratic nation, but was also Protestant and English-speaking. All of these traits were admirable, but American missionaries were particularly impressed with the last two. Britain and the United States would combine to make South Africa a bastion of Protestantism against the forces of Catholicism in French and Portuguese Africa, and against Islam in West Africa.[77]

Early U.S. policy did little to obstruct the development of racial capitalism in South Africa. The three areas of focus for U.S. policy were commercial relations, conflict between the Boers and the British, and race relations. The first two areas were directly related.

American policymakers were heavily influenced by the American miners and businessmen, who favored British rather than Boer control over South Africa. They believed that the imperial, industrial British had a better sense of how to run a booming capitalist economy than did the parochial, agrarian Boers. The policies of the Boer republics tended toward protectionism, and Boer leaders were opposed to the growing encroachment of the

"uitlanders" (foreigners). Boer suspicions proved
well-founded. When anti-Boer forces staged the 1895
Jameson Raid in an attempt to overthrow Paul Kruger's
Transvaal government, "Americans were in the forefront"
of the abortive rebellion.[78]
     The key test of official U.S. attitudes toward
Boer/British rivalry came in 1899 with the outbreak of
full-scale war. Although the British sent in 250,000
troops and killed some 26,000 Boer women and children in
concentration camps, the war ended somewhat
inconclusively in 1902.[79] The Boers were beaten, but not
so badly that they had to accept full surrender. The
compromise agreement recognized British ownership of the
mines and ultimate colonial control, but the Boers were
granted the franchise and "responsible government" within
the empire.
     The war also provided an opportunity for the U.S.
government to take a small but formative step on the long
climb to its own empire. "South Africa was to be the
first example where policies converged, and the United
States saw its interests reflected in British
interests."[80] The United States was in the process of
acquiring Spain's colonies in the Caribbean and the
Pacific, and British support for the United States in the
Spanish-American War helped make U.S. policymakers
sympathetic to imperial goals in South Africa. Teddy
Roosevelt commented:

          Though I greatly admire the Boers, I feel it is
     in the interest of civilization that the
     English-speaking race should be dominant in South
     Africa, exactly as it is for the interest of
     civilization that the United States . . . should be
     dominant in the Western Hemisphere.[81]

     American policy toward the Boer War consisted of
proclaiming neutrality while carefully aiding the British
war effort.[82] Washington used various diplomatic
procedures to help the British in their campaign against
the Afrikaner guerrillas. The State Department took no
action against British violations of American neutrality;
Washington rejected participation in European-sponsored
peace efforts; and the U.S. government spurned Boer
requests for assistance.
     The United States became the largest supplier to the
British army, providing equipment and personnel, mostly
muleteers who often enlisted in the British army after
arriving in South Africa. Secretary of State Hay
rationalized the sale of arms to the British by arguing
that the proper role of government was

> to expand the market for their [U.S.
> businessmen's] goods and products all over the
> world. They have a perfect right to deal with
> everybody, whether belligerents or not. We should be
> glad to see our people furnish . . . every army in
> the world, to feed and clothe them, and to supply
> them with everything they need.[83]

The duplicitous American policy drew fire at home
from Irish-Americans, German-Americans, and Democrats
eyeing the 1900 election. The "anti-imperialist" forces
saw the United States developing a policy opposed to
republicanism: an imperialist policy resisting efforts by
smaller states to withdraw from the "free-trade" network
dominated by Britain and the United States. The
laissez-faire "freedom" for capital to penetrate any area
of the globe required the denial of colonial peoples'
freedom to construct full sovereignty. In this way we can
see that later U.S. hostility toward the Russian,
Chinese, and other socialist revolutions was not based
solely on opposition to socialist doctrines. The earlier
U.S. opposition to sovereignty on the part of various
non-communist nationalists (Boers, Cubans, Puerto Ricans,
Filipinos, Native Americans, etc.) laid a base for
America's later interventionist and counterrevolutionary
policies against socialism.

During the late 19th and early 20th centuries, when
the foundations of South Africa's racial apparatus were
being laid, U.S. policy exhibited a consistent racial
bias.[84] American policymakers saw the race question as
another reason for supporting British control of South
Africa. The Boers were viewed as backward and bigoted,
and it was assumed that by England accepting its
Anglo-Saxon duty to the "inferior" races, black South
Africans would eventually prosper.

The British encouraged this view by speculating
about future black progress under British guidance and by
encouraging American missionary work among the
Africans.[85] The British also had made it clear, however,
that economic gains would have priority over black
advancement. Controls on black labor were strengthened,
not relaxed. "With the coming of a British administration
to the Transvaal after the Anglo-Boer War, the pass
system was not only retained but was more effectively
enforced than it had been by the less efficient Afrikaner
regime."[86]

A more revealing aspect of U.S. policy on the race
question was the official attitude toward black American
contact with black South Africans. There were two main
groups of black Americans who impacted on South Africa.
One was politically moderate to conservative, emphasizing
technical training and self help; the other tended toward
black nationalism. The former were influenced by Booker
T. Washington's self-help programs which emphasized

industrial education, eschewing political ambitions and
black separatist ideologies. "Washington's stress on work
and manual training was especially attractive to white
South Africans frustrated by the problems of creating a
black labor force."[87] The British, American and South
African governments facilitated the interaction of these
black Americans with their counterparts in South Africa.
    The black nationalists, usually church-based,
provided another avenue of black advancement.

        Largely under American Negro influences numbers
    of separatist or independent African Churches grew
    up in which White domination and authority were
    rejected and Black men of ability, to whom other
    paths were closed, came into their own as founding
    fathers and even bishops, some with large
    followings, much power, fervent adulation and
    sizeable incomes.[88]

    Key among these was the Ethiopianist church in South
Africa. "This sect made contact with the African
Methodist Episcopal Church of America (AME) and formed
close and lasting bonds, the Ethiopians drawing their
bishops from America."[89]
    Through journalism, political organizing and
interpreting the bible in a radically democratic way, the
black nationalists were seen as a threat by white South
Africans and white Americans alike. American government
officials, missionaries, journalists and black moderates
condemned black nationalism and the AME's doctrine of
"Africa for the Africans." When the South African
government began cracking down on black Americans in
South Africa following a 1906 rebellion in Natal in which
nearly 4,000 Blacks were killed, the U.S. government's
response was to cooperate by discouraging black Americans
from traveling to South Africa.[90]

SOUTH AFRICA: FROM UNION TO APARTHEID

    The British Act of Parliament that established the
Union of South Africa on 31 May 1910, for the first time
united the four provinces making up that country. "But
its white population, which alone was concerned, remained
divided in language, religion, attitudes to imperialism
and racial orientation, each sector secretly hoping to
come out on top. The great mass of the people was
unconsulted and unconsidered."[91]
    The Union was granted considerable independence
within the framework of Commonwealth status. The British
Governor-General chose General Botha, the Boer war hero,
to form the first cabinet. This early precedent of
Afrikaner leadership and the numerical superiority of the
Boers presaged eventual Afrikaner domination of the

state. In coming decades Afrikanerdom would use the state
to protect its working class and foster the development
of an Afrikaner bourgeoisie. The Afrikaners also began
pooling private capital to advance their economic and
political   power   vis-a-vis   the   English-speaking
population.[92]

The export-led growth fueled by World War I was
followed by a recession that cut sharply into mine
revenues. The mine owners reacted with a concerted
attempt to lower their wage bill by replacing high-priced
white labor with African and foreign indentured labor.
The white labor movement, influenced by Britain's
militant trade union tradition, mounted a campaign of
resistance that culminated in the Rand Rebellion of
1922.[93] Strikes and violence disrupted gold production,
thus threatening the entire economy. The coalition of
radical and reactionary white workers nearly gained
control of Johannesburg by the time the government
(dominated by the mine owners) declared martial law. Some
20,000 troops using machine guns and aerial bombing
crushed the rebellion, leaving hundreds dead and wounded.

Although an immediate defeat for the white miners,
the smashing of the Rand rebellion resulted in a
political alliance between white unions (the Labour
Party) and Afrikaner nationalism (the National Party)
that was to change the course of South African history.

The recession of the late teens and early twenties
had been a blow to the industrial and agricultural
sectors, threatening capital and labor in many areas.
These economic changes laid a material base for the
political alliance between white workers and Afrikaner
nationalists. In the elections of 1924 the
Nationalist-Labour Pact replaced the government of the
more liberal and internationalist Smuts with one more
focused on the problem of controlling black labor.
"General Hertzog became Prime Minister, pledged to an
all-out defence of White South Africa alike against
undercutting by the work-starved Black influx and
exploitation by profit-hungry financial powers. He found
strong support in both White groups."[94]

The Pact Government elaborated the mining color bar
and other legislation limiting the full
proletarianization of Africans. It addressed the
long-simmering poor white problem, partly by assuring
white jobs in state enterprises and partly by forcing the
young manufacturing sector to employ an increasing
proportion of whites. It was during this period that the
foundations of industrial apartheid were laid: "...the
early years of the polity in action in the new Parliament
of the Union of South Africa had made it clear that
economic change expressed through the competitive market
would never be allowed to alter the status-differentials
of White-Black relationships."[95]

The significance of the Labour-Nationalist coalition should not be underestimated. The incorporation of white worker interests into the state, allied with commercial farmers and the Afrikaner petty-bourgeoisie, permanently shattered the possibility of a viable black-white labor alliance. Legislation such as the Industrial Conciliation Act of 1924 defined white workers as a different class than non-white workers.[96] Subsequent legislation tended to incorporate white workers into the exploiting classes, providing them with material rewards and legislative guarantees similar to those of supervisors and managers in other countries.

The Pact Government's efforts to protect the nascent manufacturing sector were aided by strong growth in the world economy.[97] This expansion was abruptly curtailed in 1929 but the governments reacted by extending state controls over production and facilitating accumulation in the agricultural and industrial sectors.

> The effect of these measures, however, was to attract other capitals (including an increasing amount of 'foreign' capital) to these branches. Since the 'foreign' capitals had considerable competitive advantages over purely 'national' capitals, the latter soon found themselves once more in difficulty, beginning to demand measures, particularly in relation to the provision of financial resources, that would enable them to survive against the competition.[98]

The state erected traditional tariff barriers to protect infant import-substitution industries, such as textiles, clothing, leather and processed foods. In 1923 the South African state established the Electricity Supply Commission (ESCOM) as another subsidy to mines and manufacturers alike.

ESCOM became part of an eventual family of state enterprises encompassing railways, harbors, iron and steel, coal, oil and gas, fertilizers, ferro-alloys, armaments, shipping, nuclear power, and general industrial financing.[99] In South Africa "the market economy steadily gave way to the administered society."[100] The shift from an "open" to a "closed" economy, and the large-scale infrastructural subsidies, provided a basis or the rapid growth in industrial output that would be touched off by World War II and the postwar boom.

The South African gold industry benefited from the disruption of the world monetary system caused by the Great Depression of the early 1930s.

Abandonment of the Gold Standard by the world's major economies--led by Britain in 1931 and the United States in 1933--resulted in a rise in gold prices from 85 shillings per ounce in 1931 to 140 shillings per ounce in 1939, and resources were redeployed into gold mining wherever deposits existed.[101]

The shelving of the gold standard and the general countercyclical tendency of gold meant that the precious metal played a saviour Africa in the 1930s similar to the one it had depression of the a period of world economic price of gold was attractive to investments.
Huge amounts of low-grade ore were mined. A whole new gold field in the Orange Free State was discovered. The mining labor force nearly doubled in the decade prior to World War II, and output rose from 48.4 million British pounds in 1931 to 71.6 million pounds in 1938.[102] The external trade of southern Africa, largely due to South African gold, increased more in the period 1929-1945 than it did from 1913-1929.[103] Through its control of the state, national capital siphoned off larger amounts of gold profits to be used for local development. Between 1933 and 1934 alone, gold industry taxation increased by nearly 250 percent.[104]
With the state-run Iron and Steel Corporation and other heavy industry leading the way, the manufacturing sector registered advances in employment and output.[105] Table 2.3 shows the growing importance of manufacturing relative to mining and agriculture. South Africa expanded production of tobacco, food, construction, textiles, and chemicals while most nations' economies were stagnating.

Table 2.3
GROSS DOMESTIC PRODUCT BY TYPE OF ECONOMIC ACTIVITY,
1920-1945 (Rands, millions)

Year	Farming (%)		Mining (%)		Manufacturing (%)	
1920	102	(21)	104	(21)	52	(11)
1925	102	(22)	80	(17)	56	(12)
1930	70	(14)	88	(17)	78	(15)
1935	81	(14)	126	(21)	91	(15)
1940	101	(12)	196	(23)	151	(18)
1945	164	(12)	192	(14)	265	(20)

Source: Based on data in D. Hobart Houghton, The South African Economy (Cape Town: Oxford University Press, 1976), p. 273.

By 1939 the South African economy was in a good
position to take advantage of the disrupted trade
patterns resulting from the outbreak of world war. The
drastic decline in imports from Europe helped boost local
manufacturing output 116 percent between 1939 and
1945.[106] Building on its already substantial consumer and
capital goods industries, South Africa not only filled
the import substitution gap in its own economy and those
of the region, it also became a supplier of manufactured
goods to the war zones of Southeast Asia and the Middle
East.[107] The general impact of World War II is neatly
summarized in a yearly report by one of the big gold
mining firms.

An Industrial Census undertaken by the Union
government shows that industrial development has
been so stimulated by war conditions that South
Africa's annual value of manufactures is now...above
the value of the Transvaal gold output---a remarkable
advance. Expansion of local industries continues
apace, especially seeing that competition from other
parts of the world is eliminated owing to war
conditions.[108]

The number of Africans employed in the industrial
sector jumped from 270,000 to 457,000 between 1936 and
1946.[109] A growing number of Africans found professional
and clerical jobs opened to them by the war-induced labor
shortage.

The industrial labour force grew by 53 percent
during the war, but of the increase of 125,000
persons, only 19,000 were white, the remaining
106,000 being drawn from the other races. Moreover,
many of them moved into skilled and semi-skilled
jobs formerly performed by whites. Had it not been

Table 2.4
INCREASE IN MANUFACTURING EMPLOYMENT
OF WHITES AND BLACKS, 1938-1945 (thousands)

	1938-39	1944-45	% Increase 1939-45
Number of Whites	93	112	20
Number of Blacks	143	249	74

Source: Based on data in Houghton, The South African
Economy, p. 127.

for their contribution, South Africa could not both have expanded output and maintained its war effort.[110]

The government loosened the pass laws and influx control in order to secure more African workers, only to reimpose them more tightly after the war. The percentage of all Africans residing in urban areas rose from 18.4 to 23.7 between 1936 and 1946.[111] Table 2.4 shows how wartime expansion of manufacturing depended heavily on increasing employment of Africans.

The government outlawed all strikes by African workers. Special war measures made it illegal for black miners to meet in groups larger than twenty. Despite these added restrictions to black political activity there was a great deal of industrial ferment during the war. Between the 1942 passage of War Measure 145 outlawing African strikes, and the end of 1944, there were 60 illegal strikes.[112] In 1946 the gold mines were crippled briefly by a strike of some 50,000 African miners. The government brutally suppressed the strike.[113]

The increased rate of employment had also created conditions conducive to the political unification of various Africans. Progressive Africans were linking up with anticolonial and pan-Africanist forces gaining strength in other parts of the world. The fear generated in the white community by these developments contributed to the National Party coming to power in 1948 on a platform of strict white supremacy.

U.S. CORPORATIONS AND THE APARTHEID ECONOMY

The inflow of foreign capital into South Africa had been associated at every stage of the country's economic growth with the opening of new and vital sectors of the economy, which could never have been launched without the capital, and even more, the expertise, of overseas investment.[114]

South Africa's ability to transcend the limitations of a primary product, export economy is largely due to capital and technology from the United States and its major allies. Complex institutional linkages and dependencies have developed between the accumulation processes in these countries. The dynamics of these structural relations created limitations for U.S. policy toward South Africa by setting accumulation constraints on the U.S. state (e.g., dependence on South African minerals), and establishing personal and institutional ties between American and South African elites.

As previously noted, the primary task of U.S. government officials in South Africa was to promote American business involvement. The substance and tone of this 1921 communique from the U.S. Consul General in Cape Town is typical.

> There are splendid openings here...for energetic men with sufficient capital to finance the undertaking and employ the large forces of cheap native labor found in most parts....American capital could be put to splendid use here in the interest of American trade.[115]

The U.S. consul in Cape Town had proposed as early as 1914 that the U.S. Chamber of Commerce establish itself in South Africa, and in July 1920 a branch was established in Johannesburg. The Chamber provided a regional integrating function in that its members were drawn from U.S. companies in Portuguese East Africa, German Southwest Africa, the Belgian Congo, and South Africa. "The officers and board of directors reflected the primacy of the mining industry in 1920 before other commercial and trading interests became active."[116]

Following World War I, U.S. corporate and government leaders collaborated in expanding the U.S. merchant fleet. The American South African Line ran a regular, prosperous service from the East Coast, and by 1929 the South African Dispatch Line of San Francisco was running direct shipping from the West Coast.[117]

The rapid expansion of the mining industry gave South Africa the largest market, particularly for capital goods, in sub-Saharan Africa. By 1919 South Africa was accounting for over 50 percent of sub-Saharan Africa's external trade.[118] Although this percentage was to decline steadily as the rest of Africa developed (Table 2.5), South Africa remained a preferred market on the continent.

South Africa was particularly important as a market for key American manufactures. Baran and Sweezy have pointed to the importance of two great waves of "automobilization" that fueled industrial growth in the United States.[119] South Africa ranked fifth in the world as a purchaser of U.S. autos in 1920, and by 1929 ranked fourth as a buyer of all U.S. motor vehicles.[120] In 1927 South Africa was the seventh largest market for U.S. auto parts and accessories.[121] In the middle of the Great Depression South Africa rose to become the number one buyer of U.S. passenger cars and was also a substantial market for trucks and buses.[122]

Table 2.5
TOTAL FOREIGN TRADE WITH SUB-SAHARAN AFRICA
AND SOUTH AFRICA, 1897-1960 (millions of British pounds)

	Sub-Saharan Africa	South Africa	South Africa as % of Sub-Saharan Africa
1897	71.20	47.20	66
1913	187.92	104.93	56
1919	274.37	143.71	52
1929	355.66	168.07	47
1938	391.67	198.06	51
1945	603.39	269.50	45
1960	3,782.23	1,284.35*	34

*includes Namibia

Source: Based on data in J. Forbes Munro, Africa and the
International Economy (London: J.M. Dent & Sons Ltd,
1976), pp. 217-219.

Customarily sober Business Week referred to South
Africa in 1936 as "one of the most spectacular markets in
the world."[123] Throughout the interwar years South Africa
was a major purchaser of key American products such as
petrochemicals, machinery (particularly agricultural and
mining), metals, and manufactured goods.

Petroleum products, motor vehicles and chassis,
parts and accessories and various types of
machinery, beginning in 1925, accounted for 50
percent or more of American sales. The relevancy of
these goods to the Union's development can not be
understated; aside from the petroleum byproducts
. . . they were all capital goods.[124]

American superiority in petrochemicals proved vital
to South African industrialization. By the late 1920s the
United States was supplying South Africa with 62 percent
of its gasoline, 95 percent of its kerosene, 80 percent
of its lubricating oils, and 66 percent of its
antifriction greases.[125] South Africa was then, and
remains today, dependent on a few western corporations to
meet its petrochemical needs. The ancestors of two
American oil giants (Mobil and Caltex) who today control
over one-third of the South African market, had already
established a firm foothold by the late 1920s.[126]
Major U.S. companies that later gained prominence in
the world economy got an early start in South Africa.
These included Singer Sewing Machine (1870s), Kidder,
Peabody Co. (1870), Mobil (1897), General Electric
(1899), Ford (1905), and Kodak (1913).[127] By 1929 the
following corporations had opened branches: National Cash
Register, Armour and Co., National City Bank of New York,

Prentice-Hall,   Colgate-Palmolive,   Firestone,   B.F.
Goodrich,   American   Cyanimid,   General   Motors,   and
International Harvestor.[128]
    An early investment that was more important for its
symbolic   and   political   value   than   its   economic
ramifications was the participation of Morgan Guaranty
capital   in   the   1917   formation   of   Ernest Oppenheimer's
Anglo-American Corporation. Oppenheimer   was   intent   on
convincing   Herbert   Hoover   (then   president   of   Morgan
Guaranty)   to   participate,   not   solely   due   to   financial
need: he   also   "considered   it   very   necessary   American
identity should form part of Company's title."[129]
    Anglo-American brought   together   important   members   of
the British, American, and South African ruling classes,
giving them similar interests vis-a-vis African workers.

    Its original (and continuing) integration with
South African and international capital is clear
from the composition of its initial board members:
two white South Africans (including the ex-minister
of   finance),   three   U.S.   citizens   (including
individuals   from   Newmont   Mining   and   Morgan
Guaranty),   and   two   alternate   members,   with   British
nationality.[130]

    The   notion   that   capital   from   different   nations   is
separate and naturally prone to competition prevents an
understanding   of   the   economic   basis   of   international
bourgeois   solidarity.   In   many   cases   foreign   capital
integrates with local capital to better exploit local and
regional opportunities.

    U.S.   direct   investments   in   British   empire
countries--in   Australia,   Malaya,   India   and   South
Africa--were   often   owned   by   English   or   Canadian
corporations   affiliated   with   the   U.S.   parent.   One
American company (Sherwin-Williams) had in 1920 a
Canadian Company that in turn had sales branches in
India, China, and South Africa. . . .
    Ford operated in Australia, Malaya, India, and
South Africa through Ford Motor Company of Canada,
which was associated with Ford Motor Company in the
United   States   through   certain   common
shareholders.[131]

    These   linkages   further   integrated   South   African
capital with western capital, and conferred on South
African capital and management a status and degree of
autonomy not found in most of the Third World.

In a not atypical instance, the South African
sales subsidiary of National Cash Register--owned by
the U.S. parent--was effectively managed from London
by N.C.R.'s English subsidiary. The South African
National Cash Register Company had as its
"territory" southern Africa, including much of east
Africa. Thus, in the 1920s, an N.C.R. representative
in Kenya, who would typically be an Englishman or a
South African, would report to a manager in
Johannesburg, who in turn would report to the
company's headquarters in the States. Because of the
small investment, the distances, and such pyramided
international control patterns, there proved to be a
large degree of managerial autonomy in such business
operations.[132]

American capital also contributed to the relative
autonomy of the South African ruling class by providing
them with an alternative to dependence on British trade
and investment. American capital and technology rivaled
or surpassed that of Britain. Although the
English-speaking South Africans, especially businessmen,
opposed the shift, successive South African governments
were able to gradually reduce Britain's power over the
South African economy.

Prior to World War I Britain's share of the
Union's market was roughly 55 percent and sometimes
higher. Following the war and for the entire
interwar period, Britain's share declined, averaging
approximately 45 percent of imports. The main
beneficiary of this decline was the United States.
In 1913 its share of imports was 9.5 percent.
Throughout the 1920s it gradually but consistently
increased so that by 1929 the United States provided
19 percent of the Union's import requirements.[133]

To summarize, in the decades leading up to the
National Party victory of 1948 major corporations of the
U.S. monopoly sector established firm roots in the South
African economy. They were well placed to take advantage
of post-war conditions: a booming world economy, the
United States rising to world dominance, and a South
African regime committed to the repressive, cheap-labor
policies that would come to be known as apartheid.

AFRIKANER STATE CAPITALISM

As previously mentioned, World War II had a major
impact on the South African economy. Industrial expansion
resulted in a rapid increase in the proletarianization of
the African population. A key concern for the white
polity in the post-war period was how the state would

respond to the large, war-induced influx of Africans into urban areas.

The party in power at the end of the war, the United Party (UP), was unable to live up to its name. Representing segments of different business sectors (commercial, agricultural, mining, manufacturing), the UP was unable to develop policies that would suit everyone in its power base. Some members of the UP were leaning toward accepting Blacks as a permanent part of the urban workforce and granting them limited freedoms normally associated with proletarian status (e.g., union rights, and de jure freedom of movement and residence). In 1947 the Minister of Native Affairs posed this central question.

> Can we develop our industries when we have the position that the Native only works for a few months and then returns to the Reserves for a couple of years? No, the Native must be trained for his work in industry, and to become an efficient industrial worker, he must be a permanent worker. On that account, he must live near his place of employment.[134]

The manufacturing sector, particularly big capital, needed and could afford a more stable and well-trained African workforce. But at the same time, agricultural capital was confronting a labor shortage in the countryside.

The three classes most directly threatened by a policy that would recognize the African as a permanent proletarian, joined forces to block such a development. Small industrial capital unable to afford increases in the cost of African labor, white workers fearful of black competition, and agricultural capital needing to retain a rural labor force, united in bringing the National Party (NP) to power in the 1948 parliamentary elections.

The NP was a tenuous grouping of semi-autonomous, regional Afrikaner parties united by several factors: a belief in the God-given nature of their status vis-a-vis Africans, opposition to British imperialism, and class interests favoring tighter control of black workers.[135] A founding document states the NP goal of "a free, independent, republican, Christian-National state, based upon the word of God, eschewing all foreign models . . . with a Christian-National educational system...and the strongest emphasis upon the effective disciplining of the people."[136]

Opposed to humanist notions that the state is created by people for their own use, Afrikaner Calvinism views the state's authority over the individual as a gift of God. The emphasis is on discipline and obedience to this higher authority. The parallels to German Nazism were direct and explicit.

During World War II the extreme Afrikaner
nationalists were opposed to South African entry on the
side of the Allies. To block South African participation
in the war against Nazism, the most militant Afrikaner
groups (New Order and Ossewabrandwag) carried out
terrorist actions such as dynamiting railway lines,
telegraph poles, and theatres, and assaulting the police
and military.

These militant supporters of Nazism later achieved
prominence under National Party rule. Dr. Voerwoerd, the
editor of an influential Afrikaner newspaper that openly
propagandized for the Nazi cause, became Prime Minister.
Future Presidents Swart and Diederichs were Nazi
sympathizers. Prime Minister Vorster, a former commandant
in the Ossewabrandwag, declared in 1942: "We stand for
Christian Nationalism, which is an ally of Nazism."[137]

This Afrikaner nationalist party would rule South
Africa from 1948 onward, overseeing the country's
industrial expansion during the postwar boom. It was this
leadership that would develop strong mutual ties and
dependencies with the ruling classes of the West, as the
forces of African nationalism gradually pressed in on all
sides.

There were too dominant trends in post-1948 South
African development: state-sponsored industrialization
and a sharp increase in the integration of western
monopoly capital into the leading sectors of the South
African economy. By tracing the course of these two
trends we can see how they were mutually reinforcing. The
changes in class relations that made apartheid necessary
for some classes and possible to be foisted on others
also created conditions favorable to foreign capital.

Although its initial hold on state power was
somewhat tenuous, the National Party moved quickly to
implement a wide range of repressive measures aimed at
breaking African resistance to the system of labor
control. Africans were prohibited from leaving jobs
without the permission of their employers. They could not
get employment or even move about without a "pass" or
"reference" book which contained vital information about
them and was required to be shown to the police on
demand. Being caught without one's pass or being in an
area without proper authorization were, and remain,
criminal offenses. The movement of Africans from rural to
urban areas ("influx control") was tightened. A system of
labor bureaus was established to ensure that labor needs
in any particular rural district were sufficient before
releasing Africans to the city.

In its most far-reaching program, the NP began
transforming the rural areas reserved for Africans
("native reserves") into what are today known as
bantustans ("homelands" in government jargon).[138] The
basic idea underlying the bantustan system was older than
colonialism itself: divide and rule. Not only would

Whites, Coloreds (mixed race), Indians, and Africans be separated from one another, but now the black population would be divided into ten ethnic "nations", each with its own territory and administrative apparatus. From the earliest part of the century when African leaders were calling for unity under the banner of African nationalism, the Whites knew that black unity would mean the end of their privileged position. By giving each African "citizenship" in a particular homeland, the numerical superiority of Africans became less problematic for a political system with democratic pretensions.

The leaders of the bantustans are tribal chiefs handpicked and payed by Pretoria. Comprising only one-eighth of the area of South Africa, the bantustans are desolate pieces of earth, lacking in infrastructure, industry or major mineral deposits. This ensures their economic dependence on South Africa. The bantustans produce subsistence crops that increase the surplus value accumulated in capitalist industry by allowing capital to pay workers less than their actual reproduction costs. This fact was not lost on mine owners and state managers. The Chamber of Mines testified:

> It is clearly to the advantage of the mines that native labourers should be encouraged to return to their homes after the completion of the ordinary period of service. The maintenance of the system under which the mines are able to obtain unskilled labour at a rate less than ordinarily paid in industry depends upon this, for otherwise the subsidiary means of subsistence would disappear and the labourer would tend to become a permanent resident upon the Witwatersrand, with increased requirements.[139]

Concentrating the Africans in barren, rural reserves was also a long-term political precaution against the type of guerrilla war that was proving effective in other countries. Forced removals of Africans to the bantustans totalled 3.5 million persons between 1960 and 1982.[140]

The sluggish performance of the economy during most of the 1950s, combined with intensified repressive measures, produced "almost continual disturbances."[141] Race riots that rocked numerous towns in 1949 and 1950 were followed by the Suppression of Communism Act, which in effect outlawed all opposition to apartheid. The Defiance Campaign of 1952-53, led by the African National Congress, saw thousands of Africans arrested for purposeful violation of apartheid regulations before the protest was finally crushed by stricter legislation and enforcement.

African resistance crested in 1960 when police fired on a peaceful demonstration at Sharpeville, killing 67 and wounding 186. A massive crackdown followed in which African political organizations were smashed and thousands of people were arrested. From 1964 until the early 1970s African opposition went into eclipse.

Alongside the regulation and repression of black workers, the state's industrialization program proceeded apace. Partly a continuation of earlier plans, and partly an expansion into wholly new areas such as armaments and nuclear power, state-sponsored industrialization was seen by the NP leadership as the fundamental answer to several problems. Growth in the manufacturing sector was seen as a way to:

* provide productive jobs for rural Whites displaced by the concentration and centralization of agricultural capital;
* diversify the economy away from its dependence on the extractive sector, thus decreasing reliance on non-renewable resources and insulating South Africa from fluctuations in the world economy;
* calm the rebelliousness of Africans via increased job opportunities; and
* inculcate the discipline of the capitalist workplace in the African population.

By means of tariff barriers, government financing, expansion of government corporations ("parastatals"), and various types of direct and indirect subsidies, the apartheid state fostered rapid growth in manufacturing. Manufacturing as a percentage of national income grew from 6.7 percent in 1911-12 to 31 percent in 1971. Table 2.6 shows the healthy rate of growth in manufacturing during the period 1955-1970.

A closer look at the details of postwar manufacturing growth reveals an important trend. Hampered by a small domestic market but desirous of achieving necessary economies of scale in key industrial sectors, the South African state facilitated mergers and monopolization in order to more effectively compete on domestic and international markets. Houghton shows that in the period 1954-1970 the average number of employees per firm nearly doubled and the average net product more than tripled, yet the total number of manufacturing firms declined 4.4 percent.[142] This trend toward industrial concentration continued through the 1970s. In 1976 Houghton reported that "the total number of firms has tended to decline in recent years but the average size firm has quadrupled in terms of labour and increased nineteenfold in terms of capital."[143]

Table 2.6
GROWTH IN SOUTH AFRICAN MANUFACTURING

	1954-55	1969-70	% increase 1955-70
Number of establishments	10,126	13,142	30
White workers (thousands)	158	278	76
Non-white workers (thousands)	452	886	96
Value of net output (R millions)	852	2,398	181

Source: Based on data in Houghton, The South African Economy, p. 128.

This rapid industrial growth and concentration of ownership was occurring in many parts of the world during the postwar period. What set South Africa apart was the level of state participation in economic development. From early in the 20th century the Afrikaners sought to offset the economic power of the English-speaking population by pooling their capital.[144] This effort met with little success, however, until the Afrikaners gained control of the state apparatus. Although some government corporations had been established in the 1920s and 1930s, it was in the post-1948 period that the parastatals came into their own as a major economic force.[145] During the post-war period government enterprise overtook private business as the major contributor to gross fixed investment (Table 2.7).

Key sectors of the economy are dominated by these state-run corporations. With over 25,000 employees and capital assets exceeding $8 billion, the South African Railways and Harbours (SAR&H) is the largest enterprise in the country.[146] The Electricity Supply Commission (ESCOM) provides some 80 percent of the country's electricity.[147] The Industrial Development Corporation (IDC) finances a broad range of enterprises: aircraft manufacturing, shipping, mining, textiles, printing, and agriculture, among others.[148]

The Armaments Corporation (ARMSCOR) employs 25,000 people in eleven wholly-owned subsidiaries and has contracts with some 800 domestic firms.[149] In 1981 ARMSCOR was budgeted to receive $1.8 billion, about 70 percent of South Africa's military expenditures.[150]

State corporations are also involved in uranium production, nuclear power, iron and steel, oil exploration, coal-to-gas conversion, and shipping. One of the practical effects of this high level of state economic activity is that foreign capital investing in South Africa necessarily develops diverse institutional linkages to the South African state.[151]

Table 2.7
POST-WAR TRENDS IN GROSS DOMESTIC
FIXED INVESTMENT (GDFI), at current prices

	Public enterprise (R millions)	As % of GDFI	Private enterprise (R millions)	As % of GDFI
1946	99	37	171	63
1950	194	35	362	65
1955	315	36	554	64
1960	437	41	624	59
1965	855	43	1,122	57
1970	1,380	43	1,797	57
1976	4,631	53	4,105	47

Source: Nedbank Group Economic Unit, South Africa: An Appraisal (Johannesburg: Nedbank Group, 1977), pp. 97-98.

MONOPOLY STAGFLATION AND THE BLACK PROLETARIAT

The phenomenal growth of manufacturing industry has brought riches for the white corporate class and misery for the black proletariat. As several theorists have demonstrated in the case of the United States, the concentration and centralization of capital produces a structural tendency toward unemployment and inflation.[152] This dynamic is clearly visible in South Africa.[153] The same postwar economic growth that produced concentration of capital also resulted in double-digit unemployment rates for urban Blacks.

The leading sectors of the economy are capital intensive. They grow via technological innovation, not expanded employment. In recent years the job market for Blacks has been stagnating. In 1976 black employment (excluding agriculture and domestic service) was 2,659,325; it declined to 2,611,608 in 1977, 2,572,136 in 1978, and 2,604,073 in 1979. Only in the second quarter of 1980 did it regain the 1976 level, amounting to 2,676,657. This stagnation is "due primarily to the increasing capital intensification of most sectors of the economy, and the fact that much of the growth in 1979-1981 has come from the utilisation of spare capacity."[154]

In the mid-1970s the University of Cape Town estimated that of a black proletariat numbering roughly five to seven million workers, as many as two million were unemployed.[155] A July 1981 special survey by the Financial Times surmised that in urban areas "as many as 42 percent of black males in their 20s may be jobless."[156] This is despite the government's forced removal of most of its surplus labor population to the desolate bantustans where unemployment is far worse than in urban areas.[157]

This failure to produce adequate employment must be viewed against an inflation rate that has been averaging well over 10 percent. The market dominance of monopoly sector companies, and their political influence on state policies, allow them to pass on increased costs to the rest of the population. No less radical a source than South Africa's Nedbank Group points out the role of noncompetitive pricing and the western monopoly sector in this inflation. "Throughout the postwar period oligopolistic, or follow-the-leader, business pricing policies tended to make the markets bear what they could."[158]

The acceleration of inflation after the late 1960s, particularly, was accompanied by an increasing importance of 'imported inflation'. In the 1970s the exchange rate policy chosen exacerbated this pressure, the higher priced imports--being mainly capital goods--setting off a cost-push ripple.[159]

Added to this structural squeeze on the black proletariat is the fact that the government's investments in social services have steadily declined over the past decade (Table 2.8).

Average black earnings in industry increased both absolutely and as a percentage of white earnings. But this was all premised on an extremely low black wage to begin with. Thus, although the black-white wage gap appears to be improving when viewed in percentage terms (and is always portrayed that way by apartheid's defenders), in real terms the wage gap has widened considerably. For example, in manufacturing the black-white wage gap increased from R1,575 in 1960 to R4,852 in 1975.[160]

As professor Jeremy Keenan points out, there are several mitigating factors to consider when viewing government data on black wage increases. First, the data usually highlight sectors such as manufacturing and mining where pay rates are considerably higher than in sectors such as agriculture and domestic service. Second, the data do not factor out overtime wages although these can account for as much as 18 percent of total earnings. Third, the government also lumps employers' and employees' pension fund payments into statistics on black earnings even though many workers are eventually denied these funds.[161]

Table 2.8
SOUTH AFRICAN GOVERNMENT FIXED INVESTMENT
IN COMMUNITY SOCIAL AND PERSONAL SERVICES
(percent change from previous year at constant prices)

1972-78*	1976	1977	1978	1979
-2.3	-8.0	-8.6	-10.4	-2.3

*Compound annual rate.

Source: International Monetary Fund, South Africa: Recent
Economic Developments, 20 May 1980, p. 15.

In the postwar period South African Gross Domestic
Product increased more than 2,000 percent. Yet by 1975,
with an official poverty income level for a family of six
set at $127.65 per month, some 63.5 percent of black
families had monthly incomes of less than $92.[162] Blacks
comprised 71 percent of the population in 1976 and
accounted for 23 percent of national income, whereas the
16 percent of South Africans with white skin took home 67
percent of all earned wealth.[163] This extreme inequality
is a direct result of the partnership between the ruling
white coalition and western capital.

FOREIGN CAPITAL PENETRATION

Over R100 million in foreign investment was entering
South Africa every year of the immediate postwar period
and that rate did not slow down until the late 1950s. The
flight of capital in the early 1960s coincided with the
intensified African resistance discussed earlier.

The outflow of capital would have been greater
had it not been for controls. A change came in 1965,
and large amounts of capital began to enter the
country again. The trend of the capital movements
would appear to indicate a lack of confidence in the
political and economic stability of South Africa on
the part of the foreign investor during the years
immediately preceding and following 1960. The
subsequent demonstration of renewed confidence must
be attributed to the manifest strength and growth of
the South African economy and, perhaps, to the
realization that its government was unlikely to
capitulate to the forces of African nationalism.[164]

Other significant declines in private foreign investment occurred in 1973 (the Durban strikes) and 1976 (the Soweto uprising). The bulk of capital flight in these situations, however, consists of indirect investment, i.e., shares in the stock market and short term credit.[165] Direct foreign investment, while responsive to political turmoil, has proven more stable (Table 2.9).

This historical record shows that whereas some industrial capital has favored reforms that would benefit black workers, foreign finance capital in general has voted with its investments in favor of repression. In each case that capital fled due to political turmoil (early 1960s, 1973, 1976), state repression followed. When "stability" was restored, finance capital flowed back into the country.

The size of international loans, and rates at which they are loaned, act to strengthen or weaken the confidence of other capital. A recent example was in 1980 when Pretoria made two significant breakthroughs by securing a $50.8 million Eurobond and a $250 million syndicated credit involving big American banks. The rates for both credits were far better than Pretoria was able to get just a few years earlier when the turmoil of Soweto was still fresh in investors' minds.

It is not difficult to find the reason for U.S. and other western capital making substantial investments in South Africa. The rate of return on direct investment in the apartheid economy has tended to outstrip other areas of the world (Table 2.10). The sector that served as the original lure for foreign capital, mining, has sustained a rate of return for U.S. businessmen that far exceeds that of similar investments in other countries (Table 2.11).

Table 2.9
U.S. DIRECT INVESTMENT IN SOUTH AFRICA,
1970-1978 (millions of dollars)

1970	1972	1974	1976	1978
778	941	1,463	1,668	1,994

Source: Testimony of Abraham Katz, Deputy Assistant Secretary of Commerce for International Economic Policy and Research, before the House Subcommittee on Africa, 12 October 1979.

Table 2.10
AVERAGE RATE OF RETURN
ON U.S. DIRECT INVESTMENT ABROAD (percent)

Year	South Africa	Total, all areas
1960	17.3	10.9
1961	19.6	11.0
1962	19.9	11.4
1963	20.0	11.3
1964	18.6	11.4
1965	19.1	11.1
1966	20.6	10.4
1967	19.2	10.4
1968	17.3	10.8
1969	16.8	11.4
1970	16.3	11.0

Source: Ian Mackler, Pattern for Profit in Southern Africa (New York: Atheneum, 1975), p. 38; and Ruth First, et al, The South African Connection: Western Investment in Apartheid (Harmondsworth, England: Penguin, 1972), p. 336.

Table 2.11
RATE OF RETURN ON TOTAL BOOK VALUE,
U.S. FIRMS' DIRECT FOREIGN INVESTMENT
IN MINING AND SMELTING (percent)

	Canada	Latin America & Caribbean	South Africa
1953-57	8.3	10.4	25.7
1958-62	5.9	14.5	20.8
1963-67	9.9	19.9	43.3
1968-72	5.3	12.8	31.6

Source: Robert Pollin, "The Multinational Mineral Industry in Crisis," Monthly Review, April 1980, p. 28.

Not only was the rate of return in South Africa attractive to foreign capital, the absolute amount of earnings was also an important lure. In 1975 the major industrial powers were receiving the following yearly amounts from their corporate investments in the Republic of South Africa: United States--$450 million, France--$138 million, West Germany--$300 million, Britain--$975 million, EEC--$1,702 million.[166]

The importance of these investments is not solely quantitative. The largest and most influential banks and corporations of the major industrial powers dominate foreign investment in South Africa. The following chart, organized by country of incorporation, is only a partial

listing of the largest and most well-known transnational
corporations operating in South Africa, often in
partnership with South African capital and the apartheid
state.167
Japan: Akai, Bank of Tokyo, Canon, Fuji, Hitachi, Honda,
Japan Airlines, Mitsubishi, Nissan, Sanyo, Sony, Toyota,
Yamaha.
West Germany: AEG Telefunken, BASF, Bayer, BMW,
Daimler-Benz, Demag, Deutsche Bank, Hoechst, Kloeckner
and Co., Krupp, Siemens, the state-controlled STEAG
corporation, Volkswagen.
France: Aerospatiale, Banque D'Indochine, Citroen,
Credit Lyonnais, Dassault, Framatome, Michelin, Peugeot,
Renault, Rhone-Poulenc, Total.
Britain: Babcock and Wilcox, Barclays Bank, British
Airways, British Leyland, British Oxygen Ltd., British
Petroleum, British Steel Corp., Charter Consolidated,
Imperial Chemical Industries, Metal Box, Rio Tinto Zinc.
United States: Allis Chalmers, American Cyanamid, Black
and Decker, Bethlehem Steel, Boeing, Bristol Myers, Cat-
erpillar, Chase Manhattan Bank, Cities Service, Colgate
Palmolive, Control Data, Dow Chemical, Dupont, Eastman
Kodak, Firestone, Fluor, General Electric, General
Motors, Goodyear, IBM, ITT, Mobil, Motorola, National
Cash Register, Newmont Mining, Otis Elevator, Rockwell
International, Sperry Rand, Squibb, Standard Oil of New
Jersey, Tenneco, Union Carbide, Uniroyal, US Steel, W.R.
Grace, Xerox.
    Although penetrating nearly every sector of the
South African economy, these transnational corporations
focus crucial capital and technology in areas of
particular concern to the South African state:
transportation equipment, electrical machinery, metal
fabricating, armaments, nuclear technology, computers,
petroleum and other chemicals.168 The Managing Director
of Burroughs South Africa put it this way:

> We're entirely dependent on the U.S. The
> economy would grind to a halt without access to the
> computer technology of the West. No bank could
> function; the government couldn't collect its money
> and couldn't account for it; business couldn't
> operate; payrolls could not be paid. Retail and
> wholesale marketing and related services would be
> disrupted.169

    The U.S. stake is highly concentrated--13 companies
hold roughly three-fourths of all U.S. direct
investment--and it is centered in the most advanced
industrial sectors.170 The importance of this technology
cannot be underestimated. In hearings before the U.S.
House of Representatives, Professor John Suckling of

England's York University provided a detailed analysis of South African GNP as impacted by various factor inputs such as labor, domestic capital formation, foreign capital formation, etc. The findings:

> Foreign investment is the most significant factor in explaining the 1957-72 increase in GNP. Foreign investment has carried with it about two-thirds of the increase in GNP ascribed to technological changes (that is 3.2 out of 4.8 percent per annum). The most important factor contributing to the growth of GNP was "exogenous technical change."[171]

A 1978 study by Andrew Nagorski found that "56 percent of the South African economy depends on trade, 75 percent of which is with the West."[172] The influential Financial Times sums it up simply: "Foreign know-how is crucial to the country's economic future."[173]

CONCLUSION

This chapter has demonstrated a few basic points. South Africa's system of coerced-labor industrialization was a product of that country's integration into the world capitalist economy. As part of that process the U.S. economy developed links to South African state capitalism, with powerful members of America's corporate bourgeoisie acquiring a stake in the survival of their South African counterparts. This cross-national bourgeois "alliance" has reaped great material rewards for Whites and systematic impoverishment for Blacks.

This chapter provides a basis for the analysis of postwar U.S. policy presented in the next four chapters. As Poulantzas demonstrated in his book Political Power and Social Classes, the economic ties binding two countries do not directly cause government policy in all cases, but the economy is determinant in the sense that contradictions in the functioning of the economic system (class contradictions) pose problems that must somehow be dealt with by the political actors.[174] Having examined the nature of the South African economy, its class structure, and its integration with the West, we now possess an understanding of the root contradictions that constrain the behavior of U.S. policymakers.

The links between the process of capital accumulation in the two countries produced two types of constraints on U.S. policy, one structural and the other instrumental. The instrumental constraint is that many of America's largest banks and industrial corporations have a direct interest in preserving the status quo in South Africa. These bourgeois interests are either directly represented in the policy apparatus, or indirectly

represented via lobbying organizations and the funding of private policy studies.[175]
The structural constraints find expression in the fact that any policy that would disrupt capital accumulation in such a "friendly" and lucrative country as South Africa is simply a non-starter in the policy apparatus. Practically all policymakers are staunch defenders of the capitalist system, and even those who do not have a direct interest in the profitability of apartheid know that the kind of policies capable of fostering basic social change in South Africa would carry high political costs domestically.
If not pursued beyond this level our analysis would conclude that U.S. policy toward South Africa is without internal contradictions and there is little or no hope of fostering official action against apartheid. The following chapters show, however, that U.S. policy toward South Africa has become more contradictory over the years. The same need for access to labor and material resources that pushes transnational capital to invest in South Africa has also resulted in a growing U.S. stake in countries governed by regimes hostile to apartheid.
In addition, the postwar proletarianization of Blacks in South Africa and the United States, and the decolonization of Black Africa, swelled the ranks of those with some objective interest in the overthrow of apartheid.
In response to these changing circumstances the U.S. government developed a more contradictory policy: attempting to placate critics of apartheid by taking symbolic actions against that system, while at the same time striving to protect U.S. strategic and economic interests that are safeguarded by the white supremacists.

NOTES

1. J. Forbes Munro, Africa and the International Economy, 1800-1960 (London: J.M.Dent and Sons Ltd., 1976), p. 79.
2. Ibid.
3. Bernard Magubane, The Political Economy of Race and Class in South Africa (New York: Monthly Review Press, 1979), p. 103.
4. Robert V. Kubicek, Economic Imperialism in Theory and Practice: The Case of South African Gold Mining Finance, 1886-1914 (Durham, NC: Duke University Press, 1979), p. 40.
5. "During the fifty years from 1862 to 1912 the number of persons employed in mining had risen from practically zero to 325,000 and they formed the first large body of wage-paid workers in the country." D. Hobart Houghton, "Economic Development, 1865-1965," in Monica Wilson and Leonard Thompson, eds., The Oxford

History of South Africa, Vol. II (New York and Oxford: Oxford University Press, 1971), p. 19. For numbers of blacks and whites employed in the early gold mining industry see Robert H. Davies, Capital, State and White Labour in South Africa, 1900-1960 (Atlantic Highlands, NJ: Humanities Press, 1979), p. 70.

6. The mine owners' association (the Chamber of Mines) in a 1924 statement acknowledged the dependence on African labor: "it cannot be too strongly emphasized that the Witwatersrand gold mining industry has been made possible by the low cost of native labour, and that its existence on a large scale depends on obtaining an adequate supply of that labour." Cited in Stanley B. Greenberg, Race and State in Capitalist Development (New Haven and London: Yale University Press, 1980), p. 164.

7. See Davies, Capital, State and White Labour..., and Robert Davies, et al, "Class Struggles and the Periodisation of the State in South Africa," Review of African Political Economy, 7, September/December 1976.

8. Barbara Rogers, White Wealth and Black Poverty: American Investments in Southern Africa (Westport, CT: Greenwood Press, 1976), p. 94.

9. Kubicek, Economic Imperialism..., gives a detailed breakdown of percentage ownership held by Europeans and Americans in various mines.

10. For details on gold mining profits see Davies, Capital, State and White Labour..., p.46; and Frederick A. Johnstone, Class, Race and Gold(London: Routledge and Kegan Paul, 1976), p. 94.

11. Freda Troup, South Africa: An Historical Introduction (Harmondsworth, England: Penguin, 1975), p. 218.

12. Greenberg, Race and State..., p. 75.

13. Francis Wilson, "Farming, 1866-1966," in Wilson and Thompson, The Oxford History..., p. 117.

14. Greenberg, Race and State..., p. 391.

15. See W.A. de Klerk, The Puritans in Africa (Harmondsworth, England: Penguin, 1975), and T. Dunbar Moodie, The Rise of Afrikanerdom (Berkeley: University of California Press, 1975).

16. See Colin Bundy, "The Emergence and Decline of a South African Peasantry," African Affairs, 71, 285, October 1972; Sheila van der Horst, Native Labour in South Africa (London: Oxford University Press, 1942), and Francis Wilson, "Farming...."

17. George M. Frederickson, White Supremacy: A Comparative Study in American and South African History (New York and Oxford: Oxford University Press, 1981), p. 199.

18. For a comparison of white farmers' interests and industrialists' interests vis-a-vis African labor see Greenberg, Race and State..., Chapters 4, 5, 8 and 9.

19. Frederickson, White Supremacy..., p. 211.
20. Frederickson draws an important comparison to the situation in the United States: "Many white Americans were fully aware that the history of black craftsmanship and industrial employment under slavery made the black worker potentially competitive with the white." White Supremacy..., p. 211.
21. See Greenberg, Race and State..., Chapters 12, 13, and 14.
22. Ibid., p. 292.
23. Ibid., p. 293.
24. Martin Murray, "The Development of Capitalism in South African Agriculture: The Class Struggle and Capitalist State During the 'Phase of Transition'," unpublished manuscript.
25. Greenberg, Race and State..., p. 322.
26. W.M. Freund, "Race in the Social Structure of South Africa, 1652-1836," Race and Class, XVIII, 1, 1976; p. 53.
27. Greenberg, Race and State..., p. 386.
28. See Harold Wolpe, "Capitalism and cheap labour power in South Africa: from segregation to apartheid," Economy and Society, 1, 4, November 1972.
29. Munro, Africa and the International Economy..., p. 111.
30. The same process was responsible for impoverishing rural areas in Zimbabwe. See the author's "Operation Turkey Comes Home to Roost," Southern Africa, September 1980.
31. Magubane, Political Economy of Race and Class..., p.83.
32. Basil Davidson, Report on South Africa (London: Jonathan Cape, 1952), p.93.
33. Munro, Africa and the International Economy..., p. 112.
34. M. Harris, "Labor Migration Among the Mozambique Thonga: Cultural and Political Factors," Africa, 29(1), 1959.
35. Munro, Africa and the International Economy..., pp. 112-113.
36. Ibid., p. 140.
37. Ibid., p. 142.
38. Greenberg, Race and State..., p. 31.
39. Karl Marx, Capital: A Critique of Political Economy, Volume I (Chicago: Charles H. Kerr and Co., 1906), p. 102.
40. Ibid.
41. Arlene Wilson, "The Role of Gold in the International Monetary System," Congressional Research Service, 5 March 1980.

42. For background see: Timothy Green, The World of Gold (New York: Simon and Schuster, 1970); Roy W. Jastram, The Golden Constant: The English and American Experience, 1560-1976 (New York: John Wiley and Sons, 1977); and Thomas W. Wolfe, "Report on the Production, Marketing and Use of Gold, Including Recommendations on the Disposition of the U.S. Gold Stock," submitted to the U.S. Treasury Department, September 1976.

43. Wilson and Thompson, The Oxford History..., p. 13.

44. Munro, Africa and the International Economy..., p. 81.

45. Ibid., p. 106.

46. Ibid., p. 81.

47. Ibid., p. 106.

48. Ibid., p. 106.

49. Ibid., p. 106-7.

50. Ibid., p. 107.

51. Magubane, Political Economy of Race and Class..., p. 194.

52. Munro, Africa and the International Economy..., p. 87.

53. Ibid., p. 107.

54. Kubicek, Economic Imperialism..., p. 201.

55. Ibid., p. 111.

56. Ibid., Appendix A.

57. Ronald Robinson, "Non-European foundations of European Imperialism: sketch for a theory of collaboration" in Robert Owen and Bob Sutcliffe (eds.) Studies in the Theory of Imperialism (London: Longman, 1972), p. 118.

58. Arghiri Emmanuel, "White Settler Colonialism and the Myth of Investment Imperialism,' New Left Review, 73, May-June 1972, p. 40.

59. Robinson, "Non-European foundations...", p. 117.

60. Manfred Bienefeld and Duncan Innes, "Capital Accumulation and South Africa," Review of African Political Economy, 7, September-December 1976, p. 41.

61. Ward Anthony Spooner, United States Policy Toward South Africa, 1919-1941: Political and Economic Aspects (Ph.D. dissertation, St. Johns University, 1979), p. 70.

62. Edward W. Chester, Clash of Titans: Africa and U.S. Foreign Policy (Maryknoll, New York: Orbis Books, 1974), p. 60.

63. A useful description of the U.S. contribution to South African development, especially in mining, is contained in "Stevenson to the Bureau of Foreign and Domestic Commerce, May 10, 1922, South Africa-General, File #480.2," National Archives, Washington, D.C. Also see Mary W. Gary, Some Americans and Their Achievements in South Africa (Johannesburg: Kenneth B. Dickinson, 1926); Clarence Clendenen, et.al., Americans in Africa, 1865-1900 (Palo Alto: Stanford University Press, 1966);

and Clement T. Keto, American Involvement in South Africa, 1870-1915 (Ph.D. dissertation, Georgetown University, 1972).
64. Thomas J. Noer, Briton, Boer, and Yankee: The United States and South Africa, 1870-1914 (Kent State University Press, 1978), p. 44.
65. Ibid., p. 31.
66. Chester, Clash of Titans..., p. 59.
67. Ibid., p. 60.
68. Noer, Briton, Boer, and Yankee..., 31.
69. Ibid.
70. Ibid.
71. Ibid.
72. Ibid., p. 186.
73. Myra S. Goldstein, The Genesis of Modern American Relations with South Africa (Ph.D. dissertation, State University of New York at Buffalo, 1972), p.19.
74. Spooner, United States Policy..., p. 250.
75. Wolfe, "Report on the Production...," p. 6.
76. On this point see Spooner, United States Policy..., p. 39. Also see A. Dachs, Missionary Imperialism in Bechuanaland, 1826-1890 (Ph.D. dissertation, Cambridge University, 1968).
77. Noer, Briton, Boer, and Yankee..., p. 38.
78. Ibid., pp. 44-45.
79. Troup, South Africa..., p. 190.
80. Spooner, United States Policy..., p. 74.
81. Theodore Roosevelt to Henry White, 30 March 1896, cited in Noer, Briton, Boer, and Yankee..., p. 55.
82. For a detailed account see John H. Ferguson, American Diplomacy and the Boer War (Philadelphia: University Press, 1939).
83. Hay to Senator James McMillan, 3 July 1900, cited in Noer, Briton, Boer, and Yankee..., p. 74.
84. The early U.S. record on the race situation in South Africa is questionable not only with regard to Blacks. Following the Boer War the mine owners attempted to lower labor costs by importing indentured workers from China and paying them starvation wages. The Chinese received particularly bad treatment, proved too rebellious, and the plan was eventually scrapped. The United States at the time was experiencing serious anti-Asian violence in California.
"Certain members of the State Department, particularly those in the Far Eastern Affairs Division, felt America could use South Africa's problems with the Chinese to its diplomatic advantage. They argued that the mistreatment of the Chinese in South Africa and the brutal conditions in the mines made American discrimination against the Japanese seem minor by comparison. Washington ordered American consuls in South Africa to prepare detailed descriptions of the conditions of Chinese workers on the Rand. These were relayed by the State Department to the American ambassador in Tokyo to

illustrate the more moderate American policies." (Noer, Briton, Boer, and Yankee..., p. 131)
85. Ibid., p. 111.
86. Frederickson, White Supremacy..., p. 219.
87. Noer, Briton, Boer, and Yankee..., p. 112.
88. Troup, South Africa..., p. 174.
89. Ibid., p.175.
90. Noer, Briton, Boer, and Yankee..., p. 132.
91. Troup, South Africa..., p. 213.
92. See W. A. de Klerk, The Puritans in Africa...,
Chapter Eleven: "The Rise of Afrikaner Capitalism." Also
see Troup, South Africa..., pp. 236-238.
93. See Robert Davies, "The 1922 Strike on the Rand
and the Political Economy of South Africa" in P. Gutkind,
R. Cohen, and J. Copans, eds., Labour History in Africa
(Beverly Hills: Sage, 1978).
94. Troup, South Africa..., p. 243.
95. Ralph Horwitz, The Political Economy of South
Africa (New York: Praeger, 1967), p. 298.
96. Greenberg, Race and State..., p. 155.
97. See Brenda Bozzoli, "Origins, Development and
Ideology of Local Manufacturing in South Africa," Journal
of Southern African Studies, 1, 2, 1975.
98. Simon Clarke, "Capital, Fractions of Capital and
the State: 'Neo-Marxist' Analyses of the South African
State," Capital and Class, Summer 1978, p. 61.
99. Ann and Neva Seidman, South Africa and U.S.
Multinational Corporations (Westport, CT: Lawrence Hill
and Co., 1977), pp. 59-67.
100. Horwitz, The Political Economy..., p. 7.
101. Munro, Africa and the International Economy...,
p. 165.
102. Ibid., p. 166.
103. Ibid., p. 173.
104. Bienefeld and Innes, "Capital Accumulation...",
p. 47.
105. See the tables in Horwitz, The Political
Economy..., pp. 264-265.
106. Wilson and Thompson, The Oxford History... p.
36.
107. Munro, Africa and the International Economy...,
p. 172.
108. Consolidated Goldfields of South Africa report
cited by Bienefeld and Innes, "Capital Accumulation...",
p. 46.
109. Wilson and Thompson, The Oxford History..., p.
451.
110. Ibid., p. 36.
111. Ibid., p. 451.
112. Ibid., p. 455.

113. Ibid., p. 455.
114. Barbara Rogers, White Wealth and Black Poverty:
American Investments in Southern Africa (Westport,
Connecticut: Greenwood Press, 1976), p. 93.
115. Quoted in Spooner, United States Policy..., p.
194.
116. Ibid., p. 105.
117. Ibid., p. 103.
118. Munro, Africa and the International Economy...,
pp. 218-219.
119. Paul A. Baran and Paul M. Sweezy, Monopoly
Capital (New York: Monthly Review Press, 1966), pp. 235
and 244.
120. Spooner, United States Policy..., p. 178.
121. Ibid.
122. Ibid., p. 314.
123. Business Week, 6 June 1936, p. 44, cited in
ibid., p. 248.
124. Ibid., p. 180.
125. Ibid., p. 124.
126. Mira Wilkins, The Maturing of Multinational
Enterprise (Cambridge: Harvard University Press, 1974),
p. 87. The source for Mobil and Caltex controlling 38
percent of the South African petroleum market is The
Financial Mail, 22 July 1977.
127. Spooner, United States Policy..., p. 215; and
Seidman and Seidman, South Africa and U.S. Multinational
Corporations, p. 109.
128. Wilkins, The Maturing of Multinational
Enterprise, pp. 143-144; and Spooner, United States
Policy..., pp. 215, 219, 220, and 221.
129. Cited in Magubane, Political Economy of Race
and Class..., p. 197.
130. Michael Tanzer, The Race for Resources (New
York: Monthly Review Press, 1980), p. 178.
131. Wilkins, The Maturing of Multinational
Enterprise, p. 139.
132. Ibid., p. 140.
133. Spooner, U.S. Foreign Policy..., pp. 179-180.
134. Davies, et. al., "Class Struggle and
Periodisation of the State...", p. 26.
135. See Rene De Villiers, "Afrikaner Nationalism,"
in Wilson and Thompson, The Oxford History...; Hermann
Giliomee, "The National Party and the Afrikaner
Broederbond," in Robert M. Price and Carl G. Rosberg,
eds., The Apartheid Regime (Berkeley: Institute of
International Studies, 1980); de Klerk, The Puritans in
Africa...; and Moodie, The Rise of Afrikanerdom.
136. Brian Bunting, The Rise of the South African
Reich (Harmondsworth, England: Penguin, 1964), p. 94.

137. Cited in John Laurence, Race Propaganda and South Africa (London: Victor Gollancz Ltd., 1979), p. 141. For background on Ossewabrandwag see G.C. Visser, Traitors or Patriots? (South Africa: MacMillan, 1976); and Hans van Rensburg, Their Paths Crossed Mine (Johannesburg: CNA, 1956).
138. For background on the bantustan system see Barbara Rogers, Divide and Rule: South Africa's Bantustans (London: International Defence and Aid, 1980); Martin Legassick and Harold Wolpe, "The Bantustans and Capital Accumulation in South Africa," Review of African Political Economy, 7, September/December 1976; Donald Moerdijk, Anti-development: South Africa and its Bantustans (Paris: The Unesco Press, 1981); and Roger Southall, South Africa's Transkei: The Political Economy of an "Independent" Bantustan (New York: Monthly Review Press, 1983).
139. Cited in Harold Wolpe, "Capitalism and cheap labour-power in South Africa: from segregation to apartheid," Economy and Society, 4, November 1972, p. 434.
140. South African Council of Churches/Southern African Catholic Bishops Conference, Relocations: The Churches' Report on Forced Removals in South Africa (London: Catholic Institute for International Relations, 1984).
141. Troup, South Africa..., p. 329.
142. Houghton, "Economic Development...", p. 129.
143. Ibid.
144. Magubane, Political Economy of Race and Class..., Chapter 7; and de Klerk, The Puritans in Africa..., Chapter 11.
145. See Ruth Weiss, "The Role of Para-Statals in South Africa's Politico-Economic System" in John Suckling, Ruth Weiss, and Duncan Innes, The Economic Factor (Uppsala, Sweden: Africa Publications Trust, 1975).
146. Department of Foreign Affairs and Information, South Africa, 1980/1: Official Yearbook of the Republic of South Africa (Johannesburg: Chris van Rensburg Publications, 1980), pp. 80-81, and 368.
147. Weiss, "The Role of Para-Statals...", p. 64.
148. Ibid.
149. "Embargo Spurs S. Africa to Build Weapons Industry," Washington Post, 7 July 1981; and "Behind the Secrecy Shroud," Financial Mail, 11 September 1981.
150. "Embargo Spurs...."
151. Weiss, "The Role of Para-Statals...."
152. See Baran and Sweezy, Monopoly Capital; and James O'Connor, The Fiscal Crisis of the State (New York: St. Martin's Press, 1973).

153. For detailed data on these trends see Jeremy
Keenan, "The Nature of Economic Growth in South Africa:
Monopoly Capital and the Erosion of Black Living
Standards," paper read at the 12th Congress of the
Anthropological Society of South Africa, Grahamstown, 1-3
July 1981.
154. Ibid., p. 16. The yearly black unemployment
figures cited in the preceding paragraph are averages
based on Keenan's quarterly figures.
155. Ibid.
156. The Financial Times World Business Weekly, 6
July 1981, p. 32.
157. See Rogers, Divide and Rule...; and Moerdijk,
Anti-development....
158. Nedbank Group, South Africa: An Appraisal
(Johannesburg: Nedbank Group, 1977), p. 258.
159. Ibid., pp. 257-58.
160. Ibid., pp. 67-68.
161. Keenan, "The Nature of Economic Growth...."
162. Elizabeth Schmidt, Decoding Corporate
Camouflage: U.S. Business Support for Apartheid
(Washington, D.C.: Institute for Policy Studies, 1980),
p. 6.
163. Ibid.
164. Wilson and Thompson, The Oxford History..., pp.
39-40.
165. Ruth First, Jonathan Steele, and Christabel
Gurney, The South African Connection: Western Investment
in Apartheid (Harmondsworth, England: Penguin, 1972), p.
25.
166. Richard E. Bissel and Chester A. Crocker, eds.,
South Africa Into the 1980s (Boulder: Westview Press,
1979), p. 192.
167. For details on the operations of these TNCs,
see: Ann Seidman and Neva Makgetla, Activities of
Transnational Corporations in South Africa (New York:
U.N. Centre Against Apartheid, 1978); and U.N. Economic
and Social Council, Activities of Transnational
Corporations in Southern Africa: Impact on Financial and
Social Structures, Document E/C.10/39, 16 March 1978.
168. See Seidman and Seidman, South Africa and U.S.
Corporations...; Richard Leonard, Computers in South
Africa: A Survey of U.S. Companies (New York: The Africa
Fund, 1978); Karen Rothmyer, U.S. Motor Industry in South
Africa (New York: The Africa Fund, 1979); Ann Seidman and
Neva Makgetla, Transnational Corporations and the South
African Military-Industrial Complex (New York: U.N.
Centre Against Apartheid, 1979); and Truman Dunn, U.S.
Corporations in South Africa: A Summary of Strategic
Investments (New York: The Africa Fund, 1980).

169. Quoted in IBM in South Africa (New York: National Council of Churches, 1972), p. 3.
170. "Activities of Transnational Corporations in Southern Africa and the Extent of their Collaboration with the Illegal Regimes in the Area," U.N. Commission on International Corporations, 6 April 1977, p. 15.
171. U.S. Congress, House, United States Private Investment in South Africa (Washington, D.C.: Government Printing Office, 1978), p. 42.
172. Andrew Nagorski, "U.S. Options vis-a-vis South Africa" in Jennifer Seymour Whitaker, ed., Africa and the United States: Vital Interests (New York: in several South African gold mines, as well as stock in U.S. companies doing business in South Africa.
173. The Financial Times World Business Weekly, 6 July 1981, p. 32.
174. Nicos Poulantzas, Political Power and Social Classes (London: New Left Books, 1975).
175. The best example of a direct conflict of interest is Chester Crocker, Ronald Reagan's Assistant Secretary of State for African Affairs. Crocker's financial disclosure form shows that he and his wife own over 1,000 shares in several South African gold mines, as well as stock in U.S. companies doing business in South Africa.

3
U.S. Policy Toward
South Africa, 1948-1975

American policy toward South Africa and its
white-ruled neighbors during the pre-1975 period can be
characterized as "non-crisis policy."[1] Only once during
the period covered in this chapter did Washington take an
activist approach toward Africa: during the Congo crisis
of the early 1960s. Other than this one episode there
were no developments domestically or in southern Africa
to cause Washington to upgrade the region as a policy
priority. Because of the relatively free hand enjoyed by
U.S. policymakers, and the general consistency of the
policy, this chapter focuses on U.S. state activity,
providing only essential details on changes in southern
Africa and domestic U.S. politics.

There are two basic reasons for U.S. policy being
non-crisis policy during this period: 1) the domestic
political actors, state and non-state, who had an
interest in a more progressive policy toward South Africa
were lacking in economic and political power, and 2) the
white regimes of southern Africa remained relatively
stable throughout the period.

LACK OF IMPACT BY PROGRESSIVE FORCES

Traditionally there have been two sources of
progressive domestic opposition to U.S. relations with
the white regimes: liberal members of Congress and
private Africa support groups. Although these forces have
had little direct impact on U.S. policy, we must give
some consideration to the reasons for their
ineffectiveness.[2]

Early in the post-war period there were
antiapartheid groups advocating a more progressive policy
toward South Africa. The Council on African Affairs
(CAA), formed in 1937 by Paul Robeson and black
sociologist Max Yergan, was the group furthest to the
left ideologically. The following excerpt from a 1952
editorial is representative of the CAA's position that

racial oppression was part of a larger system of class
exploitation.

South Africa is part of President Truman's
"free world." Yes, dozens of America's biggest auto,
oil, mining and other trusts have highly profitable
holdings in that country.
Hence it is clear that in raising our voices
against the Malan regime we simultaneously strike a
blow at reactionary forces in our own land who seek
to preserve here, in South Africa, and everywhere
else the super profits they harvest from racial and
national oppression. United support for our
brothers' struggles in Africa is an integral part of
our task in achieving freedom for all Americans and
peace for the world.[3]

The anticapitalist content of the CAA's work was
sufficient to have it put on the Attorney General's list
of subversive organizations in 1948. The group's fate was
sealed by a cyclical process of government harrassment,
steady radicalization of its perspective, and defection
of its more moderate members.[4] The CAA folded in 1955
without having been more than an irritant to the policy
apparatus.
A group closer to the ideological center, and more
influential than the CAA, is the American Committee on
Africa (ACOA). Founded in 1953 by civil rights activists,
the ACOA has remained one of the most important
antiapartheid organizations in the United States.[5]
Through its literature, speaking tours, demonstrations,
and lobbying, ACOA has criticized U.S. corporate and
government ties to Pretoria.
ACOA's members and supporters have included such
influential figures as Hubert H. Humphrey, Walter
Reuther, Roy Wilkins, Martin Luther King Jr., Eleanor
Roosevelt, and A. Phillip Randolph. Although ACOA has had
a considerable impact on public opinion regarding South
Africa, its record on directly influencing U.S. policy
has been weak.
The two most detailed studies of the policy impact
of domestic antiapartheid groups found them to be largely
without influence. Based on extensive research, Anthony
Lake concluded: "With one or two exceptions, it cannot be
said that pressures from outside the government have ever
shaped either the general or specific course of U.S.
policy on South Africa."[6]
John Seiler's research on establishment
organizations such as the Carnegie Endowment and the
Council on Foreign Relations, as well as groups more
critical of U.S. policy, shows that with regard to
southern Africa "neither set of organizations had any
sustained impact on policy-making."[7]

Like the private antiapartheid groups, Congress has
also failed to shape policy toward South Africa. A
member's major concern is keeping his/her job, that is,
getting reelected. Since few Americans know or care much
about Africa, most members of Congress do not find it in
their interest to spend time on African issues. A veteran
Senate staffer reported in all seriousness that "Congress
doesn't know a damn or give a damn about Africa."[8]
     Constitutionally there are several ways for Congress
to influence U.S. policy toward South Africa:
legislation, hearings, appropriations, ad hoc pressures
on the Executive, and Senate clearance of treaties and
diplomatic appointments. During the period in question
none of these was used to great effect.
     It was not until 1971 that both houses voted on any
legislation regarding South Africa. The case in question,
an unsuccessful attempt by antiapartheid groups and
congressional liberals to revoke the South African sugar
quota, was more symbolic than real in its effects, but
the case provides a clear example of the international
class character of the conflict.
     In the midst of the 1971 effort by liberals to send
a message to Pretoria by terminating America's yearly
purchase of South African sugar, the State Department
sponsored a U.S. visit by Chief Gatsha Buthelezi. As
leader of the KwaZulu bantustan in Natal Province,
Buthelezi's constituency includes sugar farmers who would
have been hurt by repeal of the sugar quota. The Zulu
leader not only lobbied successfully against the effort
to repeal the sugar quota, he also called for a general
increase in U.S. investment in South Africa, a position
directly opposed to the divestment posture of American
antiapartheid groups.[9]
     Members of Congress place low value on Senate and
House Africa Subcommittee posts due to the small amount
of financial and staff resources accruing to these
subcommittees. The Senate African Affairs Subcommittee
was "altogether ineffective until 1975, when Senator
Richard Clark (D-IA) became its chairman."[10] A similar
weakness afflicted the House Africa Subcommittee until
1969 when Charles Diggs (D-MI) took over the
chairmanship. But even under Diggs' militant guidance the
subcommittee exercised only indirect influence on policy
via hearings and letters to the executive branch. No
piece of antiapartheid legislation introduced in either
Africa subcommittee has ever gone on to become law.
     The executive policy apparatus is not only insulated
from public input, internally it is very hierarchical
with only top officials having the power to significantly
alter existing policy. Lower and mid-level officials keep
their jobs by conserving current policies, not by
innovating.

Lesser officials have influence via their involvement in the formulation of policy reviews examining options for consideration by higher officials. Lower officials also have influence on the day-to-day implementation of policy. The author's own research, however, as well as the extant literature, reveals that on the question of South Africa lower officials do not deviate significantly from the norms set by top policymakers.[11]

Furthermore, Africa in general and southern Africa in particular have not only ranked low as policy priorities, they have also scored very low in terms of career potential for bureaucrats. As in Congress, State Department employees who are bright and ambitious shun Africa assignments for more important posts dealing with European affairs or East-West strategic questions. This is another example of how the international interests of America's big bourgeoisie (i.e., owners/managers of the major banks and transnational corporations) shape the structure and policies of the state. Areas of low capital penetration such as Africa are given low priority by the state, which in turn results in lack of attention and a failure to develop expertise.

The most important decisions setting the limits of U.S. policy toward South Africa are taken at the Assistant Secretary level and up. As the extensive research of Philip H. Burch, Jr. reveals, this top echelon of the policy apparatus has been dominated by members or associates of the big bourgeoisie.[12] The executive branch during the period in question was rife with top officials who had personal interests in companies exploiting the unfree black labor force of South Africa.[13] Hence it is not surprising that policymakers failed to question the most fundamental and most problematic aspect of U.S.-South African relations: the big U.S. corporate stake in apartheid. After years of detailed research, one conservative author concluded: "One policy area never became a matter of conflict for policymakers, despite sporadic rhetorical gestures: overall economic policy toward the region. Judging from available evidence, it was not even seriously considered."[14]

These instrumental constraints on the policymakers, combined with the broader structural constraints we elaborated in Chapter Two, create a situation in which some of the most important policy questions cannot even be raised within the policy apparatus.

STABILITY OF THE WHITE REGIMES

During most of the post-war era the white minority regimes of southern Africa were remarkably stable. Although the conflicts that exploded in the mid-1970s were slowly gestating during preceding decades, there were relatively few incidents stark enough to cause U.S. policymakers to surmise an impending power shift.

From the early 1960s on, there were guerrilla insurgencies in the Portuguese colonies but U.S. officials did not see these as a threat. The white settlers were well-armed; international efforts at sanctioning Portugal via the United Nations were blocked by the NATO powers; and U.S. policymakers had a very low opinion of the African nationalist forces.

There were sporadic episodes of violence in South Africa, usually consisting of state repression of mass demonstrations, but these only caused temporary lapses in business confidence and U.S. policymakers did not view them as regime-threatening conflicts. South African state violence made it more difficult for the U.S. government to maintain open and cordial relations, but the level of conflict never reached a point where policymakers would consider breaking official ties.

There was an important process underway in some white-ruled states, however, that was laying the foundation for future revolutionary change. The white settler classes in Angola, Mozambique, and Rhodesia had developed economic and political structures that blocked the development of a black business class, and prevented an orderly transition to the type of neocolonialism predominant in the rest of Africa.

The U.S. government, in addition to lacking experience in colonial transfers of power, was confronted with a unique class configuration: the settler regimes were friendly to western corporate and security interests but by their intransigence toward power-sharing with Blacks, they were plowing fertile ground for black radicalization.

One faction of the U.S. policy establishment (people like John F. Kennedy, Chester Bowles, and G. Mennen Williams) recognized this dilemma. The following statement by Williams, Kennedy's Assistant Secretary of State for Africa, is representative of this perspective. Here referring to Ian Smith's regime in Rhodesia, Williams noted:

> Since the regime's policies and actions are designed to perpetuate minority rule, they would create exactly the kind of situation in which the Communists could greatly extend their influence in Southern Rhodesia . . . policies looking toward social advancement, responsible majority rule and political stability--are far more effective weapons

against Communism, in the long run, than any of the repressive methods the Smith regime might devise.[15]

The long-standing integration of the settler classes with western interests in the region constituted a structural blockage against a policy of reform. To force the white settlers into power-sharing with moderate Blacks would have required a concerted effort by western officials to develop public and elite support for such a policy. Given the fact that U.S. corporations and the national security state had a considerable stake in the settler regimes, reform-oriented politicians would have had to make massive expenditures of political capital in order to check the polarization occurring in the settler societies.

The peculiarities of the accumulation process linking southern Africa and the United States produced a political configuration that prevented forward-looking imperial thinkers from implementing anything more than a short-term strategy. By the time radical insurgencies in Angola, Mozambique, and Rhodesia reached the regime-threatening proportions necessary to gain official American attention, the conflicts had become highly polarized and thus were more resistant to U.S. solutions.

THE TRUMAN ADMINISTRATION, 1945-1953

While the Truman administration was preoccupied with the cold war in Europe, there were important changes taking place in South Africa that presaged the future dilemma of U.S. policy. There were several trends in the early post-war period which, when traced down through the years, reveal how U.S. policy reached its current state of crisis.

The first trend has been steady polarization over the issue of apartheid. As the South African state hardened its rule under National Party leadership, the mass opposition, gaining international support from socialist states and newly emerging nations of the Third World, moved away from accomodationist politics toward a more confrontational strategy. This polarization did not produce sufficient conflict, however, to interfere with another trend: the growing involvement of U.S. capital and agencies of the U.S. state.

The low wages, rich natural resources, and modern infrastructure of the South African economy were powerful attractions for corporate giants of American banking and industry. In addition, South Africa's strategic facilities and solidly pro-West stance provided fertile ground for an American security apparatus that was rapidly developing an imperial role in world affairs. These corporate and security interests were dominant forces in shaping U.S. foreign policy.

     South African political turmoil duing the Truman
years went largely unnoticed in the United States. In
1946, the largest black mineworkers' strike in South
African history shut down 32 of the Rand's 45 mines.[16]
During the war years the black mineworkers' union had
been following the prevailing leftist strategy of labor
peace to avoid weakening the war effort against fascism.
But the combination of depressed living conditions and an
optimistic appraisal of international developments,[17]
brought some 75,000 miners out on strike. Within days
"the police cordoned off the individual mine compounds,
isolating the mines from each other and the miners from
their leaders and drove them down the mines back to work,
often with batons and rifles. Thirteen strikers were
killed and 1,200 injured, and fifty trade union officials
and leading Communists were put on trial."[18]
     The impact of the mineworkers' strike was limited
mainly to South Africa. Another struggle, however,
centering on the country's Indian population, was to have
ramifications that marked "a new phase of international
involvement in South African race relations."[19]
     In 1946, by passing the Asiatic Land Tenure and
Indian Representation Act, Pretoria violated a
long-standing agreement with the government of India to
eschew discriminatory legislation against its Indian
population. The "Ghetto Act," as it was promptly dubbed
by opponents, sharply restricted the property rights of
Asians and provided a limited franchise for the Indian
population.
     In opposing this legislation the South African
Indian Congress not only mounted a passive resistance
campaign in which some 2,000 people were arrested, they
also sent delegations to India and the United Nations.
The bitter struggle that ensued at the United Nations
produced the first open rift among the Commonwealth
nations. It was also the first in a long series of
conflicts that put the United States and its major
European allies on the side of Pretoria against the
emerging third world bloc and the communist states.
     Debate hinged on the question of the extent to which
the U.N. Charter allows for outside involvement in the
domestic affairs of a member state. South Africa, backed
by France, England, and the United States, cited Article
2(7) which abjures any right "to intervene in matters
which are essentially within the domestic jurisdiction"
of a member state.
     But as Pretoria's critics hastened to point out, the
Charter explicitly states that this principle of
non-interference should not inhibit the U.N.'s Chapter
VII obligations to uphold international peace and
security. Proponents of action against South Africa also
stressed Articles 55 and 56, which authorize the U.N. to
actively promote "universal respect for, and observance
of, human rights and fundamental freedoms for all without

distinction as to race, sex, language or religion."
The controversy between India and South Africa
dragged on for years. The U.S. government supported
direct negotiations rather than U.N. involvement.
Washington's position on this issue was not particularly
costly in itself. When contrasted to other situations,
however, such as the Korean War and the Congo crisis
where the United States tried to wrap its interventions
in the cloak of U.N. legitimacy, this stress on
non-interference with regard to South Africa proved
damaging to U.S. credibility.

Another episode at the United Nations during this
period has been ignored by diplomatic historians but
reveals a basic component of U.S. policy. The U.S.
position regarding South Africa's presence in Namibia
("South West Africa") has been more in line with majority
U.N. opinion than has the U.S. position on South Africa
itself. This has been due largely to the different legal
conditions surrounding Namibia's mandate status. As early
as 1950-51 the United States voted for resolutions aimed
at facilitating a South African withdrawal from the
territory. When it came to the question of Namibian
representatives addressing the United Nations, however,
Washington played a role that can only be termed
obstructionist.

In early 1952, Namibian chiefs were invited to
address the U.N.'s Trusteeship Committee but Pretoria
refused to issue travel documents. A resolution was
hammered out expressing the U.N.'s regret over South
Africa's lack of cooperation, but the United States
abstained.

When Reverend Michael Scott, a human rights activist
in Namibia, sought to address the United Nations in place
of the chiefs, the U.S. Ambassador to the United Nations
opposed the move. When Rev. Scott was invited to address
the body anyway, Washington delayed issuing a visa. Only
after Rev. Scott was named an advisor to India's U.N.
delegation, and domestic groups such as the NAACP lobbied
in favor of his admittance, did Washington issue the
visa. Even then the U.S. government confined Rev. Scott
to the vicinity of U.N. headquarters, and enjoined him
against "extracurricular, subversive or propaganda
activities or agitation."[20]

As we will see in later sections, this particular
episode forms part of a larger pattern: Through various
devices, the U.S. state blocks the interaction of those
forces who side with the black majority, and facilitates
contact between those South Africans and Americans who
favor the maintenance of white minority rule.

The research of William R. Cotter and Thomas Karis
reveals that the U.S. government has been highly
selective in its visa policies toward South Africa.[21]
South African leftists have often been denied admission,
had their passports mysteriously lost, or been restricted

to within 25 miles of the United Nations.[22] Yet South
African business leaders and government officials have
had ready access to the people and government of the
United States. Even South African military and
intelligence officers, despite the U.N. arms embargo,
have been able to visit their American counterparts.[23]
     More important is official U.S. acquiescence to the
highly restrictive visa policies of Pretoria. Although
South Africa exercises tight control of its citizens'
travel privileges and has denied entry visas to scores of
Americans, "the State Department has failed to take
effective action."[24]
     In 1948 the National Party won its first
parliamentary majority. Within the next five years the
ultraconservative Afrikaner nationalists succeeded in
implementing a legislative revolution. The myriad of laws
passed in those early years divided and controled the
population to an unprecedented degree.[25] The sharp swing
to the right by the South African state elicited
increased militancy by the opposition.
     Ever since its formation in 1912, the African
National Congress (ANC), the oldest and most popular
opposition movement in South Africa, had relied on
peaceful methods to pressure the government.[26] In 1949,
largely due to the influence of its younger members who
were impatient with the tactics of passive protest, the
ANC adopted a more militant policy of confrontation,
using strikes, boycotts, and civil disobedience. During
the Defiance Campaign of 1952--in opposition to new,
stricter racial legislation--some 8,000 protestors were
jailed.
     It was in response to the Defiance Campaign that
white and black Americans active in the civil rights
movement formed a group called Americans for South
African Resistance, later to become known as the American
Committee on Africa. Yet there is nothing in the
documentary record to indicate that U.S. policymakers
were worried by the fact that South African society was
polarizing due to the program of the National Party: a
party that just a few years earlier had supported the
Nazi war effort.[27]
     As the South African state was moving to the right
and the major opposition movement, the African National
Congress, was becoming increasingly militant, the U.S.
state was expanding its ties to South Africa. On 23 March
1949 the United States was one of the first nations to
upgrade its diplomatic representation in South Africa to
the ambassadorial level.[28] The Truman administration
permitted top South African military officials to consult
with counterparts in the Pentagon.[29] Pretoria
reciprocated during the Berlin airlift of 1949 by being
one of the first countries to send its air force to
participate.

In 1950 the South African military again assisted
the United States, this time in Korea. The fighter planes
and crews Pretoria contributed were not needed militarily
but they added substance to America's diplomatic
camouflage that this was not a unilateral inetervention.
Declassified secret documents reveal that on 15
November 1950 the Joint Chiefs of Staff made the
following assessment: "in event of global war, there
would be both offensive and defensive roles for the South
African armed forces . . . the ability of the Union of
South Africa to defend itself or to participate in the
defense of the area of which it is a part is of
importance to the security of the United States."[30]
In 1951 Washington approved the Mutual Defense
Assistance Act, providing reimbursable military
assistance to Pretoria. South African leaders had their
sights set on formal inclusion in the NATO alliance but
the western governments, despite close military
cooperation, politically could not afford an open pact
with Pretoria.
It was during the Truman administration that the
Central Intelligence Agency (CIA) began its long and
cordial relationship with the South African secret
police. Pretoria's intelligence apparatus was viewed by
the CIA as a "reliable, FBI-style operation."[31]
One of the most important institutional linkages
binding key sections of the U.S. state to the South
African status quo centered on nuclear development. In
order to build up its strategic arsenal Washington
required large, dependable supplies of uranium. British
and U.S. authorities began negotiations with their South
African counterparts immediately after World War II. This
resulted in an agreement to provide capital and nuclear
expertise in exchange for a monopsony on South African
uranium oxide. All the capital requirements for expanding
South African production (R66 million by 1956) were met
in the United States and England.[32]
Over the next several decades, the U.S.
Export-Import Bank, in coordination with the White House,
the Atomic Energy Commission, the Pentagon, large
industrial corporations, and major banks, allocated
nearly a billion dollars worth of credit to expand South
African uranium production.[33] Not only did this program
further integrate the interests of large U.S. banks and
industrial corporations with their counterparts in South
Africa, it also gave the U.S. national security apparatus
an important stake in the maintenance of the South
African status quo.[34]
South Africa as an issue in itself was of little
concern to the Truman administration. American policy was
determined by larger considerations of the Cold War,
relations with Europe, and the need to expand
opportunities for American business. Waldemar Nielsen
points out that "the Truman foreign policy was bold,

innovative, and effective--but not on African
questions."[35] It was not until the latter years of the
Eisenhower administration that circumstances would
require a more direct consideration of the political
ramifications of apartheid.

THE EISENHOWER ADMINISTRATION, 1953-1961

American policy under Eisenhower remained much as it
had been under Truman. Only in its final years did the
Eisenhower administration make a slight shift to a more
contradictory policy. There is no evidence that anything
resembling a serious policy review on South Africa ever
took place during the Eisenhower years.
    With U.S. trade and investment steadily increasing,
the Commerce Department in 1953 began a new
service--regular reports on the South African
economy--for American businesses interested in South
Africa. In addition to reporting on South Africa's
impressive natural resources and rapid growth, these
market surveys advised businessmen to take cognizance of
the political tension produced by that country's system
of racial inequality.
    Military ties continued along the lines laid down
during Truman's term in office. A declassified memorandum
from the Joint Chiefs of Staff to the Secretary of
Defense, dated 11 December 1956, reads in part:

> The United States does have an interest in
> developing a military capability in the South
> African Air Force which would be immediately
> available for use in collective defense, in the
> event of Communist aggression. Accordingly, it is
> recommended that the Union of South Africa be
> encouraged to purchase military aircraft, including
> fighter-bomber types, from the United States.[36]

A major antisubmarine exercise ("Operation Cape") in
1959 included American, British, French, Portuguese, and
South African naval forces. Ships of the U.S. Navy made
regular use of South African port facilities.
    On at least one occasion--a 1955 visit of the U.S.
aircraft carrier Midway--there was domestic opposition to
U.S.-South African military ties. The NAACP, supported by
opinion makers such as the New York Times and Commonweal,
argued that unless the U.S. Navy could guarantee equal
treatment of black and white sailors while on shore leave
in South Africa, the Midway visit should be cancelled.
The Navy rejected these demands.

If the United States government attempted to
accede to the NAACP demand, it would have been put
in the incongruous position of demanding of Cape
Town, South Africa, something it could not demand of
the Midway's home port of Norfolk, Virginia, or of
other naval installations at Charleston, New
Orleans, and other locations in the South.[37]

Another link strengthened during the Eisenhower
years involved America's burgeoning space program. In
1957 Washington and Pretoria reached agreement on the
establishment of a radio tracking station in South
Africa. The following year a camera optical tracking
station was established, and in 1960 a general agreement
was signed covering these two earlier facilities as well
as a deep space probe radio tracking station.[38]
Part of the agreement was that these facilities
would not hire Blacks. Until domestic pressure in the
mid-1970s forced a U.S. withdrawal from these tracking
stations, they constituted an important material interest
of U.S. national security planners.
Although nuclear relations between the two countries
had begun with South Africa playing a limited role as raw
material supplier, the United States was soon assisting
Pretoria in the development of its own nuclear power
industry. The main objective of the U.S.-South African
Agreement for Cooperation Concerning Civil Uses of Atomic
Energy, signed in 1957, was the construction of the
SAFARI-1 research reactor.
The initial agreement and subsequent amendments
provided for the training of South African personnel and
the sale of American power reactors and large quantities
of enriched uranium.[39] The agreement, subsequently
extended to the year 2007, facilitated contracts for
Allis-Chalmers, Gulf Oil, Foxboro, U.S. Steel,
Kerr-McGee, and many other U.S. corporations. Also
integrated into the program were important research
institutions such as the Massachusetts Institute of
Technology, New York University, the University of
Illinois, Rochester University, the Reno Research Center,
and the Argonne, Brookhaven, and Oak Ridge National
Laboratories. "In effect, the entire range of US research
and development on nuclear power was made available to
the South Africans for SAFARI-1."[40]
Dr. A.J.A. Roux, President of the South African
Atomic Energy Board, summed up nearly three decades of
cooperation: "We can ascribe our degree of advancement
today in large measure to the training and assistance so
willingly provided by the United States of America during
the early years of our nuclear programme.[41]

The U.S.-South Africa nuclear relationship provides a good indicator of how much more difficult the U.S. "straddle" on South Africa has grown over the years. Because the initial motivation behind U.S. nuclear cooperation was military, and due to the gradual isolation of the white settler regime, it was inevitable that Pretoria would take an interest in the weapons potential of its budding nuclear power industry. The Pentagon was not inimical to these aspirations of a trusted ally.

In 1950 South African scientists were allowed to participate in the monitoring of U.S. nuclear weapons tests in the South Atlantic.[42] That such cooperation could have been carried out without causing a stir, whereas today such a venture would be practically impossible, testifies to how much more contradictory U.S. policy has become over the years.

Planners in the U.S. national security apparatus may have foreseen that military intervention on the side of Pretoria in a future conflict would be politically costly, and therefore facilitated the development of sufficient South African weaponry to deter any aggressor. The authors of the most detailed study of South Africa's nuclear development draw the following conclusion.

The record of full technical cooperation, plentiful supplies of equipment and material, the training of South Africa's nuclear scientists and co-operation on highly sensitive projects related to nuclear weapons testing all indicate that the US Government, through at least some of its agencies, has indeed been pursuing a policy of total collaboration in the nuclear sphere, military as well as civilian.[43]

The first divergent steps in the U.S. policy straddle occurred in the final years of the Eisenhower administration. With a growing number of African countries gaining political independence, it became less practical for Washington to deal with Africa indirectly through the European powers. In 1958 the State Department initiated a separate Africa Bureau. This bureau, though certainly one of the weakest in the policy apparatus, added another bureaucratic voice to the "left" side of the internal debate over South Africa. Because the staff of the Africa Bureau, like colleagues in International Organization Affairs, have more contact with African leaders, they are more sensitive to the political costs of official friendship with Pretoria.

Like any agency, the Africa Bureau tends to favor policies that maintain smooth relations with its "clients". Though not capable of being captured by its constituency like many other government bureaucracies, the Africa Bureau has taken positions on South Africa

that are consistently more liberal than those of the
business-oriented departments (Treasury, Commerce) and
the national security apparatus.
    Another action in 1958 that strengthened the
antiapartheid side of the U.S. policy straddle came on
the perennial U.N. resolution castigating South Africa
for its racial policies. Previously the American
delegation at the United Nations had abstained on
resolutions concerning South Africa's internal affairs.
But on this occasion Washington dropped the
non-interference rationale and went along with the
majority. The vote was a compromise, however, in that
American objections to stronger language "condemning"
South Africa resulted in this phrase being deleted from
the resolution.
    Judging from the official rationale for the change
in the U.S. voting pattern, it is clear that developments
in domestic race relations were as much a factor as
conditions in South Africa. "Much of the announcement
declaring the American position was devoted to the race
problems in the United States and explaining how the
government was moving to a multiracial society without
discrimination."[44]
    These were the first subtle signs of how the
breakdown of the old racial order, domestically and
internationally, was setting U.S. policy on two divergent
tracks: one aimed at making the U.S. government "look
good" on the race question, the other linked to the
corporate need for profits and the national security
state's need for dependable allies in the war against
communism. During Eisenhower's term of office twenty-two
African countries gained their independence and took
seats in the United Nations. These changes could not be
ignored if Washington hoped to secure the cooperation of
these states on other issues.
    Domestically, even a Republican president with few
political debts to the black community could not ignore
the gains being made against racial oppression. The
Supreme Court's 7 May 1954 ruling in Brown v. The Board
of Education struck an important blow against racial
segregation by declaring that separate educational
facilities are inherently unequal. The Civil Rights Act
of 1957 contained provisions for protecting black voting
rights, established the Civil Rights Commission to
investigate voter discrimination complaints, and laid the
groundwork for a civil rights division in the Department
of Justice. The boycotts, sit-ins, and voter registration
drives of the 1950s began to have an impact on local
politics.[45] Although there was considerable backlash from
white racists, by the end of the Eisenhower
administration the domestic racial order was cracking.

The emerging U.S. policy straddle became more contradictory during the final year of the Eisenhower administration in direct response to intensified conflict in South Africa. On 21 March 1960 South African police fired on Africans protesting the pass system. At Sharpeville some sixty-seven persons were killed and nearly two hundred were wounded. At Langa township the police killed two and wounded forty-nine.[46]

The next few weeks saw mass demonstrations, some numbering in the tens of thousands, in various parts of the country. The government declared a state of emergency; the ANC and PAC were banned; thousands of activists were arrested and many fled into exile. In early April an attempt was made on the life of Prime Minister Verwoerd.[47] This turmoil created a perception of generalized crisis to most outsiders, but it was the massacre at Sharpeville that became the focus of international attention.

In some ways the Sharpeville affair seemed to have more profound effects beyond the country's borders than in South Africa itself. Already the target of European and American liberal criticism and of the Afro-Asian block, on account of its policy on apartheid, the South African government now found itself even more unpopular.[48]

This was to be one of the very few cases when events in South Africa caused a shift in U.S. policy. A State Department spokesman announced that although "the United States, as a matter of practice, does not ordinarily comment on the internal affairs of governments with which it enjoys normal relations," in this case it was necessary to express official regret over "the tragic loss of life resulting from the measures taken against the demonstrators in South Africa."[49]

Being careful to point out the difference between public discussion of South Africa's internal affairs and active intervention, the State Department came out in favor of U.N. Security Council consideration of recent events in South Africa. This was in contrast to NATO allies England and France who feared that a dangerous precedent was being set by U.N. action regarding the internal affairs of a member state. On 1 April 1960 the Security Council passed by a vote of 9 to 0 (England and France abstaining) Resolution S/4300, which not only "deplored" recent events in South Africa but also called on Pretoria to abandon its policy of apartheid. The U.S. government confined its response to the Sharpeville massacre to participation in this multilateral gesture. There is no evidence that U.S. policymakers considered taking any bilateral punitive actions.[50]

At the time of this intensified racial violence in South Africa, the U.S. Congress was haggling over the Civil Rights Act of 1960, and many cities in the South and Northeast were experiencing antidiscrimination protests. Many southern congressmen and conservative periodicals were quick to equate the State Department's criticism of South Africa with Washington's "meddling" in domestic racial affairs.[51]

At the other end of the spectrum on this issue, several groups faulted Washington for not going beyond verbal criticism of Pretoria. AFL-CIO President George Meany suggested that the United States should push for a full U.N. investigation of the Sharpeville murders.[52] Groups such as the National Council of Churches, Americans for Democratic Action, and the American Committee on Africa called for punitive measures against Pretoria such as cutting back on trade and investment.[53] Neither southern congressmen nor antiapartheid activists, however, possessed enough political clout to directly affect the official U.S. response to Sharpeville.

Although the State Department went on record in the United Nations as being opposed to apartheid, other powerful Americans were helping the National Party regime overcome the setbacks caused by unrest. Sharpeville and the events immediately following it shook investor confidence so badly that "South Africa faced a balance-of-payments crisis more severe than any experienced since 1932."[54]

In just six weeks the Johannesburg stock exchange registered a decline of nearly one billion dollars.[55] Between January 1960 and May 1961 gold and foreign exchanges reserves dropped by more than half.[56] The government took drastic steps to restrict the outflow of capital. Pretoria widened foreign exchange controls, strengthened import restrictions, and placed limitations on bank loans to finance stock exchange dealings.[57]

By November, 1960, U.S. companies began to express their old confidence in South Africa's future stability and profitability. Plans for expanded investment by General Motors and others became known. And after a series of economic measures taken by Pretoria in May, 1961, American capital came flowing in again. During 1961, U.S. companies increased their investments in South Africa by $23 million. Dollar loans of $150 million were received from the International Monetary Fund, World Bank and affiliates, Chase Manhattan and First National City Banks, and other unidentified private sources, including ten other U.S. banks. By 1962, South Africa's economic crisis was over.[58]

The Eisenhower administration's criticism of
Pretoria at the United Nations had far less impact than
the activities of corporate actors and agencies of the
national security state. Support for the U.N.'s
disapproval of South Africa's internal conditions did
mark a departure from previous U.S. policy, but it had
little effect compared to that of the military
cooperation, nuclear agreements, trade, and investment.
The Eisenhower administration's response to Sharpeville
constituted another step down a forking road: growing
symbolic opposition to apartheid, coupled with powerful
corporate and state actors wedded to the status quo.

THE KENNEDY ADMINISTRATION, 1961-1963

The presidential campaign of 1960 was the first in
which Africa played a role. Whereas Eisenhower had seemed
indifferent to African affairs, Kennedy displayed a
personal interest in the the changes sweeping the
continent. As early as 1957 Kennedy had blasted the
Eisenhower administration for its policy of supportihg
the colonial powers against Africa's legitimate
aspirations for independence. In a 2 July 1957 Senate
speech "which was to have a profound impact," Kennedy
drew attention to basic contradictions in U.S. policy
toward the developing world.[59]

The speech amounted to far more than a partisan
blast. It was a fundamental criticism of the ideas
and judgements which through the whole postwar
period had governed American policy in those
situations where concrete economic and strategic
interests and alliance commitments had to be weighed
against American political interests in the emerging
areas of the world where independence and human
freedom were the issues.[60]

In words that would prove relevant to later crises
in southern Africa, Kennedy criticized American attempts
to straddle a polarizing political struggle. He
characterized this policy as

tepid encouragement and moralization to both
sides, cautious neutrality on all real issues, and a
restatement of our obvious dependence on our
European friends, our obvious dedication
nevertheless to the principles of self-
determination, and our obvious desire not to become
involved. We have deceived ourselves into believing
that we have thus pleased both sides and displeased
no one with this head in the sand policy--when in
truth, we have earned the suspicion of all.[61]

In charging that Eisenhower's policy toward the
Algerian independence war amounted to support for
colonialism, Kennedy utilized a line of reasoning that
was to become a mainstay of the antiapartheid movement.

No matter how complex the problem posed by the
Algerian issue may be, the record of the United
States in this case is as elsewhere a retreat from
the principles of independence and anti-colonialism
regardless of what diplomatic niceties, legal
technicalities, or even strategic considerations are
offered in its defense.[62]

Kennedy realized that African nationalism would play
an important role in future developments, and that some
accomodation should be made with non-communist
independence movements. "The strongest force in the world
is the desire for national independence. . . . That is
why I am eager that the United States back nationalist
movements, even though it embroils us with our friends in
Europe."[63]

To a large extent, Kennedy's position on Africa
foreshadowed that of the early Carter administration.
Both realized that the structures of class rule in Africa
were changing, and maintenance of American interests
would require adjustments in Washington's class alliances
on the continent. In both cases the general goals of
liberals and conservatives did not differ. Kennedy, like
Carter, made it clear that he favored a policy more
sensitive to African realities because it seemed more
likely to prevent the growth of communism and protect
American economic and security interests.

The anticommunist motivation behind Kennedy's policy
toward southern Africa is illuminated by his
administration's response to the 1961 nationalist
rebellion in northern Angola. The brief African uprising
was met by a wave of brutal repression by Portuguese
colonial forces.[64] Waldemar Nielsen cites estimates of
75,000 to 150,000 African deaths by burning,
machine-gunning, and bombing during a six-week period.[65]

When the issue came up for discussion in the United
Nations it was Kennedy, with support from liberal
staffers such as Bowles, Williams, and Adlai Stevenson,
who decided to acquiesce to third world demands for
verbal condemnation of Portuguese behavior. As John
Seiler points out, however, this decision "took place en
vacuo, with no serious policy analysis preceding it, and
with no serious attention to the dynamics of political
response either in Portugal or in her African
colonies."[66]

A substantive policy review was begun several months later. It was prompted, not by the slaughter of Africans at the hands of the Portuguese, but by reports of Soviet assistance to Angolan exiles in Europe. Upon learning that Angolan students were being offered scholarships in communist countries, Kennedy immediately took action. National Security Action Memorandum #60 ordered a full report on the situation. It also authorized U.S. diplomats in Europe to offer the Angolans scholarships and other financial inducements to dissuade them from taking up residence in the East. Kennedy appointed General Maxwell Taylor to oversee an interagency task force to ensure the implementation of NSAM 60.

This episode captures a key element of U.S. policy toward settler colonialism in southern Africa. An activist response by Washington was prompted by the threat of Soviet involvement rather than by the injustice being perpetrated on the Angolan people. This is a consistent pattern in U.S. policy: African suffering evokes words of sympathy, Soviet involvement elicits substantive action.

A declassified document of the Kennedy years provides insight into the underlying premises of the liberal Democratic strategy in Africa. Entitled "Africa: Guidelines for United States Policy and Operations," this 1963 study notes the importance of enunciating an official stand against racial oppression at home and abroad.

> The most helpful things we could to to enhance our image and obtain the friendship of the African peoples are (a) to make our commitment to freedom in Africa clear without peradventure of doubt in such cases as Angola, Algeria and South Africa; and (b) to move more quickly to solve our problem of according dignity and equal opportunity to our own African-descended population.[67]

The authors of the document posit the encouragement of "free enterprise economics" as a basic objective of U.S. policy in Africa. They acknowledge the economic role of the state in most African countries and note that keeping these nations within the capitalist orbit will depend on the "gradual emergence or growth of a middle class capable of creating and managing a private enterprise sector in a mixed economy."[68] This would not only help ensure U.S. access to the workers and material resources of Africa, it would also facilitate another objective: "Denial to the Sino-Soviet Bloc of military bases, and to the maximum extent practicable, of military influence in any African country."[69] The document ascribes to Africa the dubious distinction of being "probably the greatest open field of manuever in the worldwide competition between the [communist] bloc and

the non-Communist world."[70]
     As the liberal Kennedy administration was to
demonstrate in other areas of foreign policy, its
commitment to cold war competition with the Soviets was
as strong as any Republican administration.[71] Kennedy's
recognition of third world nationalism was a tactical
difference, subordinated to bipartisan unity on the need
to prevent the erosion of capitalist relations of
production.
     There is also a little known aspect of Kennedy's
congressional career that helps put his African rhetoric
into perspective. Between 1956 and 1960 Kennedy served as
the chairman of the Senate's Africa Subcommittee. While
he held this position the subcomittee did not hold a
single hearing, and met only a few times.[72] "Kennedy did
try for political capital from his subcommittee post
during his 1960 Presidential campaign, referring often to
the need for a deeper moral commitment by the U.S. to
African decolonization, but these references were general
in language and skirted Southern African issues."[73]
     South Africa remained an issue of low priority
throughout the Kennedy years. Conflict in South Africa
and in the surrounding territories had not reached the
levels necessary to evoke an active American response.
Kennedy's foreign policy team was preoccupied with events
in Cuba, Berlin, Southeast Asia, and the Congo.
     There was only one issue involving South Africa--the
arms embargo--that received careful attention from the
White House. This issue also reveals the contradictory
nature of U.S. policy toward South Africa.
     Liberal defenders of the U.S. record on South Africa
point with pride to the fact that Washington not only
supported the 1963 U.N. arms embargo, but even declared a
unilateral arms embargo prior to U.N. action. This fact,
it is asserted, proves that the United States has been
willing to take tough action against apartheid. But
critics have suggested that the timing of Washington's
announcement of a unilateral arms embargo--immediately
preceding the U.N. embargo--reflected an American desire
to avoid seeming to take action against Pretoria only
when forced to do so by U.N. pressure.[74] Supporting this
judgement is the fact that American spokesmen at the time
emphasized the "voluntary" nature of Washington's
embargo, and asserted that it would have been implemented
even if no U.N. embargo existed.[75] As it turns out, the
Kennedy administration's strategy in this episode was
more complex than either of these portrayals suggest.
     Traditional U.S. policy toward Portuguese
colonialism had avoided a critical stand due to
Portugal's membership in NATO and American dependence on
use of the Azores as a military depot.[76] In the early
1960s approximately 75 percent of normal U.S. military
traffic to Europe and the Middle East was going via the
Azores.[77] During the early Kennedy administration some

symbolic actions were taken that led observers to believe a new policy was emerging.[78]

In 1963, however, Kennedy was faced with the task of renegotiating the Azores agreement with Portugal while at the same time trying to get congressional approval for the nuclear test ban treaty. Kennedy reasoned that a breakdown in the talks with Portugal would weaken congressional support on the strategic accords and it was therefore necessary to soften the U.S. stand on Portugal's Africa policies.[79] In order to win Portugal's cooperation, while averting any damage to the administration's anticolonial image, Kennedy decided on a dual strategy: 1) have U.S. officials publicly deny that Washington was softening its stand on Portuguese colonialism, and 2) announce a unilateral U.S. arms embargo against South Africa.

On 2 August 1963, just five days before the U.N. Security Council would pass its arms embargo, U.N. Ambassador Adlai Stevenson announced that the United States had decided to unilaterally cease arms sales to South Africa. Stevenson claimed that Washington had "carefully screened both government and commercial shipments of military equipment" in order to ensure that the embargo was "rigorously enforced."[80]

We expect to bring to an end the sale of all military equipment to the government of South Africa by the end of this calendar year in order further to contribute to a peaceful solution and to avoid any steps which might at this point directly contribute to international friction in the area.[81]

But the ambassador added an important caveat. Noting that the United States had "many responsibilities in many parts of the world," Stevenson pointed out that his government reserved

the right in the future to interpret this policy in the light of requirements for assuring the maintenance of international peace and security. If the interests of the world community require the provision of equipment for use in the common defense effort, we would naturally feel able to do so without violating the spirit and intent of this resolve.[82]

The most important paragraph of Stevenson's address was one that received relatively little attention. "There are existing contracts which provide for limited quantities of strategic equipment for defense against external threats, such as air-to-air missiles and torpedoes for submarines. We must honor these contracts."[83]

Based on a June 1962 bilateral military agreement,
the United States had established a Defense Department
space tracking station in South Africa, in return for
which Pretoria was permitted to sign contracts for
American weapons. By the time of Stevenson's speech
announcing the U.S. decision to halt new arms deals,
nearly all the contracts Pretoria wanted had already been
signed.[84]

The main type of American equipment that hadn't been
contracted by 1963, i.e., submarines, were provided by
the French. Also, "by 1963 South Africa was producing the
full range of munitions needed by her ground forces."[85]
Over the following years South Africa developed its own
arms manufacturing capability, acquired many advanced
weapons through production licensing agreements or
evasion of the arms embargo, and generally built up a
modern, well-equipped military despite the 1963 ban on
arms sales.[86]

Support for an arms embargo against South Africa was
not without cost to U.S. policymakers. Although the
Security Council embargo was only voluntary, with no
enforcement mechanism, it once again branded South Africa
as a pariah and increased its isolation from those forces
in the West who desired continued access to the country's
resources.

Between 1963 and 1966 American corporations lost "at
least $60 million in sales of civilian equipment that
might be used for military purposes, in addition to
losses on sales of military equipment."[87] It is hard to
imagine that U.S. policymakers were not mindful of
potential economic losses when they made the arms embargo
decision. This particular episode is a clear example of a
bourgeois policy apparatus making a tactical decision
that hurts some bourgeois interests in exchange for the
political credibility needed to preserve general
bourgeois rule.

The Kennedy administration's handling of the arms
embargo exemplifies a contradiction that has plagued U.S.
policy in the United Nations. By the early 1960s when
many newly independent African nations were becoming
members, the United Nations was moving beyond verbal
disapproval of apartheid to more concrete measures aimed
at weakening the political and economic power of South
Africa's white minority.

American diplomats have had the difficult task of
participating sufficiently in the condemnation of
apartheid to maintain credibility, while at the same time
preventing U.N. action that would disrupt the
international bourgeois networks that have preserved
white rule and guaranteed access to South Africa's human
and material resources. The U.S. record in the United
Nations on this issue is consistent. When proposals are
symbolic, Washington supports them. When corporate or
security interests are threatened, standard U.S. policy

is to block such proposals.[88]
There were two other symbolic actions taken by the
Kennedy administration that deserve mention. In June 1963
the American embassy in South Africa announced that its
July 4th celebrations that year would include black
guests. The South African government responded by
refusing to send official representatives to the event.
Another gesture came in late 1961 when Albert
Luthuli was awarded the Nobel Peace Prize for his work as
President General of the banned African National
Congress. If this was not enough to irk the South African
government, the U.S. ambassador praised Luthuli. When the
ANC leader addressed a press conference before receiving
the award, he called for international sanctions against
Pretoria and then read a congratulatory message from
President Kennedy.[89] Anthony Lake provides a simple yet
accurate characterization of the Kennedy administration's
approach: "when it wouldn't hurt, the Kennedy South
African policies were firmly anti-apartheid."[90]
While Kennedy's diplomats were making symbolic
gestures against apartheid, other branches of the U.S.
state were deepening their integration into the South
African status quo. As U.S. investment and trade with the
Republic continued to climb, the Commerce Department and
State Department facilitated the involvement of American
companies. A 1963 Commerce Department study points out:

> The United States Mission in South Africa, and
> particularly the economic and commercial officers
> assigned to the Embassy at Pretoria and consular
> establishments at Johannesburg, Durban, Capetown and
> Port Elizabeth, consider the rendering of assistance
> to present and potential U.S. investors to be a
> vital part of its task in the country, and indeed,
> this commands a considerable portion of the
> officers' attention.[91]

Although official assistance to U.S. trade and
investment continued unabated, some top Kennedy officials
were becoming more sensitive to the negative
ramifications of U.S. corporate ties to apartheid. This
concern was precipitated by South Africa's separation
from the British Commonwealth, and the outbreak of armed
rebellion in Angola. In a classified 1961 memo
instructing the State Department to conduct a policy
review, Kennedy's Special Assistant for National Security
Affairs, McGeorge Bundy, stated:

> We need to have a particular look at the
> provisions with respect to the encouraging of
> American private capital to seek investment outlets
> in South Africa and with respect to the purchase of
> gold and other raw materials that provide a major
> source of economic support for the South African

economy.[92]

Military cooperation between the two countries
continued. On at least one occasion U.S. military
personnel had a direct impact on internal South African
politics. In 1961 the U.S. Navy sent a five-ship squadron
on a courtesy call to Durban immediately prior to a
general strike being organized by the opposition Congress
Alliance.[93]

> United States Marines went ashore and
> demonstrated their weapons (such as flamethrowers
> and machine guns) to the South African Army.
> Helicopters were flown at low altitudes over African
> "locations", much as the South African police does
> to spot and disperse crowd concentrations.
> Obviously, almost all Africans interpreted the
> American visit as a show of force in favour of
> [Prime Minister] Verwoerd.[94]

The U.S. squadron then went on to Lorenco Marques
(now Maputo), Mozambique to carry out the same
demonstrations in cooperation with the Portuguese
colonial forces.

Nuclear cooperation continued. Agreements remained
in force allowing American companies to supply South
Africa with advanced technology, and permitting South
African scientists to study at U.S. nuclear facilities.
In 1961 the U.S. government awarded a $100,000 grant to a
branch of the University of Witwatersrand to conduct
research on methods for monitoring atomic bomb tests.[95]

In sum, U.S. policy during the Kennedy years
continued along a bifurcated path. In its symbolic acts,
such as at the United Nations, the administration
distanced itself from white minority rule. But during the
same period the entire spectrum of debate had also
shifted, leaving U.S. policy in the same relative
position of lagging behind the U.N. majority.

Important members of the Kennedy team were more
sensitive to African nationalist aspirations than any of
their predecessors. Yet even these policymakers could not
foresee how the growing polarization in southern Africa
was infusing U.S. policy with deeper contradictions that
would only become more difficult to manage as time went
by.

The white minority regimes, strengthened by military
and economic support from the West, were able to repress
opposition forces and ignore calls for reforms. This
effectively narrowed the ground for moderate opposition
and strengthened the hand of more radical elements. In
the early 1960s African nationalist forces, confronted by
the futility of nonviolent strategies, embarked on the
course of armed struggle. The development of their
military capability increased Soviet influence in the

region and gave the liberation movements the potential to alter capitalist relations of production: the two developments U.S. policymakers wanted most to avoid.

THE JOHNSON ADMINISTRATION, 1963-1969

During the Johnson years U.S. policy continued its drift away from the high-profile support of African aspirations during the early Kennedy administration. Johnson never developed an interest in African affairs, and his top policymakers were consumed by the escalating conflict in Vietnam.

Much of the political capital raised in Black Africa by Kennedy's enlightened diplomacy was depleted by two developments: a bitter African response to the U.S. intervention at Stanleyville in 1964, and congressional opposition to continued foreign aid.[96] The Johnson administration's room for manuever was also limited by an unprecedented level of domestic conflict. Racial disturbances were erupting in cities all across the country, and public opposition to U.S. involvement in foreign conflicts reached an all-time high.

This section focuses on two issues—South Africa's occupation of Namibia and Rhodesia's unilateral declaration of independence—which illustrate the basic contradictions of U.S. policy in southern Africa. Once again a familiar pattern emerges: U.S. policymakers mildly pressure the white minority for change but fail to take any actions that would weaken white minority rule.

In a 1950 Advisory Opinion, the International Court of Justice (ICJ) ruled that legitimate authority over Namibia, once held by the League of Nations which had authorized South Africa to temporarily govern the territory, should be transferred to the United Nations. Pretoria's response was to reject the decision on the grounds that an Advisory Opinion was not binding. In November 1960 Ethiopia and Liberia, the only Black African states to have held seats in the League of Nations, filed briefs with the ICJ seeking an authoritative ruling against South Africa's presence in Namibia. It was not until July 1966 that the Court issued its decision: in an extremely close vote, the Court dismissed the case on the grounds that Liberia and Ethiopia lacked the legal standing to receive a judgement on the merits of this case. The ICJ had taken six years to make a non-decision.

During the years of litigation the United States followed a policy of coaxing both Pretoria and the United Nations to refrain from any action on the question of Namibia until the ICJ reached a decision. This was a convenient position for the United States to adopt but it was not simply a cynical attempt to stonewall the majority at the United Nations. While the ICJ case was

being litigated the State Department quietly reminded
Pretoria that under Article 94 of the U.N. Charter,
member states are obligated to comply with rulings of the
ICJ. In a message delivered to the South African
government just three days before the ICJ ruling, the
U.S. Embassy in Pretoria warned that: "the United States
assumes that all parties to the case, including the South
African government, will respect the rule of law and
comply with the terms of the Judgement."[97]
    This and other documents show that the Johnson
administration wanted to avoid an international showdown
over South Africa's presence in Namibia. Intransigence by
Pretoria would widen the gap between America's corporate
and security interests in the South African status quo,
and the need to uphold the rule of law internationally.
    A secret document authored by Johnson's original
National Security Advisor, McGeorge Bundy, illustrates
the extent to which top U.S. policymakers were willing to
pressure the National Party to moderate its policies.
Titled "U.S. Policy Toward South Africa" and dated 24
April 1964, National Security Action Memorandum (NSAM)
295 reveals several aspects of U.S. strategy and deserves
to be quoted at length.
    NSAM 295 was an order to other agencies to
coordinate contingency plans for the ICJ ruling on
Namibia. "The State Department should as a matter of
urgency develop a comprehensive program of diplomatic
activity" aimed at convincing Pretoria to accept the
eventual ICJ ruling. In the meantime, Pretoria should
hold off on its plan (the Odendaal report) to institute
an apartheid system in Namibia. The document advises the
State Department to encourage "parallel actions by other
interested governments, particularly those in western
Europe," with the goal of "assuring that the
implementation of the Odendaal report is deferred as long
as possible and, hopefully, until the decision on the
merits of the case in the International Court of
Justice." In pursuing these objectives the State
Department is also directed to give "particular attention
. . . to exploring the possible bases for accomodation
and understanding with more moderate members of the South
African white community."[98]
    The memorandum orders that "existing policy
regarding military sales to South Africa will be
continued" but calls for postponement of any decision
"regarding possible sales of submarines or any variations
in existing policy" until Namibia's status is clarified
by the ICJ decision. NASA and the Department of Defense
(DOD) were ordered to "immediately undertake such
planning for and construction of alternaticve stand-by
facilities in South Africa on six months notice." Bundy
ordered that the program "be carried out in such a manner
as to avoid its coming to public notice as long as
feasible."

As another precautionary move, NSAM 295 instructs "US government lending agencies" to temporarily "suspend action on applications for loans or investment guarantees with respect to South Africa. There should be no avoidable disclosure of this policy to interested parties, however, and agencies should continue to accept and process applications."

It is clear from the tone and substance of the memorandum that the White House was expecting an ICJ ruling unfavorable to South Africa's presence in Namibia.[99] The final item of the memo even instructs the State Department to "immediately undertake a comprehensive analysis of the various sanctions that could be considered if South Africa does not accept the ICJ decision on South West Africa." Much of the contingency planning of NSAM 295 was rendered unnecessary by the ICJ's refusal to rule on the substance of the issue, but the Johnson White House was prepared to apply selective pressure on the National Party to cooperate on the Namibia question.

Following the ICJ's 1966 refusal to rule, the United States sided with the U.N. majority in warning South Africa that it should accede to U.N. supervision of Namibia. Ambassador Arthur Goldberg took a tougher stand than any previous American official. Arguing that South Africa had effectively forfeited its authority over Namibia, Goldberg supported the establishment of a U.N. commission "to recommend practical means by which South West Africa should be administered."[100]

The State Department was opposed to the ambassador taking such a strong stand against Pretoria. They reasoned that this might establish a precedent for future U.N. intervention of a type that would be unsupportable by Washington. In fact, Goldberg had avoided clearing the initiative with the State Department by getting approval directly from Johnson.[101]

While the Afro-Asian group pushed for the United Nations to assume real authority over Namibia, the United States postponed substantive action by proposing an official study of the situation and a dialogue with Pretoria, even though this had proven fruitless in the past. In May 1967 when the General Assembly established the U.N. Council on Namibia and mandated it to "do all in its power to enable independence to be attained by June 1968," the United States and its NATO allies abstained.[102] Over the years the U.S. government has refused to join the Council on Namibia, thus depriving it of the political muscle needed to obtain South Africa's cooperation.

The political residue of this episode was to reinforce the U.S. reputation for taking admirable stands in the symbolic realm but backing down when it came to substantive action. While the United Nations had been wrangling over the Namibia question, the National Party

had increased its parliamentary majority to 126 of 166
seats. By steadfastly rejecting U.N. authority over
Namibia, and spurning U.S. diplomatic pressure on the
issue, Pretoria made it clear to U.S. policymakers that
the costs to the West of forcing South Africa out of
Namibia would be unacceptably high.

Washington's preoccupation with the land war in
Indochina, and the severe political and economic
disruptions that would be caused by any intervention
aimed at ousting South Africa from Namibia, prevented the
Johnson administration from taking actions outside the
symbolic realm. Thus as U.S. policy continued to drift,
Pretoria consolidated its hold on Namibia and instituted
an apartheid system, and the Namibian nationalist
movement turned to armed struggle.

Another episode that reveals dynamics sinmilar to
the Namibia dispute is the case of the 1965 white settler
rebellion in Rhodesia. Rather than accede to impending
majority rule, Ian Smith and his five percent white
minority declared a Unilateral Declaration of
Independence (UDI) from Britain on 11 November 1965. This
white settler rebellion against colonial authority, and
the reaction of both the West and the local black
population, laid the basis for a conflict that would
disrupt the region for fifteen years, taking more than
30,000 lives in the process.

Britain's Prime Minister Harold Wilson was caught in
a straddle similar to that of successive American
leaders. In the international arena he had third world
countries, particularly the Commonwealth nations,
pressing for tough action to put down the rebellion. At
the same time, his NATO allies were urging restraint.
Within his own government there was insufficient support
for either action that could have ended the rebellion:
simply declaring Rhodesia legally independent, or
intervening militarily to force majority rule on the
white rebels.[103]

Wilson produced a compromise policy: he denounced
the rebellion as treasonous and supported selective
economic sanctions. Full economic sanctions, including a
stoppage of oil that could have paralyzed the Rhodesian
economy, were ruled out because they would have required
a costly confrontation with Smith's main external ally,
the National Party regime in South Africa.

The U.S. position was to let the British take the
lead: they were the colonial authority, and the White
House did not want to antagonize the British while their
backing for the U.S. war in Vietnam was deemed
crucial.[104] The Johnson administration's stand put
constraints on London's ability to halt the rebellion.

Speaking officially [Under Secretary of State George] Ball told British officials that they could not count on America's bailing them out if they took measures against Rhodesia that seriously damaged their own balance of payments position--already in a shaky position. This meant, of course, avoiding any action that might bring Britain into economic confrontation with South Africa.[105]

While following Britain's lead, the United States cautioned London against going too far too fast. Important sections of the U.S. state (Commerce, Treasury, CIA) and influential corporations were opposed to sanctions against Rhodesia.[106] Treasury Department officials responsible for overseeing U.S. compliance with international sanctions are reported to have argued:

A sanctions program against Rhodesia could not prove successful and would damage the concept of sanctions. This could, in turn, interfere with Treasury's sanctions programs against Albania, Cuba, the People's Republic of China and other Communist nations. Treasury was also concerned about the effect on the American balance of payments and gold position if American relations with South Africa became involved.[107]

Also opposed to sanctions were the same right-wing forces in Congress who opposed civil rights reforms in the United States, and who generally displayed sympathy for white minority regimes in southern Africa.

Relevant sections of the State Department and the White House realized the necessity of cooperating with the British-backed U.N. plan for selective sanctions. Overall, "the weight of opinion within the American government was cautiously in favor of sanctions--provided they did not mean total confrontation with South Africa."[108]

Once again Washington found a compromise position: it bent to world opinion by disrupting some economic ties to Rhodesia, yet did not pressue, U.S. relations with South Africa during these turbulent years remained much as they had been. Trade and investment continued to flourish (Tables 3.1 and 3.2). By the end of the Johnson administration the U.S. balance of trade surplus with South Africa had passed the $250 million mark.[109]

Table 3.1
U.S. TRADE WITH SOUTH AFRICA, 1960 AND 1970
(millions of dollars)

	1960	1970	Percent Change 1960-70
Exports	277	563	+103
Imports	200	288	+44

Source: Francis C. Ogene, Group Interests and United
States Foreign Policy on African Issues (Ph.D.
dissertation, Case Western Reserve University, 1974), p.
278.

Table 3.2
VALUE, EARNINGS, AND RATE OF RETURN
ON U.S. DIRECT INVESTMENT IN SOUTH AFRICA,*
1960-1970 (millions of dollars)

Year	Total Book Value	Total Earnings	Rate of Return (%)
1960	286	50	17.5
1961	311	61	21
1962	357	72	23
1963	411	82	23
1964	467	87	21
1965	529	101	22
1966	597	224	23
1967	666	128	21
1968	696	111	17
1969	755	127	18
1970	864	141	18

*includes Namibia

Source: Ogene, Group Interests and United States Foreign
Policy..., p. 277.

Government agencies of both countries continued to
facilitate mutual dependence of their respective business
classes. Regular articles in Commerce Department
publications provided detailed marketing information. A
typical piece written in 1964 by the Senior U.S.
Commercial Officer in Johannesburg reported that "the
green light is on. Both parties are committed to an
expanding economy and greater productivity. However,
aggressive and alert salesmanship will be necessary to
exploit the full potential of this market."[110]

Particularly damning are the results of several
opinion polls from the late 1960s that tested the
attitudes of American businessmen operating in South
Africa. The surveys, jointly conducted by U.S. News and
World Report, a church-based group, and a private
research firm, found that roughly two-thirds of the
American businessmen viewed apartheid as a legitimate
attempt to solve the country's problems, and if given the
opportunity they would vote for one of the political
parties supporting apartheid. Less than ten percent of
those polled found apartheid "altogether incorrect."[111]
One study

> concluded that the American businessmen not
> only supported the South African government and its
> apartheid policy but also observed apartheid laws in
> their own social and economic conduct: they see
> their profits and self-interest tied up with the
> entire system. Even the minority of businessmen who
> resented apartheid still believed that majority rule
> would usher in chaos and instability in South
> Africa.[112]

It was in the area of military relations that U.S.
policy changed most during the Johnson years. In 1964 the
United States extended its voluntary arms embargo against
South Africa to cover goods used in the production of
weapons. Washington blocked the sale of light aircraft
possessing obvious military capabilities, and in 1966 the
United States halted the sale to South Africa of French
jetliners equipped with General Electric engines. But
sales of civilian aircraft, which could be pressed into
military service in an emergency, were still
permitted.[113]

For decades it had been a standard practice of U.S.
Navy vessels to make port calls in South Africa. In April
1965, however, President Johnson decided to divert the
U.S. aircraft carrier Independence from a scheduled stop
in Cape Town because the South African government had
refused to allow planes with black crew members to land
at South African airstrips. In November 1965 the carrier
Enterprise was also diverted from a scheduled visit to
South Africa for similar reasons. The issue lay at rest
for two years.

In early 1967 the Joint Chiefs of Staff and the
Secretary of Defense obtained authorization for the U.S.
aircraft carrier Franklin D. Roosevelt to stop in Cape
Town for several days on its way home from a tour of duty
off the coast of Vietnam. These plans were reported in
the press two weeks before the visit was to take place.
This provided enough time for congressional and civil
rights opposition to be mobilized.[114] Numerous black
leaders and forty-seven members of Congress worked with
allies in the State Department to pressure the Defense

Department and the White House to cancel the visit.
Proponents of the visit argued that to divert the
ship from a South African replenishing stop would cost an
extra quarter of a million dollars. They also claimed
that South Africa had made special arrangements to lessen
the impact of apartheid restrictions on U.S. Navy
personnel taking shore leave. A compromise was reached in
which the captain of the Roosevelt was ordered to allow a
modified shore leave which was to include only integrated
activities. The captain, in consultation with the U.S.
embassy in South Africa, decided that under these
constraints it was best to cancel shore leave entirely.
Although the ship did dock at Cape Town and over one
hundred crew members went ashore despite orders to the
contrary, the outcome represented a minor victory for
antiapartheid forces in the United States. Largely as a
result of this incident the Defense Department adopted a
formal policy of not allowing its naval vessels to dock
at South African ports. But this change in policy was a
minor increment and mainly symbolic. The relationship
between the two countries was not significantly altered.
In conclusion, the Johnson administration's policy
on South Africa was mainly a continuation of existing
policy. Some tactical nuances were added but nothing was
done to halt the growing rift between the two divergent
planks of U.S. policy toward South Africa. The policy of
symbols (official pronouncements, non-substantive votes
at the United Nations) was opposed to apartheid, and
State Department officials quietly urged Pretoria to
follow policies that would cause less international
outrage. Yet as the symbolic acts became entrenched into
a tradition, the institutional links binding the American
bourgeoisie and its South African counterpart steadily
expanded. The Johnson administration had neither the
ideological inclination nor the political base to alter
this drift in U.S. policy.

THE NIXON ADMINISTRATION, 1969-1974

During the Nixon administration U.S. policy toward
South Africa moved steadily to the right. As part of the
Nixon team's initial set of policy reviews, National
Security Advisor Henry Kissinger ordered an
interdepartmental study of U.S. options in southern
Africa. This directive from the White House, National
Security Study Memorandum #39, and the study produced in
response to it, were to serve as the Nixon policy
blueprint for southern Africa. NSSM 39 has been public
for many years now and has been analyzed extensively,
hence the discussion here will be limited to its
essential features.[115]

The NSSM 39 policy review listed five basic objectives of U.S. policy, "arranged without intent to imply priority."[116]

* To improve the US standing in black Africa and internationally on the racial issue.
* To minimize the likelihood of escalation of violence in the area and the risk of US involvement.
* To minimize the opportunities for the USSR and Communist China to exploit the racial issue in the region for propaganda advantage and to gain political influence with black governments and liberation movements.
* To encourage moderation of the current rigid racial and colonial policies of the white regimes.
* To protect economic, scientific and strategic interests and opportunities in the region, including the orderly marketing of South Africa's gold production.[117]

These objectives are then followed by perhaps the most insightful, yet most underplayed line of the entire study. "These objectives are to a degree contradictory--pursuit of one may make difficult the successful pursuit of one or more of the others."[118]

The drafters of NSSM 39 recognized the difficulty of securing U.S. economic and strategic interests--requiring cooperation with Pretoria--while simultaneously improving American standing on the race issue. Yet nowhere in this lengthy policy review is there serious consideration of why these objectives are contradictory, how the particular contradictions developed, or how they might be resolved rather than glossed over.

The three basic points on which there was general agreement were: 1) the United States had no vital security interests in the region; 2) racial oppression in southern Africa had been made into an international issue and U.S. policy, for practical reasons, had to be sensitive to the international reaction to white supremacy; and 3) racial conflict would probably increase, perhaps leading to serious upheavals and increased communist state involvement.[119]

The differences of opinion among the various agencies centered on three questions:

Was violence inevitable, or was peaceful change still possible? did the U.S. have any significant influence to bring to bear toward peaceful change? did the political interests which argued against extensive contacts with the white governments outweigh the more tangible economic, military, and scientific interests which required some continuing official contact?[120]

On the first question it was agreed that some level
of violence was inevitable. The final policy document,
however, incorrectly concluded that black nationalist
forces in southern Africa would not be able to sustain
the level of military activity needed to bring down the
white regimes.

On the second question differences of opinion were
also narrowly circumscribed. No faction argued that the
United States had extensive leverage to promote peaceful
change. The question was resolved as a fait accompli: The
only means of encouraging peaceful change--international
pressure on the whites--would elicit greater resistance
from the whites and was therefore an unacceptable
strategy.[121]

On the third question the more liberal bureaucrats,
especially those of the State Department's Africa Bureau,
emphasized the importance of the race issue in future
international relations. They argued that any perceived
U.S. friendliness toward the white regimes would provide
a political windfall for the communist powers. This
position was effectively opposed by those arguing for the
primacy of more immediate material interests. Their
cynical yet accurate view was that many countries were
dependent on the United States and would not be willing
to suffer the consequences of penalizing America for its
relations with South Africa.

Roger Morris, a National Security Council aide to
Kissinger and one of the principal authors of NSSM 39,
reports that the positions taken by different agencies
were determined more by "clientism" than by lofty
logic.[122] The CIA position as presented by Director
Richard Helms was "so transparently pro-white . . . so
disdainful of black African opposition," that even the
cynical Kissinger was appalled by the Agency's lack of
objectivity.[123] As usual, Treasury and Commerce were
opposed to any policies that would impede their task of
facilitating corporate expansion. Yet even State
Department officials, usually the bureaucratic actors
more critical of apartheid, failed to resist the
rightward momentum of the policy review process. In one
typical meeting

> Secretary of State Rogers interjected that the
> issues could not be all that hard since so many of
> them around the table--John Mitchell, Vice President
> Agnew, [Under Secretary of State Elliot] Richardson,
> Rogers himself, and the President--were "lawyers who
> must have had clients in South Africa. . . . I know
> I did."[124]

Assistant Secretary of State for Africa David Newsom, one of the officials with the most to lose from a policy favorable to Pretoria, gave a rather duplicitous performance. Although he later claimed that the State Department had fought for a tough line on the white minority regimes, Newsom failed to resist the rightward tendency of Nixon's top officials, and even assured them that African opposition in the United Nations was "containable."[125]

Internal evidence suggests that the Nixon administration was motivated by personal prejudice as well as by organizational interests. Alexander Haig, then an NSC aide to Kissinger, pretended to beat drums on the conference table whenever African issues came up for discussion.[126] Kissinger was openly perplexed as to how one particular African tribe could be more Negroid than another and at the same time be more intelligent and accomplished.[127] Agnew confused Rhodesia and South Africa, and publicly disparaged black Americans during a tour of Africa.[128] Nixon casually referred to black people as "jigs."[129] These and other bits of evidence constitute a pattern of private behavior inimical to majority interests in southern Africa. As a Nixon White House staffer pointed out: "it is impossible to pretend that the cast of mind that harbors casual bigotry did not have some effect on American foreign policy toward the overwhelming majority of the world which is nonwhite."[130]

The policy option eventually chosen as a result of the NSSM 39 review called for the "selective relaxation of our stance toward the white regimes," in the hope that this would "encourage some modification of their current racial and colonial policies."[131] This was to be balanced by "substantial economic assistance" (an additional $5 million annually!) to the black states in the region.[132] It was hoped that this would "draw the two groups together and exert some influence on both for peaceful change."[133]

The National Security Decision Memorandum signed by Nixon in February 1970, which officially launched the new policy, contained other more specific guidelines.

* "The embargo on arms sales to South Africa should be relaxed generally to favor any U.S. firm applying for a license."

* Namibia "should not be made an issue in bilateral relations" between the United States and South Africa.

* On Rhodesia, the U.S. Consulate-General office should be kept open, the Union Carbide request to import Rhodesian chrome should get "further study," and U.S. agencies responsible for sanctions enforcement should formulate plans for ending U.S. compliance.

* The arms embargo against Portugal should be
relaxed to permit sales of "non-lethal equipment
which has dual civilian and military use."
* Policy on U.S. investment should be altered to
provide full Export-Import Bank financing while
"avoiding conspicuous trade promotion."[134]

The administration argued that this policy could
coax changes out of the white minority regimes. But this
would have required high level support for a coherent
policy implemented by professionals with knowledge of the
region. Such a policy was not forthcoming.
     In practice, the new policy was largely one of
continuing the contradictory drift of U.S. policy. But
now the white regimes received even more favorable
treatment without having to listen to token denunciations
of racism. South Africa remained a low priority for an
administration preoccupied with waging war in Southeast
Asia and fashioning the new triangular diplomacy of
detente with China and the Soviet Union.
     With regard to military ties, a confidential
National Security Decision Memorandum (NSDM) signed by
Kissinger on 17 August 1970 reveals the complex and
contradictory nature of U.S. military support for
apartheid. Entitled "Implementation of Arms Embargo on
South Africa and Portuguese African Territories," NSDM 81
lays out specific guidelines designed to allow U.S.
companies to make money selling equipment to South Africa
while keeping the government within defensible limits
regarding the arms embargo.[135] "Non-lethal dual-use items
which are preponderantly employed for civilian use"
(Kissinger's emphasis) may be sold to military
purchasers. Similar items that are mainly employed for
military uses "but do not have a clear and direct
application to combat or to internal security operations"
may be sold to military purchasers "upon the
recommendation of the Department of State." These items
"will generally be built to military specifications."
Items with a clearly repressive functon "will not be
licensed to military buyers" but they may be sold to
civilian purchasers, again, at the recommendation of the
Commerce and State Departments.
     The confidential memo specifically approves Lear
jets and Cessna dual-engine 401s and 402s for sale to the
South African military. It denies licenses for the sale
of several aircraft to the military, but does not
prohibit their sale to civilian buyers. Reliable studies
show that many of these aircraft possessing military
capabilities ended up in South Africa via civilian
channels.[136]

The understanding between Nixon and British Prime Minister Edward Heath to give more attention to the "Soviet threat" in the Indian Ocean probably facilitated the easing of arms sales restrictions to South Africa. Washington acquiesced to Britain's February 1971 decision to sell Pretoria seven Wasp helicopters.[137] The sale of French jetliners containing American engines, previously blocked by the Johnson admininstration, was given a green light.[138] The United States also continued supplying spare parts for military goods sold prior to the 1963 U.N. arms embargo. An expanded definition of "gray area" sales (i.e., goods possessing military and civilian uses) permitted South Africa to increase its repressive capacity.

Not surprisingly, the United States abstained, along with Britain and France, on a July 1970 U.N. Security Council resolution calling for tightening of the voluntary arms embargo. In other U.N. action, the Nixon administration during its first year cast a negative vote, rather than abstaining as was the U.S. custom, when the annual antiapartheid resolution came up in the General Assembly. In a precedent-setting March 1970 vote on a resolution calling on Britain to use force to halt the white rebellion in Rhodesia, the United States for the first time exercised its Security Council veto.

Symbolic rather than substantive action characterized U.S. policy on the question of Namibia. Washington voted in favor of a 30 January 1970 Security Council resolution condemning South Africa's presence in Namibia, but refused to go along with efforts to set a deadline for South Africa's withdrawal. Washington also opposed a resolution encouraging member states to take "appropriate measures" to force South African compliance with U.N. rulings on the territory.[139]

Kissinger did take steps to reduce American business involvement in Namibia. A secret National Security Decision Memorandum (NSDM #55) of 17 April 1970 reveals how the international legal status of Namibia forced Washington to take a different position on this territory than on South Africa itself. The memo calls for the U.S. government to "officially discourage investment by U.S. nationals in South West Africa."[140]

This policy would discourage new investment but would protect older U.S. investments in Namibia held by companies such as American Metal Climax (AMAX), Phelps Dodge, Bethlehem Steel, and Newmont Mining Corporation.[141] The secret document also prohibits the use of Export-Import Bank credits for trade with Namibia. Kissinger concludes the directive by emphasizing that these restrictions apply only to Namibia and not to the other white-ruled states.

The President intends that the foregoing decisions be regarded as concerned solely with South West Africa. They are not to be regarded as a precedent for application of similar restrictions and policies to South Africa or the Portuguese Territories.
The President desires that the United States continue to make clear its opposition to mandatory economic sanctions against South Africa or the Portuguese Territories and to any use of force in southern Africa.[142]

Other confidential documents regarding ExIm Bank credits for trade with South Africa reveal the subtle efforts of policymakers to balance conflicting economic and political interests. The relevant agencies (Commerce, State, ExIm Bank, and the White House) agreed on a policy of liberalizing ExIm credit authorizations for South Africa.[143] The documents refer to a policy in place since 1964 restricting direct and long-term credits to South Africa. The authors estimate that this had cost American exporters anywhere from $25 million to $100 million annually.[144] But the policy had political benefits. "By so minimizing official involvement with the South African economy, it has been easier to resist international and domestic pressures to take further measures to disassociate ourselves from economic relations with that country."[145]
Other similar statements in these memoranda provide a clear example of how state managers must sometimes sacrifice capitalist interests in order to protect the interests of capitalism. In this case the policy straddle required some firms to lose potential South African contracts as a consequence of Washington's attempt to placate critics. The policymakers hoped this would permit the continuation of business and security ties to Pretoria.
Although careful about the public image of its economic relations with Pretoria, Washington continued to facilitate business ties between the two countries. The Commerce Department "tacitly encouraged investment and trade, and both rose rapidly. Beginning in 1969, the Commodity Credit Corporation extended credit to South African buyers of agricultural products."[146]
The Nixon/Ford years were also marked by a steady increase of U.S. trade and investment in the Portuguese colonies of Angola and Mozambique. The oilfields of Angola proved increasingly attractive to numerous U.S. petroleum companies.[147] Angola's prospects as an important producer of diamonds, iron ore, phosphates, and sulphur lured U.S. mineral companies into deeper collaboration with the Portuguese colonialists.[148] In Mozambique, powerful interests such as Bethlehem Steel, Amoco, and the Hunt International Petroleum Company were

expanding their activities with the help of Portuguese
and U.S. government agencies.[149]
    The growing stake of U.S. capital in the white-ruled
states was surpassed quantitatively by the growth of U.S.
trade and investment in the rest of Africa.[150]
Policymakers were not oblivious to such trends. A
confidential 1971 State Department memo to Kissinger
advised:

> It should also be noted that American economic
> interests today are heavier in the developing
> countries of Africa than in South Africa. Over 65%
> of our total investment in Africa at the end of 1969
> was in the developing countries and only 25% in
> South Africa; almost 60% of our exports in 1970 went
> to independent black and Arab Africa, as against 35%
> to South Africa and 5% to other white-dominated
> areas.[151]

    Yet as long as the white regimes remained relatively
stable, and the black African states were unable or
unwilling to force a choice on U.S. capital, the American
corporate stake in white minority rule continued to grow.
    Under Nixon, and later under Ford, Kissinger's
policy toward southern Africa facilitated strong ties
between dominant U.S. economic and political actors and
the South African status quo. Although the
"communication" policy was ostensibly intended to coax
the whites into moderating their system of control, there
is no evidence that any efforts were made in this
direction until after the collapse of Portuguese
colonialism.
    The Republican administrations of Nixon and Ford
maintained friendly ties with South African officialdom.
Before he took on the job of Secretary of State in 1973,
Henry Kissinger allowed only one African ambassador to
have access to him: Johan Botha of South Africa.[152]
"During the Nixon and Ford administrations, General
Hendrik van den Bergh, the then-head of the intelligence
agency . . . used to visit Washington frequently and
enjoyed close ties with the then-director of the CIA
George Bush."[153]
    Because they relied so heavily on the intelligence
organizations of South Africa and Portugal, U.S.
policymakers underestimated the turmoil looming on the
historical horizon.[154] Although the liberation movements
of southern Africa were making steady progress militarily
and diplomatically, Kissinger was scornful of their
abilities and made no plans for potential crises in the
white states.

Within South Africa the black opposition was growing increasingly restive. The Durban strikes and general labor unrest of the early 1970s marked the beginning of a resurgent black labor movement that by the late 1970s would grow strong enough to force concessions from the government. The black consciousness movement was expanding to include more African, Indian, and Colored youth. The movement was also developing a distinctly anticapitalist flavor. Already by 1972 a leading black consciousness group, the South African Students' Organization (SASO), called for foreign capital to get out of South Africa. "SASO sees foreign investments as giving stability to South Africa's exploitative regime and committing South Africa's trading partners to supporting this regime."[155]

But the Nixon and early Ford administrations were too busy with other areas of foreign policy to take much notice of these developments. Because the black opposition had not reached regime-threatening proportions, and there was not substantial communist state involvement, policy toward southern Africa remained in a non-crisis mode. Problem areas such as Vietnam, Chile, the Middle East, and the Soviet Union drew primary attention while southern Africa policy was kept in a holding pattern.

The policy of relying on repressive regimes, despite the domestic opposition they engendered in their working classes, was not limited to southern Africa. It was part of a larger strategy that came to be known as the Nixon Doctrine. One of the lessons of the Vietnam experience was that it was too costly for the United States to intervene directly in all third world revolutionary situations. The Nixon Doctrine held that the costs of a counterrevolutionary foreign policy could be minimized by bringing regional powers (e.g., Iran, Brazil, South Africa) closer to the western alliance and equipping them to act as regional gendarmes.[156]

These powers are being given financial and technological assistance and quantities of arms. Their ability to continue dominating their respective zones of influence then ensures the protection of western interests throughout the region while avoiding the need for any direct commitment of western military power.[157]

The Nixon Doctrine had an inherent flaw. The policy did not address the gross inequalities that plague most of the Third World. Instead, it sought to repress the mass protests that were a direct outcome of these inequalities. By ignoring the actual causes of mass radicalization, the Nixon doctrine locked the United States more deeply into a dependence on authoritarian regimes with appalling records on human rights.[158] In some cases--Iran, Nicaragua, and the Portuguese colonies--the regimes were so hated, they engendered sufficient opposition to be toppled.

CONCLUSION

What is most striking about U.S. policy toward South Africa in the period 1948-1975 is its constancy. During this period Africa went from being the most colonized continent in the world to comprising the single largest bloc of votes in the United Nations. It is remarkable what little impact this sweeping transformation had on U.S. policy toward white minority rule. Denunciations of racism and symbolic actions against apartheid were in greater evidence but concrete actions that could have pressured Pretoria for reform were few and far between. This was true for Democratic as well as Republican administrations.

A similar transformation of race relations occurred within the United States, with little impact on foreign policy. Black Americans made the rough voyage into full citizenship during this period, yet there were only a few occasions, and these involving minor issues, when Afro-Americans exerted effective pressure on policy toward South Africa. The documentary evidence shows that U.S. policymakers wanted to safeguard their image on the race question, but when it came to substantive action against white supremacy Washington played a dilatory and obstructionist role. What explains this lack of change in policy during a period of significant change in the objective conditions of racial oppression?

An exclusive focus on race, and reliance on racial categories, cannot explain U.S. policy toward South Africa. Given the major changes internationally and domestically on the race question in the period 1948-1975, a racial analysis would lead us to expect significant changes in U.S. policy toward apartheid. Yet as we have seen, the changes were meager. Only by focusing on the class interests of the most powerful groups in American politics can we reach a satisfactory explanation for the conservative nature of U.S. policy toward South Africa.[159]

The power bloc that has dominated U.S. foreign policy in the post-war period is composed of the following elements:

1. Transnational capital in the form of large industrial corporations and banks have a direct interest in the South African status quo. The owners and top managers of this sector (monopoly capital) form the hegemonic class in the power bloc. Instrumentally their interests are safeguarded by the fact that top government positions are held by members or allies of this class. Structurally their interests are safeguarded by the

importance of large corporations to the general
functioning of the U.S. economy. Important banks and
corporations with numerous interlocks within the
hegemonic class have a long-standing reciprocity with the
South African bourgeoisie: the South Africans get needed
capital and technology, the U.S. coporations get handsome
profits. This hegemonic class is resolutely opposed to
any U.S. policy that weakens the South African
bourgeoisie or strengthens popular democratic forces.
     2. Agencies of the U.S. state, whether directly via
their own programs or indirectly via U.S. corporations,
have an interest in the South African status quo.
Commerce, Treasury, NASA, the CIA, the Pentagon, and the
State Department have consistently opposed policies that
could have put serious pressure on South Africa's rulers.
These agencies are run by people receiving high salaries,
whose careers depend on carrying out policy as formulated
at the upper echelons. There is nothing in the historical
record to suggest that there is even a remote chance of
this sector of the power bloc implementing policies that
would disrupt the de facto alliance between the U.S.
bourgeoisie and its South African counterpart.
     3. Classes and class fractions playing a subordinate
role in the power bloc (monopoly sector labor via the
AFL-CIO, and national/regional capital via Congress and
private lobbying groups) have had little impact on
Washington's South Africa policies. Although the
AFL-CIO's Executive Council has taken progressive stands
on the question of apartheid, the organization has relied
on symbolic rather than substantive opposition to white
minority rule.[160] Representatives of national and
regional capital have rarely affected policy toward South
Africa, and when they have it has been in a conservative
direction.
     The reason for the slow pace of change in U.S.
policy toward South Africa is quite simple. Those
elements of the U.S. population that dominate the foreign
policy process are the same forces that have the greatest
interest in preserving the South African status quo.
Transnational capital and key sectors of the state have
much to lose if revolution or prolonged instability were
to prevail in South Africa. But the racial character of
the Pretoria regime has made its integration into the
imperialist alliance problematic.
     As in many other cases of U.S. foreign policy, the
bourgeois and national security state interests that
dominate Washington's strategy toward South Africa result
in a policy that sows the seeds of its own defeat. The
short-term effect of U.S. policy is to prop up a regime
that acts as a gendarme for capitalist relations of
production. The long-term effect is to tie American
interests and reputation to the losing side of a struggle
that is steadily polarizing. As we will see in the next
chapter, the ultimate effect of this short-sighted policy

is to leave the United States ill-equipped to deal with
the revolutionary crises that inevitably arise.

NOTES

1. See Marilyn Dexheimer, American Policy Toward
Portuguese Africa: A Study in Non-Crisis Policy Formation
(Ph.D. dissertation, Boston University, 1974).
2. See John Seiler, The Formulation of U.S. Policy
Toward Southern Africa, 1957-1976: The Failure of Good
Intentions   (Ph.D.   dissertation,   University   of
Connecticut, 1976), especially chapters 3, 4, and 5. Also
see Anthony Lake, Caution and Concern: The Making of
American Policy Toward South Africa, 1946-1971 (Ph.D.
dissertation, Princeton University, 1974), Chapter 5.
Much of what follows in the next few pages is informed by
these two studies.
3. Spotlight on Africa, XI, 25 February 1952, p. 1,
cited by Patrick Henry Martin, American Views on South
Africa, 1948-1972 (Ph.D. dissertation, Louisiana State
University, 1974), p. 112.
4. Martin, American Views..., p. 113.
5. For a useful history of ACOA by its director for
twenty-eight years, see George Houser, "Meeting Africa's
Challenge: The Story of the American Committee on
Africa," Issue: A Quarterly Journal of Opinion,
Summer/Fall 1976.
6. Lake, Caution and Concern..., p. 314.
7. Seiler, Formulation of U.S. Policy..., p. 1.
8. Author's interview with staff aide to Senate
Africa Subcommittee, October 1980.
9. Seiler, Formulation of U.S. Policy..., pp.
290-292.
10. Ibid., p. 290.
11. See Lake, Caution and Concern..., Chapter 3:
"Policy Conservation in the Bureaucracy," and Seiler,
Formulation of U.S. Policy..., Chapter 6: "Bureaucratic
Perspectives and Processes".
12. See Philip H. Burch, Jr., Elites in American
History: The New Deal to the Carter Administration (New
York: Holmes and Meier, 1980); and G. William Domhoff,
The Powers That Be (New York: Vintage, 1978).
13. See Ann and Neva Seidman, South Africa and U.S.
Multinational Corporations (Westport, CT: Lawrence Hill
and Co., 1977), "Appendix to Part III: Directorships in
Other Firms Investing in South Africa and Former High
U.S. Government Posts Held by Selected Directors of
Leading U.S. Firms with Interests in South Africa, 1975,"
by David Anyiwo.

14. Seiler, Formulation of U.S. Policy..., p. 393.
15. G. Mennen Williams, Africa for the Africans (Grand Rapids: William B. Eerdmans Publishing Co., 1969), p. 120.
16. See Edward Roux, Time Longer Than Rope: The Black Man's Struggle for Freedom in South Africa (Madison: University of Wisconsin Press, 1964), pp. 336-342.
17. Much like third world nationalists in other countries, South African Blacks were attempting to put substance into the anticolonial sentiments of the Atlantic Charter and founding documents of the United Nations. As early as 1943 the African National Congress had adopted segments of the Atlantic Charter as part of a South African Bill of Rights. During the 1946 strike the African Mineworkers' Union justified its demand for a ten shilling per day minimum wage by claiming it was "in accordance with the new world principles for an improved standard of living subscribed to by our Government at U.N.O." Roux, Time Longer Than Rope..., p. 338.
18. Troup, South Africa..., pp. 281-82.
19. Monica Wilson and Leonard Thompson, eds., The Oxford History of South Africa, Volume II (New York and Oxford: Oxford University Press, 1971), p. 454.
20. See Lake, Caution and Concern..., pp. 65-66.
21. Willian R. Cotter and Thomas Karis, "'We Have Nothing to Hide': Contacts Between South Africa and the U.S." Social Dynamics, 3, 2, 1977.
22. Ibid., p. 10.
23. Ibid., p. 9.
24. Ibid., p. 10.
25. The legislation passed in those first five years of National Party rule included the following: Prohibition of Mixed Marriages Act, Population Registration Act, Native Laws Amendment Act, Suppression of Communism Act, Asiatic Land Tenure Act, Public Safety Act, Criminal Law Amendment Act, Native Building Workers Act, Group Areas Act, Unemployment Insurance Amendment Act, Native Labour Settlement of Disputes Act, Bantu Authorities Act, Immorality Amendment Act, Separate Representation of Voters Act, Native Labour Act, Prevention of Illegal Squatting Act, Bantu Persons Abolition of Passes and Coordination of Documents Act, and the Bantu Education Act. For a first-hand critique of the apartheid legal system by a South African attorney, see Joel Carlson, No Neutral Ground (London: Quartet Books, 1977).
26. For historical background on the ANC, see Roux, Time Longer Than Rope...; Gail M. Gerhart, Black Power in South Africa (Berkeley: University of California Press, 1978); and Leo Kuper, "African Nationalism in South Africa, 1910-1964" in Wilson and Thompson, eds., The Oxford History....

27. See Brian Bunting, The Rise of the South African Reich (Harmondsworth, England: Penguin, 1964).
28. Lake, Caution and Concern..., p. 50.
29. Ibid.
30. Enclosure to Joint Chiefs of Staff 2121/2, 7 November 1950. Declassified by JCS Declassification Branch, 1 February 1978.
31. Author's interview with CIA officer experienced in southern African operations, April 1980.
32. Barbara Rogers and Zdenek Cervenka, The Nuclear Axis (New York: Times Books, 1978), p. 240.
33. See Export-Import Bank Annual Reports.
34. Another indication of Washington's intentions during this formative period is evident in World Bank programs vis-a-vis South Africa. The United States has always played a dominant role in determining the policies of the World Bank and its sister organization the International Monetary Fund. Between its first loan to South Africa (1949) and its last (1967) the World Bank made eleven loans totaling $241.8 million. During the last three years of the Truman administration the World Bank loaned more to South Africa ($50m) than to any other African country except the Belgian Congo ($70m). Between 1953 and 1961 the World Bank loaned twice as much to South Africa as to any other African country. See Jim Morrell, "The International Monetary Fund and South Africa" section 6B of the Economic Sanctions Project, International University Exchange Fund, Geneva, 1981.
35. Waldemar Nielsen, The Great Powers and Africa (New York: Praeger, 1969), p.278.
36. "Memorandum for the Secretary of Defense, Subject: Fighter Planes for South Africa," dated 11 December 1956, declassified by JCS Declassification Branch, 1 June 1977.
37. Martin, American Views..., p. 114.
38. Lake, Caution and Concern..., p. 83.
39. Rogers and Cervenka, The Nuclear Axis, p. 242.
40. Ibid.
41. Cited in ibid., p. 239.
42. In 1967 South African scientists joined British and French counterparts in monitoring French nuclear weapons tests in the Pacific Ocean.
43. Rogers and Cervenka, The Nuclear Axis, pp. 258-59.
44. Martin, American Views..., p. 120. The original statement appears in the Department of State Bulletin, 24 November 1958, pp. 842-44.
45. Peter M. Bergman and Mort N. Bergman, The Chronological History of the Negro in America (New York: Mentor, 1969), pp. 559 and 562.

46. Roux, Time Longer Than Rope..., pp. 406 and 409.
47. Ibid., pp. 409-12.
48. Ibid., p. 412.
49. State Department official Lincoln White, quoted in The New York Times 23 March 1960.
50. Jonathan Wouk, United States Policy Toward South Africa, 1960-1967: Foreign Policy in a Relatively Permissive Environment (Ph.D. dissertation, University of Pittsburgh, 1972), p.87.
51. Ibid., p. 90. Also see Martin, American Views..., p. 104.
52. Wouk, United States Policy..., p. 91.
53. Ibid.
54. D. Hobart Houghton, The South African Economy (Cape Town: Oxford University Press, 1976), p. 186.
55. Wouk, United States Policy..., p. 82.
56. Ibid. A factor contributing to the deterioration of investor confidence was South Africa's withdrawal from the British Commonwealth in March 1961.
57. Houghton, The South African Economy, p. 186 provides details on these measures.
58. Lake, Caution and Concern..., pp. 82-83.
59. Nielsen, The Great Powers..., p. 268.
60. Ibid., p. 270.
61. Quoted in ibid., p. 269.
62. Quoted in ibid., pp. 269-70.
63. Quoted in ibid., pp. 285-86.
64. William Minter, Portuguese African and the West (New York: Monthly Review Press, 1972), pp. 58-60.
65. Nielsen, The Great Powers..., p. 353-54.
66. Seiler, Formulation of U.S. Policy..., p. 339.
67. Edgar Lockwood cites this document in "The Future of the Carter Policy Toward Southern Africa," Issue, VII, 4, Winter 1977, p. 11.
68. Ibid.
69. Ibid.
70. Ibid.
71. See Richard J. Walton, Cold War and Counter-Revolution: The Foreign Policy of John F. Kennedy (Baltimore: Penguin, 1972).
72. Seiler, Formulation of U.S. Policy..., p. 274.
73. Ibid., p. 275.
74. Wouk, United States Policy..., p. 114.
75. Ibid., p. 115.
76. See Minter, Portuguese Africa..., and Africa Today, July/August 1970 (special issue on the United States and Portugal in Africa).
77. April 1963 statement by Deputy Assistant Secretary of Defense Frank K. Sloan, quoted in Seiler, Formulation of U.S. Policy..., p. 114.

78. Minter, Portuguese Africa..., pp. 74-79.
79. See Seiler, Formulation of U.S. Policy..., pp. 340-41.
80. Nielsen, The Great Powers..., p. 296.
81. Ibid.
82. Quoted in Lake, Caution and Concern..., p. 96.
83. Quoted in Nielsen, The Great Powers..., p. 296.
84. Seiler, The Formulation of U.S. Policy..., p. 341.
85. Wouk, United States Policy..., pp. 100-101.
86. See International Defence and Aid Fund, The Apartheid War Machine (London: IDAF, 1980).
87. Wouk, United States Policy..., p. 124.
88. See Kevin Danaher, "Sanctions Against South Africa: Strategy for the Antiapartheid Movement in the 1980s," UFAHAMU, X, 1/2, Fall/Winter 1980-81.
89. Thomas Karis, "United States Policy Toward South Africa" in Gwendolyn M. Carter and Patrick O'Meara, eds., Southern Africa: The Continuing Crisis (Bloomington: Indiana University Press, 1979), p. 327.
90. Lake, Caution and Concern..., p. 86.
91. Cited by Ian Mackler, Pattern for Profit in Southern Africa (New York: Atheneum, 1975), p. 55.
92. National Security Council document dated 22 March 1961, National Archives, Modern Military Section.
93. This was a coalition that included the African National Congress, the (white) Congress of Democrats, the Indian Congress, the Coloured People's Organization, and the South African Congress of Trade Unions.
94. Pierre van den Berghe, South Africa: A Study in Conflict (Berkeley: University of California Press, 1965), pp. 258-59.
95. Lake, Caution and Concern..., p. 89.
96. Nielsen, The Great Powers... has a good analysis of these dynamics on pp. 308-9, 320-21, and 392-97.
97. Cited in Wouk, United States Policy..., p. 175.
98. NSAM 295 is declassified and can be found in the Modern Military Section of the National Archives. All quotes are from the document.
99. Wouk, United States Policy..., p. 174.
100. Ibid., p. 180.
101. Seiler, Formulation of U.S. Policy..., p. 343.
102. Wouk, United States Policy..., p. 187.
103. Given the lack of sophisticated air defenses in Salisbury airport, it would have been easy for British commandos to seize the capital and crush the rebellion. But the political costs of sending troops into combat against white "kith and kin" would have been quite high.
104. Anthony Lake, The "Tar Baby" Option: American Policy Toward Southern Rhodesia (New York: Columbia University Press, 1976), p. 63.

105. Ibid., p. 93.
106. Ibid., p. 96. See chapters 5 and 6 for background.
107. Ibid., p. 98.
108. Ibid.
109. Francis C. Ogene, Group Interests and United States Foreign Policy on African Issues (Ph.D. dissertation, Case Western Reserve University, 1974), p. 278.
110. Joseph L. Dougherty, "U.S. sales rise as South African economic upsurge continues; Consulate lists U.S. best sellers," International Commerce, 24 February 1964.
111. Ogene, Group Interests..., p. 281.
112. Ibid., p. 282.
113. Lake, Caution and Concern..., p. 105.
114. A detailed explanation of this incident is contained in Wouk, United States Policy..., pp. 137-43.
115. See Mohammed A. El-Khawas and Barry Cohen, The Kissinger Study of Southern Africa (Westport, CT: Lawrence Hill and Co., 1976); Seiler, Formulation of U.S. Policy..., pp. 413-26; Lake, The Tar Baby Option..., chapter 4; and Roger Morris, Uncertain Greatness: Henry Kissinger and American Foreign Policy (New York: Harper and Row, 1977), pp. 107-20.
116. El-Khawas and Cohen, The Kissinger Study..., p. 101.
117. Ibid.
118. Ibid.
119. Seiler. Formulation of U.S. Policy..., p. 416.
120. Ibid., pp. 416-17.
121. Ibid., p. 417.
122. This term refers to the tendency for bureaus to develop working relationships and vested interests in the areas they are assigned to cover. This creates a structural tendency for these bureaucratic actors to take positions favoring their clients. Hence there are frequent contradictions between policies fostering smooth relations between a bureau and its clients, and policies that best represent the national interest.
123. Morris, Uncertain Greatness..., p. 115.
124. Ibid.
125. Ibid., pp. 116-17.
126. Ibid., p. 131.
127. Ibid.
128. Aaron Segal, "The United States' Year in Africa" in Colin Legum, ed., Africa Contemporary Record (New York: Africana Publishing Co., 1972), p. A134.
129. Morris, Uncertain Greatness..., p. 131.
130. Ibid., p. 132.
131. El-Khawas and Cohen, The Kissinger Study..., pp. 105-106.

132. Ibid., p. 106.
133. Ibid.
134. Seiler, The Formulation of U.S. Policy..., pp. 425-26.
135. Colin Legum, ed., Africa Contemporary Record (New York: Africana Publishing Co., 1976), pp. C99-C100 reproduces this document. All quotes are from this version of the document.
136. Michael Klare and Eric Prokosch, "Evading the Embargo: How the U.S. Arms South Africa and Rhodesia" in Western Massachusetts Association of Concerned Africa Scholars, eds., U.S. Military Involvement in Southern Africa (Boston: South End Press, 1978), p. 160.
137. Lake, Caution and Concern..., pp. 116-17.
138. Ibid., p. 115.
139. Ibid., p. 122.
140. Legum, Africa Contemporary Record(1976), p. C97.
141. For background on these mining companies see Michael Tanzer, The Race for Resources (New York: Monthly Review Press, 1980); and G. Lanning with M. Mueller, Africa Undermined (Harmondsworth, England: Penguin, 1979).
142. Legum, Africa Contemporary Record (1976), p. C98.
143. See ibid., pp. C101-C106.
144. Ibid., p. C102.
145. Ibid.
146. Karis, "United States Policy...", p. 336.
147. El-Khawas and Cohen, The Kissinger Study..., pp. 50-51.
148. Ibid., p. 51.
149. Ibid.
150. Ibid., p. 65.
151. Legum, Africa Contemporary Record (1976), p. C103.
152. Bruce Oudes, "The United States' Year in Africa" in Colin Legum, ed., Africa Contemporary Record (New York: Africana Publishing Co., 1974), p. A40.
153. South Africa/Namibia Update, 25 March 1981, p. 1.
154. Bruce Oudes, "The United States' Year in Africa: Postscript to the Nixon Years" in Colin Legum, ed., Africa Contemporary Record(1976), p. A123.
155. Quoted in Karis, "United States Policy...", p. 334.
156. Chapter 1 of Peter Evans, Dependent Development (Princeton: Princeton University Press, 1979) has a good theoretical summary of this strategy.
157. Sean Gervasi, "Under the NATO Umbrella," Africa Report, September/October 1976, p. 13.

158. The definitive text on U.S. government support
for authoritarian regimes is Noam Chomsky and Edward S.
Herman, The Washington Connection and Third World Fascism
(Boston: South End Press, 1979).
159. See Nicos Poulantzas, Political Power and
Social Classes (London: New Left Books, 1975). Poulantzas
describes a power bloc as a contradictory unity,
"composed of several politically dominant classes or
fractions," which controls the state apparatus. "Amongst
these dominant classes and fractions one of them holds a
particular dominant role, which can be characterized as a
hegemonic role." This hegemonic class "is the one which
concentrates in itself, at the political level, the
double function of representing the general interest of
the people/nation and of maintaining a specific dominance
among the dominant classes and fractions. It does this
through its particular relation to the capitalist state"
(p. 141).
160. For relevant excerpts from the AFL-CIO
Executive Council's position see Washington Notes on
Africa, Spring 1978, p. 8.

4
The Ford Administration, 1974-1977

Longstanding U.S. complacency toward southern Africa was brought to a halt in 1974-75 with the collapse of Portuguese colonialism. The departure of the white settlers from Mozambique and Angola removed class allies who had guaranteed U.S. interests and had provided a buffer (along with Rhodesia) for the white minority of South Africa. American attention to southern Africa intensified following the Portuguese coup of 25 April 1974. The region became a high priority for the Ford/Kissinger administration as well as the Democratic administration of Jimmy Carter.[1]

During the period 1975-78 Washington gave more attention to South Africa and its neighbors than at any other time in history. American criticism of apartheid also reached its peak at this time. Never before had Washington been so vociferous in its denunciations of white supremacy.

Because the level of political conflict in southern Africa during most of the post World War II period did not reach regime-threatening proportions, U.S. policy remained in a non-crisis mode. But with the fall of Portuguese colonialism and escalating conflict in Rhodesia and South Africa, U.S. policy entered a crisis-management phase. This period was characterized by heightened attention to southern Africa, and conflict within the government over what policy to follow.

As we saw in the previous chapter, different sections of the U.S. government, reflecting various constituencies, had developed different interests and allies in southern Africa. Before 1975 these competing interests were easily accommodated. As the political situation in southern Africa rapidly polarized following the Portuguese coup, various U.S. government agencies and corporate actors found it more difficult to coordinate their approach to the region. A major focus of this chapter is to examine in detail how the escalating conflict in southern Africa exacerbated the contradictions in the U.S. policy structure.

The relationship between the conflicts in southern
Africa and the domestic struggle over U.S. policy
demonstrates two important points.
     1. The intensification of conflict in southern
Africa in the post-1974 period resulted in greater
domestic conflict over U.S. policy, producing serious
disagreements within the policy establishment.
     2. This growing struggle over the direction of U.S.
policy produced a brief shift to the left in U.S.
diplomacy.   But   the   basic   goals   of   U.S.
policy--maintaining regimes open to western capital and
not friendly to Soviet interests--remained unchanged. The
change in U.S. policy during 1976-77 was only a tactical
shift to a position giving more attention to black
African states and the revolutionary nationalist
movements.

THE AFRICAN ROOTS OF THE PORTUGUESE COUP

     Although the course of Portugal's colonial history
was changed in its metropolitan capital, the impetus of
the coup came from the twelve years of struggle against
the liberation movements in Guinea-Bissau, Mozambique,
and Angola. These guerrilla wars had not only wrecked
Portugal's economy and paralyzed its once confident
leadership; they had also worn out the Portuguese army,
whose own commanders and men returned home frustrated and
disillusioned with the wars of attrition they had been
unable to win and, ironically, carrying home with them
many of the ideas propounded by their enemy in the bush.[2]
     American policymakers had not viewed the guerrilla
movements of southern Africa as much of a threat. Aside
from continuing to provide the Portuguese with economic
and military aid, Washington took little notice of the
nationalist insurgencies that were slowly building
popular bases in Mozambique, Angola, and Guinea-Bissau.
But these movements were having an important impact on
the Portuguese armed forces. A young Portuguese artillery
captain provided the following analysis.

     Once the armed independence struggles started
     in Africa, soldiering became a dirty and dangerous
     affair--a low-prestige profession. The military
     academy was no longer stuffed with the sons of the
     rich upper class. Because of the battlefield losses
     and draft-dodging there was a real shortage of
     officers, and of candidates for the military
     academy. Entrance standards were lowered--even sons
     of the lower middle class were welcomed. Because
     social standards were lowered a big class
     differentiation developed between the captains--even
     some majors--and more junior officers, and the
     colonels and generals. This meant that in the

Overseas Territories the junior and medium-grade
officers began to feel considerable sympathy for
those waging their independence struggles as well as
a feeling of hopelessness as to any chances of a
Portuguese victory.[3]

Important leaders of the young officers' coup that
toppled the Caetano regime in April 1974 admit to having
received their political education in the colonial wars.
Captain Otelo Saraiva de Carvalho, in charge of the
military committee of the Armed Forces Movement (MFA)
during the planning of the coup, spent three tours of
duty fighting in the African colonies. He explained: "For
me and many of my comrades, an anti-colonial
consciousness was formed during such tours of duty."[4]
Major Melo Antunes, in charge of drafting the MFA's
political program before the coup and later put in charge
of the decolonization talks, explained how he had been
radicalized: "My three terms of service in Angola ...
made the strongest contribution to my real understanding
of the colonial question. Those experiences defined my
attitude toward colonialism and the fascist regime".[5]
    The leadership of the MFA favored decolonization.
Their position was that the solution to the colonial war
was political, not military. But both the President
installed by the MFA coup, General Spinola, and his
foreign minister, Mario Soares, took a conservative stand
during negotiations with the liberation movements.
Whereas MFA militants favored full decolonization,
Spinola's government was attempting to retain some of
Portugal's economic and political presence in the
colonies. Spinola received discreet support from
Washington in these efforts.

    Rather than unequivocally supporting majority
rule the United States adopted a low profile while
covertly supporting conservative elements during the
five-month power struggle between General Spinola
and militant members of the Armed Forces Movement
committed to revolutionary change within Portugal
and independence for the colonies.[6]

But the stalling tactics of the Spinola government
were only a temporary diversion. In July Colonel Vasco
dos Santos Goncalves, a staunch MFA supporter, was
appointed Prime Minister, and Melo Antunes was put in
charge of decolonization matters.
    In Mozambique the transfer of power was facilitated
by the fact that the Front for the Liberation of
Mozambique (FRELIMO) was without serious rivals to form
the new government.[7] Although the State Department and
CIA made some efforts to strengthen antiFRELIMO elements,
U.S. policymakers were eventually forced to accept
FRELIMO coming to power.[8] Since the official independence

of Mozambique on 25 June 1975, U.S. relations with the
FRELIMO government have been less than friendly, but they
have not been nearly as bad as those with Angola.

THE ANGOLA INTERVENTION

It hardly seems possible that U.S. policymakers
could fashion a policy that would not only bring about
their least preferred outcome but also anger enemies and
allies alike. This is essentially what happened in the
Angola intervention. Angola ended up with a left,
nationalist regime closely allied to the Soviet Union and
Cuba, and in the process of the civil war Washington's
reputation was dealt a severe blow, not just in black
Africa but with South Africa's white rulers as well.
The U.S. intervention in the Angolan war is well
documented and need not be reviewed in detail here.[9] This
section will focus on those aspects of the U.S.
intervention that shed light on U.S. policy toward South
Africa and the relationship between conflict in southern
Africa and conflict within the U.S. policy process.
Unlike the other Portuguese colonies in Africa where
the independence struggles were dominated by single
groups, Angola in 1974 had three nationalist movements:
The National Front for the Liberation of Angola (FNLA),
the National Union for the Total Independence of Angola
(UNITA), and the Popular Movement for the Liberation of
Angola (MPLA).[10] Although these organizations had never
managed to unify, they jointly negotiated with the new
Portuguese government. On 15 January 1975 the three
groups and the Portuguese signed the Alvor Agreement,
which established a tripartite transitional government,
called for a unified national army, and set 11 November
1975 as the date of formal independence.
Immediately after the signing of the Alvor
Agreement, Secretary of State Kissinger's Forty Committee
decided to strengthen its favored Angolan movement,
FNLA.[11] The Forty Committee authorized a direct infusion
of $300,000 to FNLA as well as stepping up arms transfers
to the Zairean government of Mobutu Sese Seko who then
passed the weapons on to FNLA.[12] This surge in American
support encouraged FNLA to seek a military victory over
MPLA.[13]
Given the FNLA's long commitment to a military
solution in Angola, its military superiority, and its
history of opposition to cooperation with the MPLA, such
an increase in U.S. aid could only have had the effect of
undermining the FNLA's adherence to the Alvor Agreements.
Indeed, in March 1975, bolstered by new shipments of U.S.
arms, the FNLA launched an attack on MPLA offices in
Luanda and expelled the MPLA from the northern
territories under FNLA control. Later that month, the
conflict was further internationalized when 1,200 regular

troops from Zaire entered Angola to fight alongside the
FNLA. These reinforcements gave the combined forces of
the FNLA/Zaire and UNITA a four-to-one advantage over the
MPLA.[14]
These initial military engagements in early 1975
began a round of escalations that quickly eliminated the
possibility of a political solution to Angola's problems.
Strengthened by the newly-arrived American weapons
and Zairean regular forces, by late March FNLA gained
control of the northern region to within thirty-five
miles of MPLA's stronghold in the capital, Luanda. MPLA
responded by requesting additional aid from Cuba and the
USSR. Moscow stepped up arms shipments, and by June over
200 Cuban military instructors had arrived in Angola.
By July the tripartite government was rent asunder,
with MPLA forces expelling FNLA and UNITA from the
capital. MPLA was also making progress toward its goal of
controlling the provincial capitals by 11 November 1975,
the date set for independence. The deteriorating position
of FNLA and UNITA in the spring and summer of 1975, and
the prospect that a Soviet ally might come to power,
produced responses from the United States and South
Africa that were to have an important impact on relations
between these two countries.
As pointed out in the previous chapter, during the
postwar period Washington had developed a dependence on a
limited group of class allies in southern Africa: Mobutu
in Zaire and the white settler regimes. There had been
numerous opportunities for Washington to build ties with
the broader-based nationalist movements, but other than
occasional covert flirtations (e.g., with Holden Roberto
in the 1960s) this option was rejected for the threat it
posed to amicable relations with Western Europe and the
white settler regimes.
During the Nixon and Ford administrations U.S.
policy had moved even further away from the nationalist
movements. Thus when the Portuguese began their transfer
of power, Washington was caught with a weak political
base among the regional black-ruled states and
nationalist movements. This left U.S. policymakers with
two options in the Angola crisis: refrain from military
intervention and enlist Portuguese, African and
multilateral cooperation in pressing for a political
solution, or intervene in cooperation with regimes (Zaire
and South Africa) that lacked legitimacy on the African
continent.
An interagency task force on Angola, headed by
Assistant Secretary of State for African Affairs
Nathaniel Davis, grasped this dilemma and recommended
that Washington pursue the diplomatic rather than the
military option.[15] The majority of Task Force members
reasoned that there were too many pitfalls involved in
supporting FNLA and UNITA in an all-out military struggle
against MPLA. The Task Force considered these major

risks:

* FNLA was known to have serious "leadership deficiencies and troop weaknesses."[16]
* UNITA was desperately soliciting arms from many sources and the South African government had expressed an interest in providing assistance. Politically, U.S. association with Pretoria in a military intervention would be the kiss of death once the involvement became known, and disclosure was likely.
* Escalation of the conflict would be exacerbated by the U.S. adopting a military strategy. This in turn would require increasing amounts of material aid which would be difficult to conceal. "The Task Force noted that such exposure would have a negative impact on our relations with other contending factions, with a number of African states, with Portugal, with socialist and Third World countries, and with large segments of the U.S. public and Congress."[17]
* The CIA acknowledged that the "Soviets enjoy greater freedom of action in the covert supply of arms, equipment and ammunition" and "can escalate the level of their aid more readily than we."[18]

Kissinger and Ford rejected the reasoning of their own Africa experts and decided to go ahead with a covert military program in Angola. Stephen Weissman's research details "a three-fold objective" of Kissinger's covert intervention:

> to avoid a precedent of Soviet expansion that could lead to pressures--and accommodationist tendencies--elsewhere in the world; to work with the "moderate" anti-Communist leaders of Zaire and Zambia who feared the consequences of a Soviet-assisted MPLA victory on their own political positions; and to prevent Soviet and MPLA-assisted black extremists from making gains in Namibia, Rhodesia and the rest of southern Africa.[19]

John Stockwell, the CIA officer in charge of the Angolan operation, reports that Kissinger rationalized his preference for covert intervention by reference to Angola's strategic location astride the sea lanes that carry most Middle East oil to the West. This was, however, merely intellectual camouflage for more basic cold war motivations.[20]

Uncomfortable with recent historic events, and frustrated by our humiliation in Vietnam, Kissinger was seeking opportunities to challenge the Soviets. . . . Kissinger saw the Angolan conflict solely in terms of global politics and was determined the Soviets should not be permitted to make a move in any remote part of the world without being confronted militarily by the United States.[21]

Kissinger explained his preference for covert methods in the following terms: "We chose covert means because we wanted to keep our visibility to a minimum: we wanted the greatest possible opportunity for an African solution. We felt that overt assistance would elaborate a formal doctrine justifying great power intervention."[22]

The CIA enjoyed friendly relations with the white minority regime in Pretoria, so when the Agency geared up its covert operation to stop MPLA it was done in full cooperation with the South African security apparatus.[23] Stockwell reports that "to the CIA, the South Africans were the ideal solution for central Angola."[24] Although the U.S. government never openly asked the South Africans to invade Angola, it is clear from the available evidence that Kissinger and the CIA led South African leaders to believe the United States would provide logistical and diplomatic support if the South African military launched an attack on the MPLA.[25]

During the course of its covert operation in Angola, the CIA shipped millions of dollars worth of arms to FNLA and UNITA, shared intelligence with the South African military, encouraged the South African army to become directly involved in the fighting, recruited western mercenaries and facilitated their entry into Angola, lied about the operation to Congress, and carried out a disinformation campaign aimed at the American public.[26] Although the CIA operated with considerable autonomy, it was not acting as a rogue elephant in this affair. The program was approved at the highest levels of the executive branch. Kissinger approved the CIA program, and had encouraged the Israelis and the South Africans to intervene militarily against the MPLA.[27]

During the summer of 1975, with fresh supplies of Soviet weapons and a few hundred Cuban military instructors, MPLA was handily defeating FNLA and UNITA. In July Ford and Kissinger authorized a large increase in U.S. covert aid to the forces arrayed against MPLA. Approximately $65 million worth of arms was granted to FNLA and UNITA.[28]

In the first week of August South African troops first entered southern Angola from their bases in Namibia. The South Africans captured several towns and began training and equipping FNLA and UNITA. MPLA responded by sending military delegations to Cuba and the Soviet Union. The Soviets were unwilling to provide anything more than material aid but the Cubans responded with several hundred additional troops.[29] MPLA did well during the intense fighting of September and October, and with less than a month until independence it appeared that MPLA would receive the reins of government from the departing Portuguese. Official U.S. policy aimed to place FNLA and UNITA on at least an equal footing with MPLA on independence day. It was hoped that this would allow a negotiated solution and less than full power for MPLA.[30]

Only a few weeks before independence there was a military development that proved to be a decisive political factor in MPLA's victory. On 23 October 1975 an estimated 5,000 heavily armed South African troops, accompanied by FNLA, UNITA, and former Portuguese forces, launched an invasion aimed at capturing Luanda. The motorized invasion force (known as the Zulu column) pushed rapidly northward, seizing major towns along the coast. MPLA troops retreated as the South African forces advanced some 500 kilometers in little more than a week. By early November MPLA forces blew up bridges to stop the Zulu column's advance 400 kilometers south of Luanda, and made an urgent appeal for assistance from Cuban regular forces.

On 8 November the first of over 18,000 Cuban troops began arriving in Luanda.[31] By mid-December the Cuban/MPLA forces turned the tide of the FNLA/Zairean offensive in the north and halted the South African advance in the south. The anti-MPLA armies never regained the initiative in the war.

While the CIA was channeling arms and mercenaries into Angola, American diplomats were also active in the attempt to halt MPLA's rise to power. Although U.N. Ambassador Daniel Patrick Moynihan admitted there was "a convergence of policy" between Washington and Pretoria, Secretary of State Kissinger attempted to obscure the South African role.[32] As late as 28 November 1975, when thousands of South African troops occupied Angola, Kissinger stated: "To the best of my knowledge, the South Africans are not engaged officially."[33]

Washington officials "pressured countries like Trinidad and Tobago and Barbados to deny refueling privileges to Cuban planes en route to Luanda."[34] Kissinger made public threats against Cuba and at one point secretly considered making a military feint at the island. On the eve of a January 1976 Organization of African Unity meeting on the subject of Angola, U.S. officials lobbied African leaders to condemn all foreign intervention rather than singling out South Africa's invasion. This effectively split the Africans into a 22 to 22 deadlock, and no resolution could be passed.[35]

With MPLA in control of the Bank of Angola and its lucrative contracts with Gulf Oil, CIA and State Department attorneys sought to block Gulf's royalty payments to the MPLA government.[36] Although Gulf could not be persuaded to hand the money over to FNLA and UNITA because these groups controlled neither the central government nor the Cabinda oil fields, U.S. officials did succeed in pressuring Gulf to put its royalty payments in an escrow account. This effectively denied MPLA hundreds of millions of dollars in operating revenues.

The State Department blocked the transfer to Angola of two Boeing 737 planes that had already been paid for. In response to appeals from the president of Boeing and two Angolan envoys to release the planes, the State Department presented the Angolans with an official statement regarding American technology transfers and their political costs.

> The MPLA would do well to heed our advice that no government can plan the reconstruction in postwar Angola without United States and western help. No government can obtain the technical and financial resources to stimulate economic development without American consent...the United States would be quite responsive and helpful to a coalition government that was not dependent on the Soviet Union.[37]

The MPLA was not impressed by the logic of this argument and continued its efforts to defeat FNLA and UNITA. The planes were not delivered.

A key turning point for the U.S. intervention in Angola was reached on 27 November when the CIA exhausted its Contingency Reserve Fund. Attempts to secure $28 million from the Department of Defense were unsuccessful. This gave congressional opponents of the Angola intervention an opportunity to pass legislation restricting funding for covert U.S. involvement in Angola. The timing could not have been much worse for those favoring an interventionist policy. With the U.S. defeat in Vietnam fresh in people's minds, there was considerable public and congressional opposition to U.S. involvement in another third world country that seemed of little strategic significance.

On 19 December 1975, the Senate passed an amendment offered by John Tunney (D-CA) to the Defense Appropriations bill prohibiting further spending on covert operations in Angola. On 27 January 1976, the House voted 323 to 99 in favor of the restrictions, and on 9 February President Ford, reticent to veto the entire Defense Appropriations bill, signed the restrictions into law.

Although it was clear as early as December 1975 that Congress was opposed to the covert program in Angola, the CIA mustered several million dollars more and continued shipping weapons into Angola. "Only after February 9, when the President's signature legalized the Tunney Amendment, did the CIA acknowledge defeat and begin to withdraw."[38]

Opposition in Congress was based as much on procedure as on substance. Throughout the covert program to assist FNLA and later UNITA, the CIA briefed numerous members of Congress but led them to believe that the operation would be carried out indirectly. Zaire would supply weapons to the insurgents and the United States would simply resupply Zaire. No U.S. personnel would be involved in the conflict, and the operation would not stigmatize the United States by cooperating with Pretoria. All of these assurances were lies.

The Pentagon had intelligence personnel in Namibia consulting with South African military officials.[39] The CIA briefed "friendly" African leaders on how to deceive Senator Clark when he made a fact-finding trip in the summer of 1975.[40] On one occasion in early December, preceding the Senate's passage of the Tunney Amendment, the Deputy Assistant Secretary of State for Africa, Edward Mulcahy, was caught lying to a Senate panel on the question of direct U.S. arms shipments into Angola. Congressional pique over being manipulated by Kissinger, Colby, and other officials played as important a role in sparking dissent as did principled opposition to an interventionist foreign policy.

If disarray in executive/congressional relations was one legacy of the Angola affair, another was the sowing of distrust among South African leaders toward their counterparts in Washington. Having received a green light from Kissinger and the CIA to intervene, and having committed itself to a venture with high political as well as military risk, by January 1976 the South African government realized that Washington would not provide anything near the levels of support that were intimated at the outset. With Cuban/MPLA forces now on the offensive, and growing international opposition to Pretoria's intervention, the Zulu column began an orderly retreat to bases in northern Namibia.[41]

Despite the CIA's camaraderie, and despite whatever reassurances the South Africans felt they had received from the Ford administration, the United States had rejected their bid for overt support. Three months later the United States joined in a critical vote against them in the United Nations Security Council. The South African military was bitter, feeling that it was discredited in the eyes of the world. The campaign had been expensive, costing the South African government $133 million. The damage to its white population's morale, the bitterness over the deaths of its soldiers in a secret, ill-conceived campaign in Angola, the humiliation of having two soldiers paraded before the Organization of African Unity in Addis Ababa, were all impossible to measure.[42]

The leader of the South African Defense Forces during this betrayal by Washington was the future prime minister, P.W. Botha. Years later, South African leaders would use this American betrayal--at the hands of a Republican administration--as a political stick with which to hit American negotiators.[43]

Another negative legacy for the United States was the way in which Kissinger's blundering on Angola alienated leaders in Black Africa. While Kissinger and other American officials fulminated against communist backing for MPLA, African states moved decisively to support MPLA's consolidation of power. As early as 27 November 1975 Nigeria--at that time America's second largest supplier of oil--had recognized MPLA and began providing substantial assistance.

On 22 January 1976 the Organization of African Unity officially denounced South Africa's intervention while refusing to condemn the Soviet Union or Cuba. The OAU's seal of approval was given to MPLA on 11 February when the new government was admitted as a member. By March, 41 of the 46 members of the OAU had officially recognized the MPLA government.

Kissinger and other conservatives were correct in arguing that the outcome in Angola was a victory for communist forces and represented part of a new, more confident strategy by Moscow.[44] If, as one analyst opined, the Soviets "gambled on paralysis in U.S. foreign policymaking machinery to make their challenge in Angola, it proved to be a good gamble".[45]

But this begs the question of what caused the "paralysis" in U.S. policy. Why did U.S. policymakers end up with a situation in Angola that was precisely the opposite of what they had intended? How could the CIA have been so politically insensitive as to ally itself with South Africa in a military intervention against black Africans far from South Africa's borders? What explains Kissinger's ignorance of Angola and his arrogance toward the U.S. Congress?

The Armed Forces Movement coup in Portugal effectively removed one of Washington's main class allies in southern Africa. For many decades America's corporate and government leaders had been content to rely on dictatorial minority regimes to secure western access to the profitable human and material resources of the region. Over the years solid ties developed between the U.S. ruling class and its counterparts in southern Africa. This alliance required the suppression of the African majority in these nations. The price the U.S. government was paying for its alliance with the white minority regimes was the alienation of black African opinion and a paucity of dependable African allies in the region. This was not a big problem as long as the white minority regimes were firmly in power, but when they began to be challenged by black insurgents U.S. policy

entered a crisis phase.
The fall of Portuguese settler colonialism, not
foreseen by American intelligence because of its
dependence on official Portuguese and South African
sources, made it necessary for the United States to
scramble for a new set of local allies. Decades of
regional neglect and acceptance of the racist status quo
had left Washington with a weak political base in
southern Africa--Kissinger's two main allies in the
Angola intervention were Mobutu's Zaire (one of the most
discredited states in Africa), and the apartheid
government of South Africa (certainly the most detested
regime on the continent). Within Angola, Washington had
little knowledge of, or leverage over, the three
contending movements. And when reliable information on
these movements was finally collected, consideration of
the political dynamics within Angola was subordinated to
Kissinger's fixation with Soviet behavior.
Starting from this weak position, U.S. policy in the
Angolan crisis was also saddled with an operational arm,
the CIA, that was incapable of representing U.S. national
interests. The CIA's close working relationship with
Pretoria, its dependence on the least viable of the three
nationalist movements (FNLA), its use of the
much-despised white mercenaries, and its systematic
deception of the American Congress and public, all
combined to guarantee a policy debacle in Angola.
Although the CIA violated aspects of its charter, it was
operating within traditional political guidelines of
opposing Soviet allies and supporting anticommunist
elements. This simple rule-of-thumb has the status of
dogma within the U.S. policy apparatus but has proven
that it is insufficiently flexible to deal with the
complex realities of third world revolutions.
The Angolan crisis was important for several
reasons. First, Angola has great potential for assisting
revolutionary forces in South Africa.[46] Second, the
Angolan conflict marked a significant turning point in
official U.S. attention and tactics toward southern
Africa.[47] Third, the defeat of U.S. and South African
forces represented a high-water mark for Cuban and Soviet
policy in Africa, while Washington and Pretoria were each
dealt a serious blow.[48] Finally, revolutionary
nationalists in Namibia, Zimbabwe, and South Africa were
given a considerable boost by the outcome in Angola.[49]

REDEFINING THE U.S. ROLE

It was not until the Cubans intervened in
Angola that Kissinger began seriously to question
any of the assumptions about U.S. policy in the
region. The ill-fated Angolan rescue operation was
the immediate reaction, and the Kissinger speech in

Lusaka in April 1976, outlining a new U.S. commitment to majority rule in Rhodesia, was the first serious step toward redefining the American role in southern Africa.[50]

The rapidity of change in Angola, and the eventual outcome, came as a shock to U.S. policymakers. Kissinger was determined that the method by which the MPLA had come to power, with the assistance of Cuban forces and massive Soviet aid, would not set a precedent for other revolutionaries in the region.[51] Washington refused to recognize the MPLA government and blocked its entry into the United Nations. Kissinger's tough line against the Angolans was based mainly on their ties to the USSR and Cuba. But domestic pressures were also pushing the Ford administration to be loudly anticommunist.

It was no coincidence that the hardening of the Administration's line on Angola coincided with the conservative challenge mounted by Ronald Reagan during the primaries. From Florida in February to California in June, Ford (with considerable help from Kissinger) tried to appeal to the right wing of the Republican Party through caustic attacks on Cuba and Angola.[52]

Kissinger's denunciations of the Cuban role in Angola served several functions. In early 1976 South African troops were still in the process of withdrawing from Angola, and Kissinger's attacks on the Cubans helped deflect media attention from the South African retreat. Kissinger also had his eye on the next conflict that would require his attention: he threatened unspecified retaliation by the United States if Cuba became more directly involved in the Rhodesian conflict.[53] Kissinger "directed his threats about Zimbabwe almost exclusively against Cuba, although they apply by implication to the Soviet Union also".[54] This unconventional twist to traditional anticommunist rhetoric was based on the fact that candidate Reagan had been blasting Kissinger's policy of detente with the Soviets. The Ford team hoped that by directing their anticommunist attacks primarily at Cuba they could still maintain an appearance of being tough on communism while not playing into Reagan's hands on the issue of detente.[55]

With the war in Rhodesia intensifying, Kissinger was concerned to prevent an outcome similar to that in Angola.[56] Kissinger explained his fears of radicalization in southern Africa in the following terms.

Events in Angola encouraged radicals to press for a military solution in Rhodesia. With radical influence on the rise, and with immense outside military strength apparently behind the radicals, even moderate and responsible African leaders--firm proponents of peaceful change--began to conclude there was no alternative but to embrace the cause of violence.[57]

There were several long-term consequences of the guerrilla war that Kissinger was trying to avert. The Zimbabwean guerrillas stood a good chance of toppling Rhodesia's white minority, thus advancing the armed struggle to South Africa's doorstep. Prolonged people's war could result in a general radicalization of the populace, and continued armed struggle provided opportunities for communist powers to increase their leverage in the region. It was also clear that if the United States was to manage a transition to bourgeois African rule in Rhodesia it would be necessary to gain the cooperation of the the Frontline Presidents,[58] the British, and South African Prime Minister Vorster, all of whom had sound historical reasons for distrusting the others.
    Kissinger saw the U.S. role as that of a go-between for groups too bitterly opposed to negotiate directly. The British were recognized by most parties as still holding colonial responsibility for overseeing the transition to majority rule, and London had already laid out a detailed set of proposals for just such a process. Kissinger intended to get all-party negotiations on the track laid out by the British proposals and then, having used American influence to get things moving, retire to a supporting role and let the British take over.[59]
    In April 1976 Kissinger travelled to Kenya, Tanzania, Zambia, Zaire, Liberia and Senegal. The key policy address of the tour came on 27 April in Lusaka, Zambia. In it Kissinger proclaimed "a new era in American policy" toward southern Africa.[60] His ten-point proposal foreshadowed many of the positions to be taken by the Carter administration. He warned the white regime in Salisbury that it should not expect U.S. support in its conflict with neighboring African states and the liberation movements.[61] Also included in the speech was a promise to provide assistance to neighboring states experiencing hardships due to the closing of their borders with Rhodesia in compliance with U.N. sanctions.
    By taking a tough verbal position against white minority rule in Rhodesia, and offering humanitarian aid to regional black-ruled states, Kissinger was attempting to gain sufficient cooperation from black elites to bring about a negotiated settlement that would be enforceable. He later described his divide-and-rule strategy in the following way:

My plan was to co-opt the program of moderate evolutionary reform, that is to say majority rule, and minority rights. At the same time we sought to create a kind of firebreak between those whose radicalism was ideological and those whose radicalism was geared to specific issues. We could meet the demands for majority rule; we never thought we could co-opt the ideological radicals; our goal was to isolate them.[62]

During the summer and fall of 1976 Kissinger shuttled around the capitals of the region. He was attempting to get the Frontline Presidents to deliver the Zimbabwean liberation movement leaders to the negotiating table. He coaxed Pretoria to do the same with Ian Smith. Kissinger had little direct leverage with the Rhodesian regime and had to rely on Vorster to pressure Smith.

Kissinger's talks with Vorster on how to bring Smith to the conference table were kept secret but some details can be pieced together. In diplomatic jargon, Kissinger relied much more on carrots that sticks. One author claims that Washington was manipulating the price of gold to put pressure on the South African economy, but this charge is based on flimsy evidence.[63] As for the carrots, the very fact that the U.S. Secretary of State was meeting openly with Vorster was a concession. This was a clear break with the U.S. tradition of avoiding public contacts with South African leaders. Although during a 17 June 1976 address to the House International Relations Committee Kissinger explicitly denied having promised any rewards to Vorster, he in fact made several friendly offerings in order to secure Vorster's cooperation on Rhodesia.

First, Kissinger invited the South African navy to send a frigate to a naval revue as part of America's bicentennial celebrations. While mainly a token gesture, it was the first visit of a South African naval vessel to the United States, and the apartheid regime has always prized military ties to the West.

Second, Kissinger reportedly presented Vorster with a proposal for the United States to sponsor and train a Namibian military force if Pretoria would cooperate with a transfer of power to a mutually acceptable, indigenous ruling group in Namibia.[64]

Third, during 1976 and early 1977 the International Monetary Fund (IMF) granted South Africa $464 million in credits. At the time, South Africa was suffering from one of its more severe balance of payments crises, and desperately needed infusions of capital (Table 4.1). Although there is no hard evidence that it was done at Kissinger's request as a bargaining chip to Vorster, considerable British and American pressure was used to overcome opposition to the credit by European and African members. The West German, Italian, Spanish, and Portuguese delegates accused the IMF of rigging its own data to favor the South African loan requests.[65]

Table 4.1
SOUTH AFRICA'S BALANCE OF PAYMENTS (millions of Rand)

	1970-74 (annual average)	1975	1976	1977
Exports	2,180	3,653	4,889	6,332
Net Gold Output	1,451	2,540	2,346	2,795
Imports	-3,533	-6,742	-7,443	-6,893
Invisible Items, Net	-712	-1,264	-1,422	-1,483
Current Balance	-613	-1,813	-1,630	751
Long-term Capital	495	1,746	989	211
Short-term Capital	25	-238	-415	-1,086
Overall Balance	-93	-305	-1,056	-124

Source: International Monetary Fund, South Africa: Recent Economic Developments, 26 April 1978, p. 17.

The amount granted was greater than the total IMF allocation to all of Black Africa during the same period and was only exceeded by record loans to Mexico and Britain. The European and African delegates opposed to the South African credits pointed out that Pretoria had created its own predicament: it was financing a huge military buildup by printing money, thus pushing up inflation rates and exacerbating the balance of payments crisis.[66] Confidential records show that in spite of these considerations British and American members of the IMF executive Board spoke out strongly in favor of giving Pretoria "some feeling of international support" in its time of economic crisis.[67] The record aid package was granted.

Kissinger wanted Vorster to pressure Ian Smith's ruling Rhodesian Front Party to make enough concessions to draw the Frontline Presidents and the guerrilla leaders into a negotiated transition to majority rule. Kissinger hoped this could be done while retaining substantial economic and political power for the whites.

President Nyerere criticized Kissinger, however, for focusing all his attention on Rhodesia and failing to pressure the South Africans to end their illegal occupation of Namibia. "Nyerere argued with Kissinger that conditions were not ripe for hasty action in Rhodesia; but they were in Namibia where Vorster had the power to ordain change. So Kissinger should concentrate on Namibia when he got to Pretoria."[68]

The guerrilla movements in Rhodesia had reached
regime-threatening proportions, so Kissinger sensed the
urgency of preventing the radicals from coming to power.
In Namibia, on the other hand, geographic and demographic
factors limited the guerrilla movement's ability to pose
a serious military challenge to South African rule. For
Kissinger and the white supremacists of southern Africa,
Rhodesia was an emergency, Namibia could wait.[69]
     If a "moderate" (i.e., bourgeois) African government
could be eased into place in Rhodesia it would not only
safeguard western economic interests in that country but
would also limit the future leverage of the radicals in
Namibia and South Africa. "Betraying" the Rhodesian
whites (as they saw it) was a price Kissinger was willing
to pay in exchange for retarding further radicalization
and Soviet influence in southern Africa.[70]

ON THE HOME FRONT

     The policy straddle confronting Kissinger in
southern Africa--establishing necessary ties with black
leaders while coaxing traditional white allies to make
concessions--was matched by a similar straddle in the
United States. Kissinger sought the support of American
black leaders for his southern Africa initiative, yet in
an election year the Ford administration was
understandably worried about a challenge from the right.

     Conservatives in particular have criticized the
     Kissinger efforts, and some Republicans believe that
     Ronald Reagan's victory in the Texas primary was
     aided by Mr. Kissinger's initial trip to southern
     Africa and his support for majority rule in Rhodesia
     that he expressed on that trip.[71]

     According to administration officials, most of the
mail coming into the State Department at the time was
opposed to Kissinger's initiative in southern Africa
because of its support for black majority rule.[72]
     In 1975 the United Nations Security Council had set
31 August 1976 as a deadline for the South African
government to show some progress toward granting
independence to Namibia. Coincidentally, on that very day
Henry Kissinger was in Philadelphia trying to convince an
important group of black Americans (Reverend Leon
Sullivan's Opportunities Industrialization Centers)[73]
that progressive change was definitely on the agenda in
southern Africa, implying that this was largely due to
his own efforts. The themes of the address were similar
to the ones stressed earlier that month in a speech
Kissinger gave to the National Urban League, and in
private conversations with black leaders such as the
Reverend Jesse Jackson, Manhattan Borough President Percy

Sutton, and William Booth of the American Committee on Africa.[74]

Although Kissinger initiated these meetings on southern Africa, the black leaders brought their own agenda. They demanded that: Washington communicate to Pretoria in strong terms its opposition to the race policies that had precipitated recent rioting; Kissinger disclose the content of his talks with Prime Minister Vorster; the U.S. grant political asylum to South African refugees; and an official black American fact-finding team visit South Africa.[75] The black politicians and civil rights leaders also suggested that Washington pressure American corporations to improve working conditions for their black South African employees.[76] Congressmen Andrew Young (D-Ga.) stressed that U.S. banks and industrial firms could play an important role in uplifting South Africa if only they would alter corporate policies.[77] But the problem that received the greatest attention and the only substantive response from the Ford administration was the issue of minority hiring in the State Department.[78]

Apart from revised hiring practices at the State Department, there were no changes forthcoming that could have altered the amicable relations between the U.S. government and South Africa's rulers. A former White House Africa specialist under Kissinger lamented that as late as 1976 there was "still no authentic sensitivity or sophisticated knowledge" of the struggles taking place in southern Africa.[79] "Nor is there a wider readiness in the administration to confront the vast American corporate interests or the cozy CIA liaison with South Africa that have always quietly mocked the official public disapproval of the racist regimes."[80]

If one of Kissinger's primary domestic goals was to gain black support for the Ford administration, his lobbying efforts were indeed a failure. Jimmy Carter won over 90 percent of the black vote in the 1976 election.

In the international arena Kissinger's diplomacy was slightly more successful. Assuming that his dual goal was to impede the advance of the armed struggle (especially in Rhodesia), and establish negotiations aimed at a transfer of power to pro-western African leaders, Kissinger's efforts were only a temporary success. His 1976 Geneva conference on Rhodesia fizzled, and he left office without having significantly changed the flow of events in southern Africa.

How was it that this extremely skilled diplomat, with the resources of the world's most powerful nation behind him, was unable to tilt the balance of forces in a small country like Rhodesia? And why, in hindsight, did Kissinger's efforts seem doomed from the start?

THE FAILURE OF KISSINGER'S RHODESIA DIPLOMACY

In the fall of 1976 Kissinger conducted a round of shuttle diplomacy in an attempt to forge agreement on his set of proposals for ending the civil war in Rhodesia.[81] Ian Smith, pressured on one side by the guerrilla armies and on the other side by Kissinger and Vorster, accepted Kissinger's proposals for a gradual transfer of power. The Frontline Presidents, on the other hand, rejected any package deal written by Kissinger, Vorster, and Smith, and held out for an all-parties conference to be convened by Britain. The Frontline Presidents still recognized Britain as the colonial authority in Rhodesia and held the British responsible for overseeing a transition to majority rule.

By late October an all-parties conference was convened in Geneva with the British presiding. Although the conference broke down in early December without a settlement, the process helped illuminate the basic contradiction that has stymied U.S. policy initiatives in the region.

The settler-colonial regimes, which for many decades facilitated western capital penetration of the region, also engendered a highly unequal distribution of wealth and political power. By 1976 opposition by black Rhodesians to white minority capitalism had grown to such an extent that the very survival of the regime was in question.

Kissinger and other U.S. policymakers understood that in order to preserve Rhodesia's political and economic linkages to the West it would be necessary to expand the popular base of the regime. Kissinger hoped to increase the Rhodesian government's domestic and international legitimacy while blocking Soviet influence and limiting the revolutionaries' power to disrupt capital accumulation. This contradiction between legitimation and accumulation was the central and ultimately unmanageable problem for Kissinger in Rhodesia. It also foreshadowed the key problem for U.S. policy toward South Africa.

The two guerrilla movements, the Zimbabwe African National Union (ZANU) and the Zimbabwe African People's Union (ZAPU), had recently formed an alliance--the Patriotic Front. The Patriotic Front was the only black Rhodesian political group to gain the support of the Frontline Presidents, the Organization of African Unity, and a majority at the United Nations. The Patriotic Front and its backers were convinced that armed struggle had played a decisive role in bringing about negotiations in the first place. During the course of the guerrilla war there had been a direct relationship between the guerrillas' increasing combat effectiveness, brutal government repression of the peasantry, popular support for the guerrillas, and international assistance to ZANU and ZAPU.[82]

As these most militant and anticapitalist of the black political groups were in the ascendant, the Rhodesian blacks who cooperated with the white minority regime were steadily losing what little credibility they had. Although there were several black collaborators--later the U.S. government would even make efforts to break Joshua Nkomo away from his alliance with Robert Mugabe--the key black ally of Smith and the West was Bishop Abel Muzorewa.[83] The Bishop owed much of his political strength to his conciliatory stance toward western capital and the white minority. His support among Rhodesian blacks was due largely to his leadership of the "No-to-the-Pearce-Commission" campaign of 1972.[84]

In recent years the Bishop's popularity had been declining due to his ever closer identification with white interests. Then, at the Geneva conference, Muzorewa suffered the humiliation of several top aides defecting to the Patriotic Front. Although the Geneva conference broke down without reaching a settlement, it helped strengthen the impression that the moderate blacks were declining as a political force, while the revolutionaries were gaining strength domestically and internationally.

Kissinger left office without having brought the Rhodesian conflict closer to a resolution. Yet this policy failure cannot be blamed on Kissinger's personal shortcomings. It is true that he was generally ignorant of African affairs.[85] For most of his career Kissinger had been concentrating on Southeast Asia, the Middle East, China and the Soviet Union. He had little time for African matters until the events of 1975 forced him to take an interest in southern Africa. Kissinger's relative ignorance about Africa fed into his ideological penchant for viewing African affairs from the perspective of East-West competition. In addition, one of Kissinger's top Africa advisers claimed that racism also clouded the Secretary's view of Africa.[86]

Kissinger's major error lay in his underestimation of the importance of winning over black African leaders (particularly the Frontline Presidents), and in his reliance on Vorster and Smith as agents of change. The guerrilla movements were dependent on the Frontline States for political and economic support as well as geographic security, and the Organization of African Unity had endorsed the Frontline Presidents as the ones responsible for African strategy in the Rhodesian conflict. This meant that for U.S. policymakers to gain leverage with the main agents of change in the region they would need to cultivate a relationship with the Frontline Presidents. Kissinger failed to do this.[87]

Yet it would be wrong to fault Kissinger personally in this regard because he was simply following a pattern that had been laid down by generations of U.S. policymakers before him. Africa had never been a high priority in Washington. Because U.S. policy was dominated by corporate and security interests, America's institutional ties were with the white minorities. When the regional balance of power began shifting with the fall of Portuguese colonialism and growing black insurgency in Rhodesia and South Africa, U.S. policymakers were caught with a narrow diplomatic base and a set of alliances that were rapidly becoming obsolete.

For decades U.S. policymakers had relied on a strategy of carefully crafted ambiguity: attempting to straddle the race question and more material interests with a dual policy of verbally attacking white supremacy while maintaining friendly ties to the white regimes. No American president, dependent as they all are on corporate support, could take decisive action against anticommunist regimes friendly to western capital.

Many decades of bourgeois dominance over U.S. policy created cross-national institutional linkages to the white regimes. These ties limited U.S. flexibility when, in the 1970s, guerrilla movements backed by the communist powers rapidly expanded their popular base. In the past, capital accumulation had been the dominant motivation for U.S. involvement in the region, but now with the growth of a radical alternative, U.S. policymakers had to pay greater attention to the legitimation of the capitalist social order.

The immediate dilemma of U.S. policy was that those forces who were gaining mass legitimacy (the revolutionaries) were the most estranged from the West, while those whose popular support was eroding (the white regimes and their black collaborators) were the ones most closely linked to western elites. One of the innovations of the early Carter administration would be to deal with this structural crisis by backing away from friendly collaboration with the white regimes and working more closely with black states and the revolutionary nationalist movements.

NOTES

1. Throughout my discussion of the Ford administration I use the name of Henry Kissinger to personify U.S. policymaking. Although Gerald Ford was nominally in command, there was little doubt as to who was really calling the shots on foreign policy. A former member of Kissinger's National Security Council sums it up well: "Ford entered the foreign affairs responsibilities of the presidency as the epitome of the uninformed, unprepared, expert-awed American politician, all with the added burden of being the unknown, unelected successor to the most corrupt administration in memory.

Without a sense of his own independent position in foreign policy. . . . Ford found Kissinger indispensable in appearance and fact." Roger Morris, Uncertain Greatness: Henry Kissinger and American Foreign Policy (New York: Harper and Row, 1977), p. 292.
2. Colin Legum, "Introduction" in Gwendolen M. Carter and Patrick O'Meara, eds., Southern Africa in Crisis (Bloomington: Indiana University Press, 1977), p. 9.
3. Wilfred Burchett, Southern Africa Stands Up (New York: Urizen Books, 1978), p. 57.
4. Ibid., p. 60.
5. Ibid., p. 61.
6. Allen Isaacman and Jennifer Davis, "U.S. Policy Towards Mozambique 1946-1976," in Rene Lemarchand, ed., American Policy in Southern Africa (Washington, D.C.: University Press of America, 1978), p. 36.
7. Isaacman and Davis provide a concise, reliable overview of the war for independence in Mozambique. Also see James H. Mittelman, "Mozambique: The Political Economy of Underdevelopment," Journal of Southern African Affairs, III, 1, January 1978.
8. Isaacman and Davis, "U.S. Policy...", pp. 37-38.
9. Useful sources on this topic are: John Stockwell, In Search of Enemies (New York: W.W. Norton & Co., 1978); Gerald Bender, "Kissinger in Angola, Anatomy of a Failure," in Lemarchand American Policy in Southern Africa; Ernest Harsch and Tony Thomas, Angola: The Hidden History of Washington's War (New York: Pathfinder Press, 1976); Burchett, Southern Africa Stands Up; Center for National Security Studies, CIA's Secret War in Angola (Washington, D.C.: CNSS, 1974); U.S. Congress, House, United States-Angolan Relations, Hearings before the Subcommittee on Africa, 25 May 1978 (Washington, D.C.: Government Printing Office, 1978); and Mohammed S. El-Khawas, Angola: The American-South African Connection (Washington, D.C.: African Bibliographic Center, 1978).
10. For background on the Angolan nationalist movements, see John A. Marcum's two volume study The Angolan Revolution: The Anatomy of an Explosion, 1940-1962 (Cambridge: MIT Press, 1969) and The Angolan Revolution: Exile Politics and Guerrilla Warfare, 1962-1976 (Cambridge: MIT Press, 1978); and the insightful review essay by W.G. Clarence Smith, "Class Structure and Class Struggles in Angola in the 1970s," Journal of Southern African Studies, 7, 1, October 1980.
11. Along guidelines established by National Security Decision Memorandum (NSDM) #40 signed by President Nixon in 1970, the Forty Committee was responsible for overseeing covert operations. It consisted of Kissinger (chairing the group), Joint Chiefs of Staff Chairman General George Brown, CIA Director William Colby, Deputy Secretary of Defense William Clements, and Under Secretary of State for Political

Affairs Joseph Sisco. The FNLA's leader, Holden Roberto, had been receiving $10,000 a year from the CIA throughout most of the 1960s. This had been cut off early in the Nixon administration as a friendly gesture to the Portuguese colonial regime.
    12. Stockwell, In Search of Enemies, pp. 265-68 provides detailed lists of the weapons delivered to FNLA and UNITA.
    13. Bender in Lemarchand, American Policy... pp. 76-77, gives a detailed appraisal of the impact of the U.S. assistance.
    14. William LeoGrande, Cuba's Policy in Africa, 1949-1980 (Berkeley: Institute of International Studies/University of California, 1980), pp. 16-17.
    15. Davis' account of the intra-state struggle over these different options is contained in his article, "The Angola Decision of 1975: A Personal Memoir," Foreign Affairs, Fall 1978. My characterization of the Angola Task Force's Report is based on Davis' account (pp. 111-13).
    16. Ibid., p. 114.
    17. Ibid., p. 113.
    18. Ibid., p. 114.
    19. Stephen Weissman, "The CIA and U.S. Policy in Zaire and Angola," in Lemarchand, ed., American Policy in Southern Africa, pp. 404-5.
    20. For more on official U.S. and South African rationales for the intervention see El-Khawas, Angola: the American-South African Connection, pp. 2-3.
    21. Stockwell, In Search of Enemies, p. 43. Stockwell reports that CIA Director William Colby also viewed the situation from a cold war perspective.
    22. Quoted by Thomas Franck and Edward Weisband, Foreign Policy by Congress (New York: Oxford University Press, 1979), pp. 456-57. The quote is taken from Kissinger's testimony in U.S. Involvement in the Civil War in Angola, U.S. Senate Subcommittee on African Affairs, Hearings, 29 January 1976.
    23. John Stockwell was the CIA officer in charge of ground operations during the CIA's covert intervention in the Angolan civil war. Much of my account is based on Stockwell's book In Search of Enemies, his House Africa Subcommittee testimony of 25 May 1978, United States-Angola Relations, and interviews conducted with Stockwell in 1979 and 1980. Also instructive on U.S. cooperation with South Africa in this intervention are the previously cited works by Weissman and El-Khawas.
    24. Stockwell, In Search of Enemies, p. 187.
    25. John Marcum, "Lessons of Angola," Foreign Affairs, 54, 3, April 1976, p. 422.
    26. In Stockwell's Congressional testimony (United States-Angolan Relations, 25 May 1978, House Africa Subcommittee) he reports "that there was close collaboration and encouragement between the CIA and the

South Africans. The CIA funded and directed the activities of two teams of propagandists inside the United States and fed them false information to be used to influence the United Nations and the American people. It also placed false stories in American newspapers" (p. 13). Why did the CIA find it necessary to deceive the American public? "The CIA Director and Mr. Kissinger were surely acutely aware that the American public would not tolerate such an operation 3 months after the humiliation of our evacuation of South Vietnam, so they lied about it. Even in secret briefings to Congress they dissembled" (p. 13). When asked if there was collaboration between the CIA and the South African Intelligence Agency, BOSS, Stockwell relied "Yes sir, indeed. Early in the conflict we gave permission to the Pretoria station to brief them fully on our program and what we were doing. We required all stations in the area to inform Pretoria of their cable traffic so Pretoria would be fully informed of everything that went on. This was obviously intended as encouragement" (p. 17). "There was close collaboration. It was intentional. During the program, one of the chiefs of the South African service flew to Washington twice and conferred with the CIA Director and with the Chief of the African Division" (p. 16).

27. Britain's conservative business journal The Economist of 5 November 1977 reports that "Mr. Kissinger in early 1975 secretly asked the Israeli government to send troops to Angola to co-operate with the South African army in fighting the Cuban-backed Popular Movement." (p. 90) The evidence of Kissinger's encouragement of South Africa's invasion comes from several sources. The first piece comes from Der Spiegel, 14 August 1978, pp. 96-101, reprinted in Foreign Broadcast Information Service (FBIS), 15 August 1978, pp. E6-E14. When Foreign Minister Roelof Botha is asked if Washington encouraged South Africa to invade Angola, Botha replied: "'Encourage' would be the understatement of the year." John Marcum, in his article "Lessons of Angola", reports on South African officials citing "an understanding with American officials that the United States would rush sufficient supplies to counterbalance the weapons superiority of the MPLA/Cuban forces." (p. 422) In a 17 May 1976 interview in Newsweek Prime Minister Vorster implicates the U.S. in encouraging the invasion. In the 1970 annual review of world events by Foreign Affairs, former U.N. Ambassador Andrew Young says that South Africa's invasion was "launched with western encouragement."

28. LeoGrande, Cuba's Policy..., p. 17. As LeoGrande points out, this is not the figure given by the CIA. The Agency was systematically undervaluing the military hardware so it would appear to be less than what was actually delivered. For example, .45 caliber automatic pistols were priced at $5 apiece and automatic rifles

were valued at $7.55 each. Some estimates of total CIA aid at this time range as high as $100 million. See Bender in Lemarchand, American Policy...
     29. LeoGrande, Cuba's Policy..., p. 18
     30. Stockwell, In Search.., p. 161.
     31. LeoGrande (p. 20) provides a detailed chart of western and Cuban/MPLA estimates of how many troops arrived during different time periods. For a dramatic, inside look at the Cuban troop movements see Gabriel Garcia Marquez, "Operation Carlota," Tricontinental, #53.
     32. El-Khawas, Angola: The American-South African Connection, p. 6.
     33. Quoted in ibid., p. 5.
     34. Ibid., p. 6.
     35. Stockwell, In Search..., p. 233.
     36. Ibid., pp. 203-204, provides details.
     37. The full text of the message appears in ibid., pp. 205-6.
     38. Stockwell, In Search..., p.234.
     39. This Pentagon intelligence officer told the author that not only was there close cooperation between the CIA and the South Africans, the Pentagon also had intelligence personnel on the ground in Namibia consulting with the South African army.
     40. Stockwell, In Search..., p. 232.
     41. The Zulu Column was not fully withdrawn from Angola until late March 1976.
     42. Stockwell, In Search..., pp. 227-29.
     43. On this point see Benjamin Pogrund, "South Africa Stalls," The New Republic, 18 November 1981.
     44. A leading conservative authority on Soviet policy in Africa, David E. Albright, argues that "the demise of Portugal's African empire in the mid 1970s first convinced Soviet leaders that significant new opportunities were opening up in the area...," "USSR and Southern Africa," African Index, 3 November 1980, p. 73. Also see Albright's edited volume Communism in Africa (Bloomington and London: Indiana University Press, 1980), particularly the essay by Jiri Valenta, "Soviet Decision-Making on the Intervention in Angola"; and Colin Legum, "The Soviet Union, China and the West in Southern Africa," Foreign Affairs, # 54, July 1976. For a well-informed Soviet view of the Angolan civil war see Oleg Ignatyev, Secret Weapon in Africa (Moscow: Progress Publishers, 1977).
     45. Colin Legum, "A Letter on Angola to American Liberals," The New Republic, 31 January 1976, p. 17.
     46. Few people realize the importance of Angola to the continuing revolution in southern Africa. Angola suffers from neither the military proximity nor economic integration with South Africa that necessarily moderates the politics of other regional states. Although the economy is severely underdeveloped, there are vast stores of oil and minerals, in addition to considerable

agricultural potential. A stable, socialist Angola would
be capable of providing crucial geographic and financial
assistance to revolutionary forces in the region, hence
the enduring South African campaign to destabilize the
Angolan economy. See U.S. Agency for International
Development,Development Needs and Opportunities for
Cooperation in Southern Africa: Annex A--Angola
(Washington, D.C.: U.S. AID, 1979); David Neigus,
"Angola," Multinational Monitor, August 1981; "Angola:
Potentially Wealthy Economy Waiting to Be Explored,"
Africa Economic Digest, 6 February 1981; "Bombs and
Bullets Fail to Shatter Angola's Economy," New African,
June 1971. Also see "The Destabilization of Southern
Africa," Washington Notes on Africa, Winter 1981.
        47. Colin Legum, "International Rivalries in the
Southern African Conflict," in Carter and O'Meara, eds.,
Southern Africa: The Continuing Crisis (Bloomington:
Indiana University Press, 1979), p. 9.
        48. "For white South Africa the result in Angola had
brought closer to reality two of its worst nightmares:
the success of a black movement of violence and the
'approach of communists' to their borders." Colin Legum
"Introduction" in Carter and O'Meara, Southern Africa in
Crisis, p. 12.
        49. See Carter and O'Meara, Southern Africa: The
Continuing Crisis, pp. 147-8, 337-8; Legum, ibid., p. 11;
and Washington Notes on Africa, 29 March 1976, p. 1.
        50. Andrew Nagorski, "U.S. Options Vis-a-Vis South
Africa," in Jennifer S. Whitaker, ed., Africa and the
United States : Vital Interests (New York: New York
University Press, 1978), p. 196.
        51. "On February 12, when it became clear that the
MPLA would be victorious, Kissinger said that Angola
would not be allowed to set a precedent for southern
Africa." Southern Africa, May 1976, p. 35.
        52. Bender in Lemarchand, American Policy..., p.
113.
        53. Southern Africa, May 1976, p. 35.
        54. Ibid., p. 36.
        55. Ibid.
        56. George Kennan, The Cloud of Danger (Boston:
Little, Brown and Co., 1977), p. 71.
        57. Quoted in Bernard Magubane, "What is Kissinger
up to in Southern Africa?" Freedomways, 16, 3, 1976, p.
165.
        58. These included Samora Machel of Mozambique,
Julius Nyerere of Tanzania, Seretse Khama of Botswana,
Kenneth Kaunda of Zambia, and Agostinho Neto of Angola.
Neto's first meeting as a frontline president was the 5-7
September 1976 meeting to discuss the Kissinger-Vorster
propositions on Rhodesia.

59. See Colin Legum, Africa Contemporary Record 1976-77 (London: Rex Collings, 1977), p. A29.
60. For the full text of Kissinger's Lusaka speech see ibid., pp. C145, and C159-C162.
61. For background on the Rhodesian conflict and the genesis of the nationalist movements see Martin Loney, Rhodesia: White Racism and Imperial Response (Harmondsworth, England: Penguin, 1975); David Martin and Phyllis Johnson, The Struggle for Zimbabwe (London and Boston: Faber and Faber, 1981); Kees Maxey, The Fight for Zimbabwe (New York: Africana Publishing Co., 1975); Charles Utete, The Road to Zimbabwe: The Political Economy of Settler Colonialism, National Liberation and Foreign Intervention (Washington, DC: University Press of America, 1978).
62. "Henry Kissinger on the U.S. and Rhodesia," Washington Post, 3 July 1979. This strategy toward the radicals of southern Africa was similar to Kissinger's privately enunciated plan "to isolate the Palestinians" in the Middle East conflict. See MERIP Reports, #96, May 1971.
63. R.W. Johnson, How Long Will South Africa Survive? (New York: Oxford University Press, 1977), pp. 216-20.
64. Review of African Political Economy, #9, May/August 1978, p. 85; and Dublin Sunday Express, 19 September 1976.
65. James Morrell and David Gisselquist, "How the IMF slipped $464 Million to South Africa," special report, January 1978, Center for International Policy, Washington, D.C.
66. Ibid.
67. Ibid.
68. Legum, Africa Contemporary Record, 1976-77, p. A33.
69. For useful background on this aspect of the Namibia question see Colin Legum, The Western Crisis Over Southern Africa (New York: Africana Publishing Company, 1979), pp. 14-17.
70. Washington Notes on Africa, 29 March 1976. For insight into Kissinger's basic motivations regarding southern Africa see Roger Morris, Uncertain Greatness: Henry Kissinger and American Foreign Policy (New York: Harper and Row, 1977), pp. 107-20.
71. "Ford Says US Must Seek an Agreement in Africa," New York Times, 9 September 1976.
72. Ibid.
73. The most comprehensive analysis of Rev. Sullivan and his Sullivan Code for U.S. companies in South Africa is by Elizabeth Schmidt, Decoding Corporate Camouflage (Washington, D.C.: Institute for Policy Studies, 1980).

74. "U.S. seeks apartheid end, Kissinger tells OIC here." Philadelphia Inquirer, 1 September 1976; "Kissinger, PUSH leader Confer", Washington Post, 4 August 1976; "Sutton Urges Ford to Speak out on South Africa," New York Times, 26 August 1976.
75. "U.S. Blacks Meet on South Africa," New York Times, 24 August 1976.
76. "Business Urged to Press South Africa," New York Times, 2 August 1976.
77. "Young Assails U.S. ties with white-ruled Africa," Washington Post, 4 August 1976.
78. "Black diplomats stressed," Baltimore Sun, 4 August 1976.
79. Morris, Uncertain Greatness..., p. 296.
80. Ibid.
81. For a detailed discussion of the Kissinger proposals and the diplomacy accompanying them see Colin Legum Africa Contemporary Record, 1976-77, pp. A28-A41.
82. See Burchett, Southern Africa Stands Up, Chapters 18 and 19; Martin and Johnson, The Struggle for Zimbabwe; and Larry Bowman, "US Policy Towards Rhodesia", in Lemarchand, American Policy....
83. For background on various Zimbabwean nationalist leaders see Diana Mitchell, African Nationalist Leaders in Zimbabwe: Who's Who 1980 (Salisbury: Cannon Press, 1980); and Barry M. Schutz, "The Colonial Heritage of Strife: Sources of Cleavage in the Zimbabwe Liberation Movement," Africa Today, 25, 1, January/March 1978. Regarding U.S. efforts to split Nkomo away from his alliance with Mugabe see Robert Rotberg, "Rhodesian 'Wallace'? Tsk-tsk," New York Times, 1 May 1978. This strategy of division was confirmed in private interviews with former government officials. One source close to the CIA reported that the Agency was covertly picking up the tab for ZAPU's propaganda operations in the United States. Be that as it may, the fact that the U.S. government clearly favored that section of the Patriotic Front sponsored by Moscow raises some question as to the alleged incompatibility of US and Soviet national interests.
84. See Carter and O'Meara, eds., Southern Africa: The Continuing Crisis, pp. 30-33.
85. One CIA officer interviewed by the author reported a briefing in which Kissinger had trouble finding Angola on a map of Africa.
86. Morris, Uncertain Greatness..., p. 131.
87. Ronald T. Libby. Toward An Africanized U.S. Policy for Southern Africa (Berkeley: Institute of International Studies/University of California, 1980), p. 89.

5
The Carter Administration, 1977–1981

The 1976 presidential campaign was the first in the U.S. in which African issues played any prominent role.[1]

In July 1976 the Foreign Affairs Task Force of the Democratic Party's platform drafting committee accepted most of the recommendations of its Study Group on Africa. The Study Group was headed by two liberals: Wayne Fredericks, formerly a top Africa advisor under Lyndon Johnson, and Goler Butcher, a former aide to Congressman Charles Diggs.[2]

The platform statement criticized the Republicans for "eight years of indifference, accompanied by increasing cooperation with racist regimes" which "have left our influence and prestige in Africa at an historic low."[3] Various aspects of the Democrats' position on Africa reflected the significant changes that had occurred in southern Africa since the collapse of Portuguese colonialism. Relevant sections of the platform recommended the following positions:

* an Africa-centered policy, and not a corollary of the kind of antiSoviet strategy that produced the Angola fiasco;
* unequivocal support for majority rule in southern Africa; non recognition of Bantustan "independence" in South Africa;
* strengthening the arms embargo against South Africa;
* withdrawal of tax credits for U.S. corporations operating in Namibia;
* enforcement of Rhodesia sanctions and repeal of the Byrd Amendment;
* normalization of relations with Angola;
* increased participation of black Americans in the formulation of foreign policy; and

* denial of tax advantages to all U.S. corporations
  in Rhodesia and South Africa who support or
  participate in apartheid practices and policies. [4]

As we will see, many of these positions would not be
implemented. The Africa Study Group of the platform
drafting committee was dominated by representatives of
the most progressive wing of the party, operating in a
political and intellectual environment that was much more
insulated from class constraints than the policy
apparatus the Carter administration would inherit.
      Candidate Jimmy Carter was aware of black Americans'
interest in U.S. policy toward Africa. He admitted that
he had "received a growing number of questions in my
political campaigning from Black Americans on the
question of Africa."[5] Carter even drew an historical
parallel to suggest that the black community should
become more active on African issues.

      It would be a great help to this nation if
      people in public life were to be made aware of the
      problems of Africa through a significant Black
      interest in Africa. Americans might not have made
      the mistakes we made in Vietnam had there been an
      articulate Vietnamese minority in our midst.[6]

      The notion that Afro-Americans should play an
important role in shaping U.S. Africa policy can be found
in the writings of one of Carter's main Africa advisors.
Anthony Lake wrote his doctoral dissertation on U.S.
policy toward South Africa and was to become Carter's
Director of Policy Planning at the State Department. He
asserted that "the key to future congressional action on
South Africa, like the key to future pressures on the
Executive, is the black community."[7]
      The high profile given to African affairs by the
Carter team was related to the backgrounds of key staff
members. Although the Georgia governor possessed little
personal knowledge of Africa, several of his advisors had
expertise on the question of white minority rule. Ruth
Schacter Morgenthau, a noted Africanist, became advisor
to the United Nations Economic and Social Council. Goler
Butcher, a black lawyer, would head the Africa section of
the Agency for International Development (AID) for
Carter. Butcher judged that "a decision on U.S. policy
towards South Africa" was "the first order of business."[8]
She also argued persuasively for instituting "a new
policy of providing no new support to the minority and of
ending present support, while providing all appropriate
support to the majority and those working for change."[9]

Andrew Young, former aide to Martin Luther King, Jr., had visited South Africa and was guardian for a child of Robert Sobukwe, one of the founders of the Pan Africanist Congress of Azania (PAC). Young was appointed U.S. Ambassador to the United Nations. Even Carter's top foreign policy advisor, Columbia University Soviet specialist Zbigniew Brzezinski, admitted that "nothing could be more destructive than for the United States to position itself as the ultimate shield of the remnants of white supremacy in Africa at a time when racial equality is coming to be accepted as an imperative norm."[10]

Another aspect of the Carter team's background figured in their position on southern Africa: that of the civil rights struggle in the United States. On several occasions Jimmy Carter and Andrew Young laid claim to special American expertise on questions of racial strife. Young asserted:

I think our country has established through our own experience in race relationships, and particularly in the South, an understanding of this very sensitive issue of black and white people within the same community . . . with the special knowledge in our country, I think we might be a help in Africa.[11]

In addition to members of Carter's staff having more sympathy for majority rule in southern Africa, influential Afro-Americans were taking a more active antiapartheid stand. In September 1976 the Congressional Black Caucus organized a Black Leadership Conference on Southern Africa. More than 100 representatives of organizations such as the National Association for the Advancement of Colored People (NAACP), the National Council of Negro Women, Africare, the Black Economic Research Center, Operation PUSH, and others issued an African-American Manifesto on Southern Africa.[12]

The manifesto went considerably beyond the Democratic party platform by endorsing armed struggle, if necessary, by the liberation movements and their seeking aid from whatever quarters available, opposing U.S. support for any settlement in Namibia and Zimbabwe that compromised the freedom of blacks, and condemning U.S. political support of South Africa "as ransom for America's hostage private corporations."[13]

The conference demanded U.S. support for comprehensive U.N. sanctions against South Africa. It also established TransAfrica, a black lobbying group for Africa and the Caribbean that went on to become the major foreign policy voice of the black community.[14]

The NAACP stepped up its Africa-related activities during late 1976 and early 1977. It established a Task Force on Africa that made study tours to Africa. It issued a 500-page report which, among other recommendations, called for economic sanctions against South Africa and withdrawal of U.S. investments.[15]

BREAKDOWN OF THE POLICY CONSENSUS

The Carter team's opposition to white supremacy was part of a general trend that was transforming the foreign policy establishment. The analytical paradigm that had dominated U.S. policy during the first twenty-five years of the post-war period was giving way to a new perspective that deemphasized U.S.-Soviet competition and focused more on third world nationalism as a causal factor in the revolutions causing Washington so much trouble. This shift in perspective resulted from basic changes in America's economic and political standing in the world.

During the period of American hegemony over the capitalist world, a policy of "containment" held sway within the U.S. policy establishment.[16] Key precepts of the dominant logic were:

* the Soviet Union is bent on world domination and must be contained, with force if necessary, by America and its allies;
* U.S.-Soviet competition is a zero-sum game--any gain for Moscow is a loss for the United States--therefore it is proper to view all foreign policy issues against this backdrop;
* socialist movements or regimes in the Third World are more or less pawns of Moscow and must be resisted; and
* an ever-expanding U.S. military, covert operations, and economic coercion are essential tools for competing with the Soviets for global influence.

This doctrine supported a policy of intervention against revolutionary nationalists in various parts of the world.[17] As James Petras points out, this interventionism was necessitated by America's far-flung business empire and was based on three factors:

1) exercise of hegemony over subordinated classes in the metropolitan countries (i.e., their support for or acquiescence in imperialism to sustain overseas involvement); 2) a worldwide armed force with capacity to defend these economic interests; and 3) an international network of loyal and supportive allies and clients among the advanced

and Third World capitalist countries capable of
collaborating in meaningful joint activity.[18]

These three props of U.S. interventionist capability
were all weakened by the debacle in Southeast Asia.
America's hegemonic position was also eroded by the
reindustrialization of Japan and Western Europe, the
victories of revolutionary forces in Cuba, Vietnam,
Angola and Mozambique, the huge flow of funds into the
oil-exporting countries, the discrediting of U.S.
political leadership following Watergate and revelations
of CIA crimes, and the long-term cyclical downturn in the
world economy beginning in the mid-1970s. These changes,
as well as growing fissures in the communist "bloc,"
effectively replaced the bipolar distribution of world
power that characterized the immediate post-war decades,
with a more multipolar distribution of economic and
political power.
      These changes set the stage for a growing debate
over the cold war precepts of U.S. policy and the
interventionist strategy they justified. By the late
1960s a process of ideological revision had begun within
the corporate liberal section of the policy elite.
      The general goal of checking Soviet influence
remained, but a whole new set of tactics and justifying
assumptions were elaborated which altered the priority of
that goal and the means for attaining it. Tom J. Farer,
writing in Foreign Policy, details these new precepts:

*   that threats to the status quo in and among Third
    World states usually spring from volatile
    political, social, and economic conditions that
    exist independently of the Soviet-American
    competition;
*   that, on the one hand, the terrible problems of
    economic growth and distribution and, on the
    other, the industrial democracies' overwhelming
    advantage in the deployment of markets, capital,
    and technology give the United States and its
    allies an enormous edge in East-West competition
    for influence in Third World states, including
    those run by ostensible Marxists;
*   that national imperatives require Third World
    governments to distribute their resources through
    international markets;
*   that most Third World states are of only trivial
    significance to the East-West strategic balance;
*   that the costs of armed intervention either to
    promote or frustrate political change are high
    because the capacity of Third World states to
    resist coercion is increasing;

* that ideas and values have material consequences and that the complex of values incorporated in the major human rights texts will therefore play a crucial orienting role for the generation coming of age in the Third World, as well as for elites in the West; and
* that the regnant image of the United States as an opponent of major Third World blocs on issues of central importance to them limits the scope of present and potential cooperation along the whole range of international issues.[19]

Since 1973, "when human rights became a byword in the battle between the legislature and the executive branch over the conduct of foreign affairs,"[20] religious organizations, humanitarian groups, and members of Congress had been expanding the political base for human rights as a main factor in determining U.S. foreign policy.[21]

When the Carter administration took office, these human rights activists were at a peak of their influence. They had put together coalitions of Congressional liberals and conservatives to push through strong human rights legislation, they had forced State, Treasury, and Defense Department officials to account for human rights consequences of official actions and decisions; they helped turn promotion of human rights into a major goal of the new administration.[22]

In addition to this pressure from outside the executive branch, numerous individuals who were to become high officeholders in the Carter administration had been contributing to the process of ideological reconstruction. People such as Charles William Maynes (Assistant Secretary of State for International Organization Affairs), Anthony Lake (Director of Policy Planning at State), Leslie Gelb (Director of the State Department's Bureau of Political-Military Affairs), and even Zbigniew Brzezinski (National Security Advisor), had been writing articles criticizing the dominant cold war paradigm.[23] Although a new approach to U.S. relations with the Third World was already "foreshadowed during the Kissinger years by such congressional action as the so-called Clark Amendment that ended US intervention in Angola," the Carter administration marked a turning point "by bringing advocates of a consistent, alternative approach to the Third World from the shadowy frontiers of respectability into the center of power."[24]

The traditional cold war paradigm, or "globalist" perspective, had been delegitimated sufficiently to be temporarily disloged by the "regionalist" perspective. The globalists, however, still had a strong political base in Congress, the executive bureaucracy, the Pentagon, the intelligence community, and the American public.[25] The regionalists had their institutional base in the U.N. staff, sections of the State Department (the Africa Bureau, International Organization Affairs, and Policy Planning), and partly in the President.

Both perspectives, "supported by different factions within the policy elite, and in some cases unreconciled in the thought of the same individual," were initially well represented in the Carter administration.[26] The regionalists included Cyrus Vance, Richard Holbrooke, Leslie Gelb, Paul Warnke, Anthony Lake, Richard Moose, Marshal Shulman, and Andrew Young. The globalists, centered in the National Security Council, included Zbigniew Brzezinski, Samuel Huntington, William Griffith, Lincoln Bloomfield, Michael Oksenberg, and Colonel William Odom.[27]

It is the struggle between these two competing perspectives and their supporters that helps explain the vacillation and contradictory policies of the Carter White House.[28] Later we will see how the evolution of this two-line struggle caused a basic shift in Carter's policy toward South Africa beginning in 1978.

The administration's early policy on southern Africa was dominated by the regionalists. People like Anthony Lake, Andrew Young, Donald McHenry, and Goler Butcher used their interest and expertise in the area to take an early lead in formulating the Carter strategy. Pretoria's brutal suppression of the riots that rocked South Africa in late 1976 made it difficult for the globalists to argue for a soft line on apartheid.

The regionalists distinguished their strategy from Kissinger's by claiming that whereas the previous administration had let Pretoria off the hook regarding apartheid and Namibia in return for cooperation on Rhodesia, the Carter administration would press for reforms on all three fronts.[29] Pretoria would be expected to assist Washington in bringing about a negotiated settlement to the Rhodesian conflict, but would also be pressured to reform the grosser aspects of apartheid and cooperate with an internationally acceptable transition to independence in Namibia. As we will see, this central aspect of the Carter strategy was to be short-lived.

Whereas the regionalists were more vocally critical of Pretoria than any previous administration, their willingness to pressure South Africa had distinct limits. As Chapter Two demonstrates, the most important structural link between South Africa and the United States is the corporate connection. As the most extensive institutional bridge between the two societies, this

economic interdependence provided the most important area
of leverage for an American president wanting to
influence South Africa's policies. Yet the Carter
administration made it clear from the outset that the
U.S.-South Africa business relationship would not be
downgraded as a punitive measure against Pretoria.

At a July 1976 press conference in Plains, Georgia,
candidate Carter said: "heavy investments that we now
have by the private sector in industrial opportunities
and banking" in South Africa could be a "possible
mechanism that we might use jointly with government" to
stimulate reform in that country.[30] In a later interview
with the Financial Mail Carter voiced a similar position,
"I think our American businessman can be a constructive
force achieving racial justice within South Africa."[31]

Later in the same interview Carter was asked if he
would "free up American investment...and otherwise
encourage an increase in private American lending and
corporate activity in South Africa." His answer: "Yes
indeed. Economic development, investment commitment and
the use of economic leverage...seems to me the only way
to achieve racial justice there."[32] This perspective was
nothing more than a reaffirmation of past U.S. policy.

Carter was not alone in asserting that U.S.
corporations could be a progressive force for change in
South Africa. Carter stalwart Andrew Young was operating
under similar precepts when he informed a group of South
African businessmen that "the free market system can be
the greatest force for constructive change now operating
anywhere in the world."[33] Young reported that "I've come
to think of the business community as in many respects
being the key to hope . . . for South Africans to live
together as brothers and with the rest of the world as
brothers."[34]

Young asserted that U.S. banks had eventually
recognized the potentially disruptive effects of
segregation and had led the way to desegregation in
Atlanta. He suggested a similar relationship with the
apartheid regime. "South Africa cannot survive without
the Chase Manhattan Bank, First National City Bank and
Morgan Guaranty Trust Co., and these banks cannot make a
profit if there is turmoil."[35]

The Carter administration, even at its most
progressive point, was not prepared to restrict corporate
activity as a way to pressure Pretoria. Whether or not
the Carter team actually believed that U.S. corporations
were a progressive force for change in South Africa is
difficult to test. There are some objective political
facts, however, that clarify Carter's reticence to
pressure the corporations.

THE CLASS CONTENT OF THE CARTER TEAM

During the early days of the Carter administration much was written about Carter's relationship with the influential Trilateral Commission.[36] Carter's Trilateral connections helped him immensely in the campaign and, once elected, he responded by appointing numerous Trilateralists to his cabinet. There were, however, other corporate political debts Carter had accumulated before he emerged on the national political scene.

It was through his connections to the Atlanta business establishment that Jimmy Carter first came to the attention of the national ruling class. Early in his Georgia political career Carter received assistance from Atlanta lawyer Charles Kirbo. Kirbo's prestigious law firm (King and Spaulding) had clients such as General Motors, Coca-Cola, Prudential Insurance, and the influential Cox Enterprises whose combined radio, television, and newspaper outlets reached 80 percent of Georgia's households.[37]

Another early backer was Philip H. Alston, whose law firm (Alston, Miller and Gaines) worked for Chrysler, Eastman Kodak, Equitable Life Insurance Co., Aetna Life Insurance Co., E. I. DuPont de Nemours, and Sears Roebuck. Other key support came from the Gambrell family, particularly David Gambrell and his father E. Smythe Gambrell.

The elder Gambrell is a former president of the American Bar Association and Georgia State Chamber of Commerce. His law firm represents corporations like Eastern Airlines, Greyhound, Allstate Insurance, Travelers Insurance, Olin-Mathieson, Uniroyal, Cummins Engine, RCA, Continental Can, and others.[38]

These millionaires introduced Carter to people like J. Paul Austin, a board member of important U.S. multinationals (General Electric and Morgan Guaranty Trust) in addition to his main job as chairman of Coca-Cola. In his 1976 campaign autobiography, I'll Never Lie To You, Carter acknowledged his debt to Atlanta-based Coca-Cola:

We have our own built-in State Department in the Coca-Cola Company. They provide me ahead of time with . . . penetrating analyses of what the country is, what its problems are, who its leaders are, and when I arrive there, provide me with an introduction to the leaders of that country.[39]

Through these contacts Jimmy Carter attracted the
attention of national ruling class institutions such as
the Council on Foreign Relations and the Rockefeller
family.[40] By May 1971 when _Time_ magazine ran a cover
story on Carter and the "New South," the president-to-be
had already met with billionaire banker David
Rockefeller, and Hedley Donovan, editor-in-chief of _Time_
and a director of the Council on Foreign Relations.[41]
It is well known that Carter was a member of David
Rockefeller's Trilateral Commission, and that much of the
Georgia governor's foreign policy education took place in
that institutional context. Less familiar, however, is
how a relatively unknown southern governor was chosen to
be one of the few politicians invited to join the
prestigious Trilateralists.

Carter was consequently no stranger to these
national leaders when they decided to form the
Trilateral Commission in the Spring of 1973. At that
time David Rockefeller, with George S. Franklin Jr.,
a Rockefeller in-law, Zbigniew Brzezinski, Henry
Owen, Robert Bowie, and Gerard C. Smith--the last
four now members of the Carter Administration--
selected members for the Commission. Franklin,
Brzezinski, Owen, Bowie, and Smith were all leading
members of a premier organization of the Eastern
Establishment: the Council on Foreign Relations. The
Council has a number of affiliated organizations,
called the Committees on Foreign Relations. . . .
Franklin called upon one of the leaders of the
Council's Atlanta Committee--a group reflecting that
city's power structure--to set up an advisory group
to recommend possible members for the Commission.
This was done and, on 13 April 1973, this body of
prominent Atlantans recommended Carter for
membership.[42]

If it had not been for Carter's acceptance by the
Atlanta establishment and their generosity in providing
the funds and national contacts necessary for a
presidential bid, it is likely that Carter would have
remained a strictly Georgian politician/millionaire.[43]
Judging from the record of his participation, Jimmy
Carter took seriously his membership in the Trilateral
Commission. He attended all the regional meetings as well
as the first plenary session in Japan in May 1976. Carter
admitted that membership on the Commission provided him
with "a splendid learning opportunity."[44] His Trilateral
connection gave Carter information on substantive issues
both foreign and domestic, and it acquainted him with
important members of the western elites who play such an
influential role in the major capitalist countries--the
same countries that are most tightly connected to the
apartheid regime.

The Trilateral Commission's membership and policy prescriptions embody "the ideological perspective representing the transnational outlook of the multinational corporation" which "seeks to subordinate territorial politics to non-territorial economic goals."[45] A significant number of Commissioners were executives from the largest multinationals of Japan, Western Europe and the United States, and many of the American members were chosen to fill Carter's cabinet.[46] In addition to the Presidency itself, many of the top foreign policy posts with relevance for U.S. policy toward South Africa were filled by Trilateralists. The backgrounds of the following personnel speak volumes about the Carter administration's positive portrayal of U.S. corporate involvement in South Africa.

Zbigniew Brzezinski was Special Assistant to the President for National Security Affairs.

Brzezinski took an early interest in Carter as a presidential hopeful and, assuming something of a tutor's role, sent him a series of articles on foreign policy over the next few years. In addition, in 1976 Brzezinski acted as head of the Carter campaign's 28-man task force on defense and foreign affairs. Hence Brzezinski clearly had the inside track for this key position. And if there is any doubt as to his ties, it need only be noted that he had served as a director of the Council on Foreign Relations for five years prior to his appointment to this high federal post.[47]

Brzezinski's position as first Director of the Trilateral Commission made him a major link between Carter and Commission founder David Rockefeller.

Carter's entire foreign policy, much of his domestic policy has come directly from the Commission and its leading members. The architect of Carter's foreign policy from 1975 to the present [1980] has been Zbigniew Brzezinski, first Commission director. Brzezinski wrote Carter's major speeches during the campaign, and as the president's national security adviser, heads foreign policy--with assists from fellow CFR leaders and Trilateral Commissioners like Vance, Brown, Blumenthal, and a few others. The watchword for Carter's foreign policy from 1975 on was "clear it with Brzezinski". Carter would always ask when given a memorandum on foreign policy, "has Brzezinski seen this?"[48]

For his Secretary of State, Carter chose Cyrus
Vance, a man described as a "thoroughly Establishment
figure."[49] Vance's law firm (Simpson, Thatcher and
Bartlett) was general counsel for many large
corporations.

> And Vance himself served up to 1977 as a
> director of IBM, the Aetna Life and Casualty Co.,
> the New York Times Co., Pan-American World Airways,
> and One William Street Fund (a mutual fund
> controlled by Lehman Brothers). Vance's most
> critical ties, though, may have been with certain
> other elite groups, since he served in the mid-1970s
> as board chairman of the Rockefeller Foundation,
> vice-chairman of the Council on Foreign Relations,
> and a member of the Trilateral Commission.[50]

Warren Christopher was Deputy Secretary of State. As
number two man to Vance, Christopher "had no experience
in diplomatic affairs and had spent only two years in the
federal government."[51] Christopher was, however, a member
of the Trilateral Commission and had spent most of his
professional career with

> one of Los Angeles's most prominent corporate
> law firms, O'Melveny & Myers. He had also been a
> director of such large regional concerns as the
> Pacific Mutual Life Insurance Co. and the Southern
> California Edison Co., and had reportedly acted as
> the Los Angeles lawyer for IBM.[52]

W. Michael Blumenthal was Secretary of the Treasury.
Because sections of the Treasury Department (e.g., the
Foreign Assets Control Division) deal with issues such as
international sanctions, this post is relevant to U.S.
policy toward South Africa. Although he had some
government work under his belt, "Blumenthal had made his
mark mainly as a businessman."[53] Blumenthal was not only
chief executive officer of the Bendix Corporation, but
also had "served in recent years as a director of the big
(New York-based) Equitable Life Assurance Society, a
trustee of the Rockefeller Foundation, a director of the
Council on Foreign Relations, and, up to 1975, a member
of the Trilateral Commission."[54]

Harold Brown was Secretary of Defense. As top
bureaucrat in the military apparatus, Brown represented
one of the major constituencies for continued U.S.
support for the apartheid regime. Although primarily a
technocrat, Brown had considerable ties to multinational
capital. He was a board member of corporations such as
IBM, the Times-Mirror Co., and Schroders Ltd., a British
banking group which owned the J. Henry Schroder Banking
Corp. of New York.[55] In addition, Brown was a member of
the Trilateral Commission.

This simple exercise could be continued but by now the point should be clear. The top policymakers of the Carter administration were very sympathetic to the needs of U.S. multinationals. Some of these individuals were former employees of corporations that have direct interests in apartheid.[56] It is not surprising that a key theme of these policymakers was that U.S. corporations in South Africa can be a progressive force and should be allowed to remain there.

CARTER'S INITIAL STANCE ON SOUTH AFRICA

Between Carter's victory at the polls and his inauguration in mid-January it became clear that a new agenda was being constructed for U.S. policy in southern Africa. South Africa had been shaken by its most turbulent year of protest in history; the antiapartheid movement in U.S. cities and colleges was gaining momentum; and the more progressive forces within the Carter administration were opting for a tougher U.S. stand against white minority rule. On 9 November 1976, insuring that Carter would get the message early, third world and socialist states in the United Nations passed ten resolutions condemning apartheid.[57] One reputable columnist reported: "The entire spectrum of debate has moved to the left: the question is no longer whether or not the U.S. should support majority rule, but how hard and how fast to push--and what losses are acceptable."[58]

In early December Andrew Young provided a preview of Carter administration thinking on South Africa. At an international conference in Lesotho that included American corporate and government leaders as well as representatives of African governments and liberation movements, Young said the new president would support "peaceful rather than militant change in southern Africa."[59] He explained to a Reuters correspondent: "South Africa is its own worst enemy. The only people who will win if change is not peaceful are the communists."[60] In press interviews, as well as in his formal address to the assembly, Young stressed several themes that were to be reiterated many times over the next few years:

* communism had little to offer the black majority of southern Africa and only capitalist expansion held a cure for white supremacy;
* this point was bolstered with references to the civil rights movement--it was claimed the corporate sector played a leading role in ending segregation; and
* Young ruled out the use of economic sanctions as a method for pressuring the South African government.[61]

The Carter team did not wait long to conduct a
formal review of U.S. policy in southern Africa. Within
two weeks of the inauguration, National Security Advisor
Brzezinski ordered an interagency task force to produce
Policy Review Memorandum #4. In early March 1977 Carter
signed a Presidential Directive (based on PRM 4) that
contained the following features:

* the problems of southern Africa should receive
  urgent action;
* because the continuation of guerrilla war equates
  with growing Soviet influence, the U.S. must
  strongly affirm a commitment to peaceful solutions
  in southern Africa;
* it is important for the U.S. to cooperate with
  European and African allies in developing its
  initiatives;
* the administration will need to take "visible
  steps" to distance the United States from the
  apartheid regime unless there is noticeable
  movement toward power-sharing in South Africa; and
* if the U.S. government does not speak out strongly
  against apartheid there will be a considerable
  loss of credibility with African states and the
  rest of the Third World.[62]

IMPLEMENTING THE PLAN

Within days of his Senate confirmation as the new
U.S. Ambassador to the United Nations, Andrew Young was
dispatched to Africa to bring the message of a new U.S.
policy to key African leaders. Other than his more
general goal of establishing a rapport with these
leaders, Young's main objective was to revive the
Rhodesia negotiations. His key meetings were with Julius
Nyerere of Tanzania, Kenneth Kaunda of Zambia, Agostinho
Neto of Angola, and Olusegun Obasanjo of Nigeria. These
were the heads of state (along with Samora Machel of
Mozambique) who had the most leverage over the Zimbabwean
guerrilla movements.
     Nyerere welcomed the professed interest of the
Carter administration but he made it clear to Young that
the U.S. government had a specific and limited role to
play in Rhodesia. The Tanzanian President pointed out
that as the colonial power Britain still held primary
responsibility for reining in the rebellious settler
colony, and the United States should play a supportive
but low key role. Nyerere told Young that the United
States should use its considerable economic clout to
wring concessions from the Rhodesian whites. At a press
conference following his meeting with Young, Nyerere gave
no sign that the Frontline Presidents were eager to have
the United States assume a major role in southern African

diplomacy. Those on the scene reported that this generally reflected the sentiments of the other African leaders Young had been meeting.

In attempting to gain the confidence of African leaders, Young was up against more than just a traditional U.S. policy of neglect. During this first official trip to Africa the Ambassador was already being sniped at by conservative forces at home. As Young was leaving for Africa the State Department saw fit to "clarify" an earlier contention by the Ambassador that Cuban troops brought "a certain stability and order to Angola" by making clear that "neither Ambassador Young nor the Secretary condones the presence of Cuban troops in Angola."[63]

In a more straightforward attempt to undercut the new policy Young was trying to get off the ground, "United States intelligence sources" chose the very day of Young's departure for Tanzania to leak a report citing an alleged movement of Cuban military advisors into Tanzania to train Zimbabwean guerrillas.[64] Young had been very purposefully trying to distance U.S. policy from its cold war legacy by minimizing the importance of the Cuban/Soviet presence in southern Africa: "One of the most wholesome things about our administration is that . . . it won't be paranoid about communism."[65]

Young's initiative was hurt on the domestic front by a prominent story published in the New York Times while the Ambassador was still in Africa. The glaring headline "7 White Missionaries in Rhodesia Slain in Raid by Black Guerrillas" topped an article that blamed the incident on the Patriotic Front. This was despite several facts: there was no evidence to prove exactly who committed the crime; the Catholics in question were noted for their friendly relations with the Patriotic Front; and a special black unit of government troops (the Selous Scouts) were known to dress up as guerrillas and carry out atrocities in order to discredit the real guerrillas. None of this was mentioned in the article.[66]

Following visits with leaders of the Frontline States, Ambassador Young concluded his trip with a stop in Nigeria, where he met Nigerian head of state Lt. General Olusegun Obasanjo and Angolan President Agostinho Neto. Young's visit to Nigeria was significant because the Nigerians had condemned the U.S. role in Angola and rejected the Rhodesia diplomacy of Henry Kissinger. They also had refused on three separate occasions to have Kissinger set foot inside their country. Young met with the Nigerian head of state for several hours. Although few details of the discussion were revealed, Obasanjo agreed to a joint press conference afterward (a rare event for the Nigerian leader) and described the talks in very favorable terms. This was enough for some observers to label the meeting a "diplomatic breakthrough".[67]

American policymakers knew that good relations with

the Nigerians were important for several reasons. First, Nigeria had been playing an increasingly important role in the fight against white minority rule in southern Africa. They were one of the first governments to recognize the MPLA government in Angola, and by the time of Young's February 1977 meeting they had donated more than $50 million to the liberation movements in southern Africa.[68] The Nigerians gave considerable support to the international antiapartheid movement, and a Nigerian, Akporode Clark, was chairman of the United Nations Special Committee Against Apartheid. Early in the Carter administration the Nigerians had warned that they were "prepared to take economic action against Western countries supplying arms and investments to white-ruled South Africa."[69]

Second, Nigeria had clout in the African community. As the most populous state in Africa (roughly 80 million people) with a rapidly expanding economy and a large military, the Nigerians could exert pressure on other African states regarding issues of importance to the U.S. government such as Black Africa's estrangement from Israel.[70]

Third, the Americans were well aware of Nigeria's growing importance to the U.S. economy as a trading partner and a field for investment. In one of his most important speeches on Africa, Secretary of State Vance told an NAACP audience in July 1977 that "trade with South Africa in 1960 was 39 percent of our commerce with Africa. Now our trade with Nigeria is double the value of that with South Africa".[71] Table 5.1 compares the long-term growth of U.S. trade with Nigeria and South Africa. Although the big jump in the figure for U.S. imports from Nigeria in 1974 is partly due to the oil price increase of that year, the long-term growth trend is clear.

Table 5.1
U.S. IMPORTS AND EXPORTS WITH NIGERIA AND SOUTH AFRICA
(millions of dollars)

	Exports		Imports	
	Nigeria	South Africa	Nigeria	South Africa
1960	26	288	40	108
1965	74	438	60	226
1970	129	563	71	290
1973	161	746	652	377
1974	286	1,160	3,286	609
1975	536	1,302	3,281	840
1976	770	1,348	4,938	925
1977	958	1,054	6,096	1,269

Source: Statistical Abstract of the United States, 1978, U.S. Department of Commerce, Bureau of the Census, p.879.

By October 1977 U.S. transnational corporations had invested over one billion dollars in Nigeria's oil-boom economy.[72] Nigeria had become the second most important foreign supplier (after Saudi Arabia) of crude oil to the United States. In addition to being closer to the United States than many other oil countries, thus cutting transportation costs, Nigerian crude is a low-sulphur variety critical in helping U.S. oil companies conform to environmental regulations.[73]

In recent years the Nigerians had been alienated by the U.S. intervention in Angola. Ambassador Young succeeded in getting relations between the two countries back on a friendly track.

THE NAMIBIA QUESTION

As Ambassador Young was busy establishing a new image for U.S. policy in Africa and trying to get the Africans to cooperate on Rhodesia negotiations, his deputy, Donald McHenry, was focusing his attention on Namibia.

The guerrilla war being waged by the South West Africa Peoples' Organization (SWAPO) against South African rule had been making headway and the Western powers saw that the time was right for negotiations.[74] With McHenry facilitating, the five western members of the U.N. Security Council (coincidentally the five countries, other than South Africa, with the most investment in Namibia) came together to plan a joint strategy. What became known as the Contact Group (England, France, West Germany, Canada, and the United States) was formed in response to the prospect that developments in Namibia would cause a majority of U.N. members to demand economic sanctions against South Africa.

In recent years it had become clear that the South African government was not going to allow free elections in the sparsely populated, mineral-rich territory. A leaked report from South Africa's own military intelligence found that if elections were held, SWAPO would win over 80 percent of the vote.[75] The strong links between the Western ruling classes and their South African and Namibian counterparts meant that any call for economic sanctions by the U.N. majority would be vetoed by the permanent Western members of the Security Council. This would be a blow to the West's legitimacy, hence, coordinated planning was necessary to postpone the showdown.

The Contact Group agreed that Security Council Resolution 385 (1976) on Namibia should serve as the basis for negotiations. This resolution called for: 1) removal of South Africa's administrative apparatus in favor of temporary U.N. control and U.N.-supervised elections in Namibia before an internationally recognized independence;   2)   an   end   to   legalized   racial discrimination; 3) allowing all exiles to return without intimidation, and; 4) release of all political prisoners.

By   arguing   that   only   its   members   had   enough legitimacy to wring concessions from the South African government, the Contact Group's initiative was accepted by the Secretary General and the Africa group at the United Nations.[76]

The   Contact   Group   sought   to   replace   the   United Nations as the mediator between the main parties to the struggle, SWAPO and South Africa. The U.N. General Assembly and the U.N. Council for Namibia[77] opposed the apartheid regime and clearly favored SWAPO. This position rested   on   a   firm   legal   foundation   that   had   been painstakingly constructed over the years.[78] In August 1969   the   Security   Council   had   endorsed   official termination of South Africa's mandate over Namibia, and in June 1971 the International Court of Justice declared South Africa's presence in Namibia illegal. If left to the United Nations the situation would have continued to polarize, with Pretoria becoming increasingly isolated and   SWAPO   gaining   more   international   support.   This scenario   would   jeopardize   economic   and   strategic interests of the five western members of the Security Council.

The Contact Group's ability to monopolize the role of neutral arbiter in this struggle is surprising if one considers   the   political-economic   positions   of   these states vis-a-vis SWAPO and Pretoria. SWAPO is opposed to corporate imperialism and is utilizing armed struggle to build socialism in Namibia. Its major backer, financially and   diplomatically,   is   the   Soviet   Union.   Its   major supporter in southern Africa is the Marxist MPLA regime in Angola, a government never recognized by the United States. On the other side, the National Party in South Africa has received the bulk of its weapons, finance, technology,   and   diplomatic   support   from   those   same western   countries   comprising   the   Contact   Group.   In addition, these nations have been the biggest violators of a U.N. decree calling for the protection of all Namibian resources until an independent government is installed.[79]

The detailed intentions of the Contact Group were clarified   in   October   1977   when   they   presented   a Declaration on Southern Africa to the U.N. Security Council. Its adoption was blocked by the Africa Group, however, which was staunchly opposed to item 15 of the declaration. The offending statement read: "The Security Council will seek to work constructively with other principal organs and with the Government and people of South Africa for a just and peaceful solution to the problems of the area."[80]

The problem with this formulation, as pointed out by

the African members of the Security Council, was that it would have required the Security Council to work with the South African government, and thus lend it legitimacy, in a country where the South African presence had already been declared illegal. In addition, the clause referring to a "peaceful solution" was seen by the African Group as an attempt to downgrade the legitimacy of guerrilla war as a political strategy.[81]

This early rebuff didn't stop the Contact Group from pressing on in the role of key negotiator on Namibia throughout the Carter administration. Senior foreign policy officials of the Western powers, led by McHenry, conducted numerous rounds of shuttle diplomacy, trying to get the cooperation of SWAPO, the Frontline States and South Africa.

The apartheid regime had reasons to be wary of Western intentions. The leaders in Pretoria knew that if instability in Namibia reached regime-threatening proportions the West would be willing to dump the white supremacists if a viable ruling class of black moderates could be eased into place. Pretoria responded with a two-track strategy: participating in negotiations in order to forestall sanctions, and continuing the war against SWAPO while cultivating a loyal multi-racial Namibian ruling group.[82] Although not providing a final solution, this strategy was to prove rather successful for Pretoria.

After a year of shuttle diplomacy the Contact Group submitted detailed proposals to the Security Council in March 1978. Pretoria conditionally accepted the proposals on 25 April and before SWAPO could respond, the South African army launched an attack on a Namibian refugee camp in Angola.[83] On 4 May 1978 an airborne raid by South African paratroops operating out of bases in Namibia, struck 150 miles into southern Angola, devastating the SWAPO camp at Cassinga. Some 1,000 Namibians and Angolans (mostly women and children) were killed in the attack. Angolan and U.N. relief workers photographed mass graves containing hundreds of unarmed civilians. Survivors related gruesome stories of mutilations and the effects of napalm and phosphorous bombs. The attack was also designed to cripple the Angolan economy by disrupting mining operations in an area known for its sizeable iron deposits.[84]

The political motivation for the South African raid was complex. The raid was intended, in part, to placate the more right-wing faction in the South African government which was angered by the dominant faction's participation in negotiations over Namibia. Also, the leadership in Pretoria knew that a brutal attack on SWAPO camps would force SWAPO President Sam Nujoma and other SWAPO leaders to back away from the negotiating process, thus making it look like SWAPO rather than Pretoria was the more intransigent party to the talks. This was in fact what happened. Immediately following the raid on Cassinga, Sam Nujoma expressed "SWAPO's continued wish for an acceptable negotiated settlement," but nonetheless cancelled new talks with the western powers and left immediately for Angola.[85]

Meeting on 6 May 1978 due to a complaint from Angola, the U.N. Security Council unanimously adopted Resolution 428 "condemning the invasion of Angola by South Africa and its utilization of the international territory of Namibia as a spring-board for such an armed invasion."[86] The condemnation could not have been taken very seriously in Pretoria because in May/June 1980 some 3,000 South African troops, backed by armor and artillery, invaded Angola from bases in Namibia.[87] South African officials denied there were heavy civilian casualties, claiming that the attack was aimed solely at "terrorist bases."[88]

By the time of the May/June 1980 raid, the Carter administration had backpedaled so far from its original policy that this flagrant violation of international law was virtually ignored. Even when it came to the perfunctory U.N. vote condemning the invasion, the U.S. and Britain abstained.[89] Andrew Young, by now a former Ambassador to the U.N., lamented the hypocrisy inherent in the fact that the continuing attacks by South Africa were met with inattention by the same western governments who were so outraged over military adventures by communist nations.[90]

In many ways the conflict in Namibia was no closer to a settlement when Carter left the White House than when he first took office. The man on the Carter team most closely identified with policy toward Namibia, Donald McHenry, complained that after four years of negotiating it still seemed like the South Africans were "stalling."[91] In response to a question regarding what was blocking a Namibian settlement, McHenry answered: "The real question I think remains that of the political will on the part of South Africa. There really is nothing to negotiate. All of the substantive objections which South Africa has raised have been met."[92]

After four years of Carter administration policy toward Namibia the balance sheet was quite lopsided:

* South Africa increased its military presence inside Namibia and in late 1980 began drafting young Namibians into an anti-SWAPO army;
* South Africa continued its attacks on Angola, hitting Angolan military and civilian targets as well as SWAPO guerrilla bases and refugee camps;
* South African and western corporations extracted billions of dollars of natural resources from Namibia, in violation of explicit U.N. resolutions to the contrary;
* the major NATO powers prevented the United Nations

from implementing economic sanctions to pressure
South Africa; and
* while tens of thousands of Namibians languished in
refugee camps, those inside the country remained
colonized and unfree with little chance for
political equality or balanced economic
development.

THE MONDALE-VORSTER MEETING

On 19-20 May 1977 Vice President Walter Mondale and
key aides met in Vienna with South African Prime Minister
John Vorster. The summit was significant in that it was
the first top-level encounter of the two regimes, and it
marked the first time that a high-level U.S. official
used the concept of one-man-one-vote to describe the
preferred future for South Africa's political system. One
seasoned commentator referred to the meeting as "the
major U.S. initiative in the period before the South
African crackdown of October 19, 1977."[93]
What actually transpired during the meeting was not
made public but Mondale gave a lengthy statement at a
press conference following the summit. He acknowledged
that there was "a fundamental and profound disagreement"
between the two governments.[94] He warned that South
African intransigence was "the surest incentive to
increase Soviet influence and even racial war."[95] Mondale
echoed earlier statements by Carter and Young when he
lectured the South Africans on "how our nation went
through essentially the same dispute and how the
elimination of discrimination and the achievement of full
political participation has contributed enormously to the
health, vitality, the stability, the economic growth, the
social health and the spiritual health of our country."[96]
Mondale reportedly warned Vorster that the United
States would not come to the aid of the white
supremacists if their apartheid policies led to violent
conflict with Africans, even if this involved outside
intervention by communist states. Mondale stressed two
basic U.S. demands for South Africa: the elimination of
discrimination, and "full political participation by all
its citizens on an equal basis."[97] The closing exchange
of the press conference went as follows:

Question: Mr. Vice-President, could you
possibly go into slightly more detail on your
concept of full participation as opposed to one man
one vote? Do you see some kind of compromise?
Answer: No, no. It's the same thing. Every
citizen should have the right to vote and every vote
should be equally weighted.[98]

This response caused a small shock wave to roll

through the world press. It was the furthest any U.S.
official had gone in demanding democratic reform in South
Africa. By the following month, however, State Department
spokesman Hodding Carter announced (with much less press
attention) that the United States was not insisting on
one-man-one-vote in South Africa. Secretary of State
Vance said that all the Carter administration wanted were
"steps" in the direction of democratic rule, and he was
quoted as saying: "We did not demand one-man-one-vote
tomorrow."[99]

Lost in the verbiage was the fact that the Americans
planned no specific actions to back up their demands.
Prior to the meeting, one State Department official
confessed that "we have a policy but we have no
program."[100] In private interviews, Carter administration
officials revealed a crucial aspect of the U.S. position
that was overlooked by the press. The policy, as
presented to Vorster, was that the Carter team was
seeking progress on any of the three fronts (Rhodesia,
Namibia and South Africa) but not all at once. The
officials failed to see a contradiction between this
position and their earlier claim that they had broken
with the Kissinger policy of going easy on internal South
African reform in order to secure Pretoria's cooperation
on Rhodesia.

Mondale reportedly warned Vorster that diplomatic
measures would be taken against Pretoria if change was
not forthcoming but he neglected to specify what these
might be. And even if there had been more specific
threats, the fact remained that the Carter administration
was following a well-worn path in U.S. policy toward
South Africa: "the approach favored is still one of
reform by the white rulers at the top, assisted by
selected Blacks, in opposition to the radical programs of
the African liberation movements."[101]

The reaction of South African officials to the
Vienna meeting was one of stern defiance. In a separate
press conference following the summit, Prime Minister
Vorster rejected the American call for change. Although
Vorster endorsed U.S. efforts to arrange a settlement to
Rhodesia's guerrilla war, he said he would resist
American pressure for dismantling apartheid.[102]

Vorster met with his European and North American
ambassadors and told them that they should work hard to
improve South Africa's image in their respective areas
but that they should be prepared for a confrontation with
the Carter administration.[103] In what would prove to be
the most prophetic statement of the entire affair,
Vorster dismissed the Carter team's tough talk by
commenting: "We'll see in six or nine months how it works
out."[104]

"DON'T GIVE ANY MORE RACIST SPEECHES"

While Vice President Mondale was meeting with Vorster in Vienna, Andrew Young was playing his part by attending a United Nations conference in Mozambique and meeting with "moderate" blacks and whites in South Africa. Considering that the Maputo conference was being held in a socialist country, to support the Namibian and Zimbabwean liberation struggles, and many guerrilla leaders were present, it was noteworthy that a U.S. ambassador even showed up. By the time Andrew Young left the conference he may have regretted his decision to attend.

Although most of the participants were clearly in support of the guerrilla movements, there was a noticeable difference of opinion when it came to practical proposals. The liberation movements and representatives of socialist countries stressed the need for concrete steps to put pressure on the ruling white minorities. Representatives of the Frontline States on the other hand were willing to moderate some of their demands in order to secure western cooperation in bringing about a transition to majority rule.[105] Late in the conference these more pliable elements collaborated with western diplomats "in a last-minute effort to soften resolutions calling for sanctions against white-ruled South Africa and Rhodesia."[106]

Despite their differences on tactical questions most participants uniformly endorsed armed struggle as a necessary component of attaining independence. This theme was expounded by Jamaica's Michael Manley, President Samora Machel of Mozambique, and Sweden's Prime Minister Olof Palme among others. Manley made the point succinctly:

> The Rhodesian racists have made one thing clear; they will not yield to moral suasion nor even to partial pressure. Unless there is dramatic change in world response, we must conclude that armed struggle provides the only realistic path to a solution.[107]

Just prior to Andrew Young's arrival at the conference, President Carter had told a television interviewer that the United States was prepared to take a tough stand on South Africa's illegal presence in Namibia. He reportedly instructed Vice President Mondale to inform South Africa's Prime Minister: "if you don't do something about Namibia, we'll take strong action against you in the United Nations."[108] The Maputo conferees were encouraged by this stand and were expecting Andrew Young to propose some concrete measures in support of the independence struggle. The expectations were not met.

Young departed from his prepared speech to give an extemporaneous thirty-minute sermon on civil rights, comprised mainly of personal anecdotes. Most of his comments were about the history of racial struggles in the United States and were admittedly intended to establish "the credibility of our policy and why I think these policies represent something of a revolution in the consciousness of the American people."[109] Claiming that the United States had overcome racism, "southern colonialism," and "domestic imperialism," Young was clearly trying to borrow from the rhetoric of the anticolonial struggle and establish a reputation of American expertise that would legitimate an increased U.S. role in the region's politics.[110] He hardly mentioned Namibia and suggested that Zimbabweans should eschew armed struggle and rely on nonviolent boycott tactics to overthrow white supremacy. In one of his few references to U.S. policy in southern Africa, Young asserted that international arms embargoes and economic sanctions would be ineffective and therefore a waste of time.

This was the first major address Young had made regarding southern Africa in front of an African audience. The reaction was almost uniformly negative. Robert Mugabe criticized Young's ignorance of Zimbabwean history and pointedly rejected the suggestion that the nonviolent tactics of the U.S. civil rights movement were an innovation for the Zimbabwean struggle. Mugabe noted that his people had already "used strikes, sit-ins, and passive resistance. We tried these methods and our people got shot. . . . We came to the conclusion that what remained to be tried was the armed struggle."[111]

Nigerian Ambassador to the United Nations and Chairman of the U.N. Committee Against Apartheid, Leslie Harriman, said he found Young's remarks irritating. "We are not talking about improving the lot of Africans. We are talking about liberation."[112] Harriman expressed regret that the U.S. Ambassador had "nothing new" to say with regard to the struggle in Zimbabwe.[113]

But Mozambican President Machel delivered the harshest reprimand to Young. Machel emphasized that the struggle in southern Africa was not primarily a racial conflict but rather a struggle against colonialism and economic exploitation. Following Young's speech Machel reportedly told the American Ambassador not to make any more "racist speeches" while in Mozambique.[114] Machel also tried to educate the U.S. Ambassador about the necessity of using armed force in the struggle for independence.

Using the drama of an effective teacher, Machel told Young ironically that the FRELIMO members with whom he was sitting had all enjoyed killing Portuguese during the war. He then stopped abruptly and explained why armed force had been a necessary component of their struggle. Young came out of the meeting visibly shaken.[115]

The critical reaction of many of the Africans to Andrew Young's stand in Maputo says much about the gulf between U.S. policymakers and the African liberation struggle. This was not a Moynihan or a Kissinger addressing the Africans, it was a black American who admitted that during Mozambique's war of independence "we gave the Portuguese guns and we gave them bandages."[116] This was an American ambassador who was painfully aware of the racism in U.S. history and in the history of America's major allies. In short, this was the most progressive, sympathetic U.S. envoy to come along in quite some time. Yet the U.S. position was so hemmed in by the need to protect corporate reputations and the social stability needed for capital accumulation that Andrew Young could not reach common ground with the people most responsible for the changes sweeping southern Africa.

From Maputo Young went to South Africa. Officials in Pretoria grudgingly approved the visit after considerable lobbying from Washington, but they refused Young's request to visit Soweto. The Ambassador's message was received more favorably than it had been in Maputo. Addressing some of South Africa's top business executives assembled at the home of mining magnate Harry Oppenheiner, Young received a "generally positive response" when he suggested "that they should accelerate the promotion of blacks to enlist black support for the free enterprise system."[117] Once again Young tapped his experience in the civil rights movement to tout the alleged progressive impact of capitalism.

When in Atlanta, Georgia, five banks decided that it was bad for business to have racial turmoil, racial turmoil ceased. Because those five banks controlled the loans to all the businesses in the community. . . . And since that day . . . everybody's enjoying the prosperity of the market system.[118]

Young also met with a group of blacks who were handpicked by the U.S. embassy. Relying on his favorite themes, though more militantly than with the white businessmen, Young recommended a reliance on nonviolent struggle and faith in the positive powers of capitalism. In urging South African blacks to restrict themselves to civil disobedience and economic boycotts the American

envoy was again ignoring a long history of nonviolent
protest that had reaped South African blacks little more
than a whirlwind of repression. On at least one occasion
Young gave a hint that he understood the inherent
contradictions in the U.S. position regarding
nonviolence. "It would be hypocritical if the United
States, which had to take up arms to get its freedom from
Britain, was to go around advising people against it."[119]

Although spurned by the more militant of South
Africa's black leaders, Young was warmly embraced by the
likes of Zulu chief Gatsha Buthelezi.[120] As head of the
KwaZulu bantustan, Buthelezi owed his status to the
apartheid government, but he was also aware that too
close an association with the racist regime was a kiss of
death for a black leader. Buthelezi's stand toward the
West involved a similar straddle. He espoused the two
main planks of U.S. policy--increased foreign investment
and nonviolent black politics--but was careful not to
distance himself too far from the position of the African
National Congress, advocates of armed struggle who were
held in great esteem by the black majority. In this
encounter with American officialdom, Buthelezi seized the
opportunity to approach Young at the podium, embrace him,
and address those assembled. "I have stated to many
fellow South Africans that you are this country's best
friend. I have said that all your efforts on the
international scene are geared toward the peaceful
resolvement of our problems."[121]

Only two months earlier, in March 1977, Buthelezi
had marked a milestone in U.S. relations with South
Africa. At President Carter's invitation, the Zulu chief
had become the first black South African leader to have a
personal meeting with a U.S. President.[122] Buthelezi had
also been one of the key blacks picked to meet with Henry
Kissinger during his shuttle diplomacy in 1976, and was a
main target of western efforts to cultivate "moderate"
black alternatives in southern Africa.

One of the black groups that refused to meet with
Young, despite two attempts by the embassy to persuade
them, was the Black Peoples Convention (BPC). As a
representative of the black consciousness movement, and
more militant than the other blacks chosen to meet with
Young, BPC charged that the ambassador was not consulting
South Africa's "true Black leaders". "Our leaders are all
either in jail, banned, or outside South Africa--people
like Mandela, Sisulu, Mbeki and Sobukwe. If Black leaders
are to be consulted, then it must be these people."[123]

THE HOME FRONT

The domestic component of U.S. policy toward South
Africa involved courting the American equivalents of
Gatsha Buthelezi, i.e., middle class blacks who had a
definite stake in the capitalist system but who
simultaneously held some legitimacy as leaders of the
black community.[124] The Carter team needed the support of
middle class blacks to fend off both right-wing attacks
(e.g., attempts in Congress to drop U.S. compliance with
sanctions against Rhodesia), and pressure from radical
supporters of the liberation movements urging punitive
measures against the white minority regimes.
A key constituency was the Black-Jewish coalition
that traditionally held a prominent place in the
Democratic Party. On his various trips around Africa
Andrew Young's two main issues were white supremacy, and
black Africa's rift with Israel stemming from the 1973
Middle East war.

Far and away the most politically significant
of Young's educational accomplishments was his work
in repairing the frayed black-Jewish relationship in
America through his frequently repeated contention
that black Africa is not inherently anti-Israel, and
that a positive US policy in black Africa is not
inconsistent with US support for Israel. In March
1977, Young said that the Administration's Africa
initiatives had already produced "some softening of
the rhetoric of African countries against Israel.
Now that Africa is getting attention, they're on the
verge of being more cooperative."[125]

Even after Young lost his job as U.N. Ambassador in
1979 he continued to lobby various African leaders to
reestablish working relations with Israel.[126]
On 1 July 1977 Secretary of State Vance made an
important speech on U.S. Africa policy to the annual
convention of the NAACP. As the Administration's first
full exposition of its Africa policy, Vance's address
listed "a number of broad points" that defined "the
general nature of our approach."[127] First, "negative,
reactive American policy that seeks only to oppose Soviet
or Cuban involvement in Africa would be both dangerous
and futile." Second, the Secretary favored a long-term
approach that would "depend more on our actual assistance
to African development...than on maneuvers for short-term
diplomatic advantage." Third, U.S. policy "should
recognize and encourage African nationalism. If we try to
impose American solutions for African problems, we may
sow division among the Africans and undermine their
ability to oppose efforts at domination by others." Vance
also mentioned the administration's intention to make
"our best effort peacefully to promote racial justice in

southern Africa."[128] Distinguishing the Carter team's
approach from that of its Republican predecessors, Vance
explained that

> this Administration has decided to pursue
> actively solutions to all three southern African
> problems--Rhodesia, Namibia, and the situation
> within South Africa itself.
> Some have argued that apartheid in South Africa
> should be ignored for the time being, in order to
> concentrate on achieving progress on Rhodesia and
> Namibia. Such a policy would be wrong and would not
> work.
> We believe that we can effectively influence
> South Africa on Rhodesia and Namibia while
> expressing our concerns about apartheid.[129]

The Secretary's address to the NAACP marked one more
occasion for the Carter administration to warn the
apartheid regime that relations with the United States
would "inevitably suffer" unless South Africa began
moving toward full political participation for all its
people.[130]
     In the early months of their reign the Carter
policymakers wasted little time in enunciating the
toughest line on apartheid yet put forward by an American
president. Liberal and left critics of South Africa were
encouraged by the administration's verbal assaults on
apartheid. It was inevitable that the white rulers in
Pretoria would challenge this strong rhetoric: the test
was to come before the first year of the Carter
administration had run its course.

"STRANGULATION WITH FINESSE"

     Following his Vienna summit with Vorster, Walter
Mondale admitted that the South Africans had made it
clear they would not make changes in response to the
talks.[131] The Vorster regime did in fact make changes but
they were not in the direction being suggested by U.S.
policymakers. Following decades of only token opposition
from Washington, the ruling National Party (NP) decided
that increased diplomatic pressure from the Carter
administration should be met head on.[132] The response
from Pretoria had several facets: strong public criticism
of American pressure, Vorster's call for early
parliamentary elections to demonstrate public support for
his policies, and a major crackdown on internal
opposition.
     Referring to Carter's pressure for reform as
"strangulation with finesse," Prime Minister Vorster
warned that Carter's policy, "if persisted with, can only
lead to one thing as I see it--namely to chaos and

anarchy in southern Africa."[133] Vorster suggested that the Carter administration was using the white minority as a convenient whipping boy to gain favor with African and other third world leaders, as well as to pay off an electoral debt to U.S. Blacks.[134] The former Nazi sympathizer claimed that American pressure would result in "the destruction of South Africa."[135]

Vorster attacked Carter's policy by emphasizing one of his favorite themes, the communist threat. "Mr. Vorster said South Africa was not prepared to take orders from any other country on her internal policy and stressed that what Africa faced was Russian imperialism and naked colonialism."[136]

In a BBC interview Vorster argued that control over southern Africa, its minerals and sea routes, was part of Soviet grand strategy. He alleged that the Carter administration was naive in that it failed to give sufficient weight to the Soviet threat.[137] Minister of Information, C.P. Mulder, joined in with charges that the western posture toward the Marxist challenge was "flabby," lamenting that this flabbiness was more disturbing than the challenge itself.[138] Mulder, later to be driven from office bacause of a scandal in the Information Department,[139] tried to justify the status of blacks in South Africa by claiming that the victories of MPLA and FRELIMO were a step backward for Africa: "In no way can the standard of living of Blacks in Mozambique and Angola be considered better than it was under the Portuguese."[140]

A somewhat more tangible hardening of South Africa's stand toward the United States came over the question of Rhodesia. The war in that country had been intensifying and western leaders were eager to halt the advance of the Patriotic Front.[141] Pretoria had been playing a key role of mediator between the white minority regime of Ian Smith and the joint efforts of British and American envoys.

As part of its generally tougher policy adopted in mid-1977, the Vorster regime let it be known that it could frustrate western efforts in Rhodesia if it so desired. In early August South African Foreign Minister Pik Botha met with Ian Smith and "pledged his country's full support" for Rhodesia's white minority, in the process "snubbing the joint Anglo-American peace initiative."[142] Just one week later Botha was in London to discuss the Rhodesian struggle with Secretary of State Vance and British Foreign Secretary David Owen. He reportedly used the occasion to criticize U.S. and British pressure on South Africa. "I told them bluntly that there was a growing conviction by the government that what Britain and the United States wanted of us would lead to our destruction."[143] The next meeting among South African, British and American diplomats to discuss the Anglo-American plan for Rhodesia took place in

Pretoria in late August. Again the South Africans proved uncooperative.[144]

In August 1977, at the same time that Pretoria was fending off accusations that it was preparing to test a nuclear bomb,[145] the Vorster regime also launched the reform component of its response to western pressures. With much fanfare, Vorster announced that his government was considering a plan that would establish "three full-fledged parliaments, one each for Whites, Coloureds and Indians, each with its own prime minister, cabinet and assembly."[146]

Although pro-apartheid propaganda stressed the ethnic division-of-power elements in the proposal, the heart of the reforms involved scrapping the parliamentary system for a presidential model that would allow the consolidation of power in the hands of a more centralized executive.[147] Touted by the government as a "new dispensation" and obviously aimed at mollifying criticism from the West, the new arrangements did little to alter the structure of apartheid.

> The new plan . . . would not disturb the existing realities of power in the country. Whites, through the presidency, would remain in ultimate control, while the other two racial groups (Coloureds and Indians) would be given a minority voice in national affairs through a multi-racial council.
>
> The blacks would gain nothing. They would be allowed political rights only in the nine tribal homelands. . . . The 10 million blacks living outside the homelands . . . would remain voteless.[148]

Because the government reform plan was "rigidly racial," it came as no surprise that black South Africans reacted in an "unrelievedly negative" way.[149] The black community was quite experienced with cosmetic reforms and rejected this latest effort. Other sectors of South African society also rejected the plan.

> Beyond initial statements of contempt...black leaders have scarcely bothered to pay it any attention. While newspapers serving the white community have been headlining it, The World, the leading paper for blacks, has treated it as a matter of minor interest. . . .
>
> Among whites who support black equality, and among representatives of the Asian and mix-race communities, who would be the principal beneficiaries of the plan, the prevailing view has been that the proposal cannot be accepted.[150]

South African government officials continued their attacks on the Carter administration in an attempt to mobilize white sentiment behind National Party policies. In September 1977 the Christian Science Monitor reported: "A new wave of defensiveness, even a siege mentality, is sweeping over South Africa--with the help of the country's politicians and military men."[151]

With white opinion primed by months of government protest over the alleged harshness of Carter's policy toward the Republic, in late September Vorster dissolved parliament and the provincial councils, and announced that early parliamentary elections would be held on 30 November 1977. Vorster and other National Party officials assumed that a strong showing in the polls would provide a solid base of domestic support that could be used to resist foreign pressure. When Vorster announced the decision, he stated explicitly that the special election was to show the Carter administration that the National Party's resistance to international pressure had the backing of the (white) electorate. "What I am asking the electorate to do is to say that they agree with my standpoint that no country has the right to meddle in the affairs of another country, or to prescribe to another country how it should run its affairs."[152]

Throughout the campaign, top government officials continued to attack the policies of the Carter administration, making "foreign interference in this country's affairs the overwhelming issue" of the election.[153] When the votes were tabulated Vorster's strategy of defiance was vindicated. The ruling National Party increased its majority in Parliament to an unprecedented level. The NP expanded its legislative share from 117 to 135 seats while the opposition parties all lost ground. The Progressive Federal Party slipped from 18 to 17 seats, the New Republic Party dropped from 24 to 10 seats, and the South African Party's share was cut in half from 6 to 3 seats.[154] But when the white voters gave their overwhelming approval to the National Party in late November 1977, they were doing more than thumbing their noses at foreign interference. They were also condoning a major crackdown on internal opposition.

THE FALL 1977 CRACKDOWN

The wave of repression unleashed by the apartheid regime in the fall of 1977 dealt a crushing blow to the black community. The premeditated crackdown also proved to be an acid test for the Carter administration's policy toward South Africa.

In mid-September Police Minister James T. Kruger
announced that Steve Biko had died while in police
detention. Although the government made strenuous efforts
to cover its tracks, evidence soon mounted showing that
Biko had been beaten to death by police.[155] A young but
very popular black leader, Biko's writing and organizing
had touched the lives of many people and his death
ignited a wave of protest.[156] His funeral brought out
thousands of Blacks who expressed their militant outrage
by skirmishing with police. In a display of solidarity,
hundreds of Whites also protested Biko's death, "calling
for Kruger's resignation, repeal of laws allowing
detention without trial, and an independent inquiry into
all 21 of the deaths in detention over the past 18
months."[157]

Biko's death in police custody put Vorster in a
bind: he could not condemn his own police force, which
the regime depended on so heavily, but a coverup would
stimulate more protest. His preferred solution turned out
to be preemptive repression.

Shortly before the results of the government's
inquest into Biko's death were announced (accidental
death, no police culpability), Vorster ordered a broad
crackdown on the opposition. Eighteen African
organizations and the multiracial Christian Institute
were declared illegal.[158] Some forty prominent black
leaders were arrested and seven white opposition figures
were banned.[159] The two leading newspapers for Africans,
The World (estimated readership 891,000) and its sister
paper, The Weekend World, (estimated readership 1.79
million) were shut down. Editors Percy Qoboza and Aggrey
Klaaste were among those arrested.[160]

Reaction within South Africa was overwhelmingly
negative. Black demonstrators clashed with police in
Queenstown, Sharpeville, Peddie, Stinkwater, King
William's Town, and in the Venda and Lebowa
bantustans.[161] The Financial Mail criticized the new wave
of repression as "another step away from the possibility
of peaceful racial reconciliation and further down the
road that leads to violence."[162]

The death of Biko and the accompanying crackdown
were met with hostile reactions in the international
community. African and Asian members of the United
Nations were quick to condemn Biko's murder as an
"atrocity".[163] U.N. Secretary General Kurt Waldheim
lamented the fact that Biko "suffered constant
persecution, imprisonment and stringent restrictions, but
was never convicted of any offense even under the
arbitrary South African laws."[164] While many speakers in
the U.N. General Assembly renewed their demands for an
arms embargo and called for "the international community
to isolate that regime," Ambassador Young sat quietly and
did not address the gathering.[165]

Biko's death prompted a flurry of activity in
Washington. Eleven members of Congress asked the South
African government to allow the International Red Cross
to be present at Biko's autopsy but South Africa's
Ambassador in Washington, Donald B. Sole, coolly rebuffed
the legislators, saying simply that this independent
verification would not be possible.[166] The House of
Representatives initiated debate culminating in a 31
October resolution (passed 347 to 54) condemning
Pretoria's campaign of repression and calling on
President Carter to "take effective measures against the
Republic of South Africa in order to register the deep
concern of the American people about the continued
violation of human rights in that country."[167]
    Initial reaction from the executive branch was also
non-substantive. The State Department said the
administration was "deeply disturbed" by the recent
events, and belabored the obvious by pointing out that
the international community would see the crackdown as an
attempt "to stifle the freedom of expression by spokesmen
for black aspirations in South Africa."[168] Prime Minister
Vorster countered by declaring that U.S. opinions were
"totally irrelevant".[169] A congressional delegation met
with State Department officials and suggested that the
administration recall the American Ambassador, William
Bowdler. Carter did temporarily recall Bowdler on 21
October 1977 but the Congressional Black Caucus insisted
on stronger measures, e.g., withdrawing certain embassy
attaches (particularly the commercial attache),
terminating U.S. tax credits for companies operating in
South Africa, downgrading the status of the U.S. embassy,
and supporting United Nations' sanctions against
Pretoria.[170]
    The Carter administration was "facing a major crisis
of credibility," according to David Ottaway of The
Washington Post:

    If it fails to take any meaningful action
    against South Africa, black African nations as well
    as the black population here are certain to question
    the substance and direction of American diplomacy
    toward the bastion of white rule.
        On the other hand, if the U.S. government does
    back economic sanctions or other measures
    unacceptable to South Africa, it may well lose South
    Africa's crucial support for U.S. initiatives to
    find a peaceful solution to the Namibia and Rhodesia
    disputes.[171]

On 24 October Andrew Young announced that he was
personally in favor of sanctions and warned that the
United States would not use its veto to block Security
Council action against Pretoria. Young added, however,
that "the President and Secretary of State will have to

decide   what   sanctions   are   appropriate   in   these
conditions."[172] The   following   day   President   Carter
announced to an impromptu press conference that he had
made a decision on U.S. support for U.N. action against
South Africa but he refused to specify what this might
include.[173] Within a few days the U.S. position became
very clear. Carter's bluff had been successfully called.

THE U.N. SANCTIONS STRUGGLE

     The first nine months of the Carter administration
had set a high-water mark for official U.S. criticism of
apartheid. A consistent backing down from this original
position can be dated from October 1977 and traced
through the remaining three years of the administration.
In late October, responding to intensifying repression in
South Africa as well as Pretoria's refusal to quit
Namibia, members of the United Nations again pushed for
punitive measures against the apartheid regime.[174] Some
observers believed that Biko's death and the newest wave
of repression sweeping South Africa would be enough to
shake the major capitalist nations from their traditional
position of blocking sanctions. During its first year in
office the Carter administration had contributed to this
perception with assorted threats against Pretoria. Carter
had told a television audience:

     We're not supporting South Africa. We are very
     eager to see, and willing to use, all the leverage
     we   can   to   bring   about   an   end   to   racial
     discrimination in South Africa and an end to the
     apartheid system. . . .
     We've   gone   to   Vorster   now   and   given   him   a
     request--a   little   bit   stronger   than   a
     request--saying that if you don't do something about
     Namibia, then we're going to take strong action
     against you in the United Nations.[175]

     But in late 1977, when a tidal wave of support for
sanctions was looming, Carter's rhetoric took on a more
conciliatory tone. In late October the administration
began placing greater public emphasis on the need to keep
"bridges open to Pretoria," and Carter himself emphasized
his desire "to work harmoniously with South Africa."[176]
     Third world members of the United Nations had heard
this "keeping bridges open" line before, however, and
they   were   not   impressed.   International   concern   over
conditions in South Africa had been building since the
very first meeting of the U.N. General Assembly. The
various   "requests"   and   "urgings"   of   those   early
resolutions seem quite tame today but they laid the
foundation for stronger action that was to follow.

Throughout the 1950s and 1960s governments, church groups, labor unions, and liberation movements pushed for various types of boycotts and other measures designed to isolate Pretoria. The latter half of the 1960s saw a relative decline in efforts to impose sanctions mainly due to the politico-military stability of the white settler regimes and "consistent Western opposition to sanctions."[177] But in the mid-1970s the climate began changing with a rapidity few observers had foreseen. The victories of MPLA in Angola and FRELIMO in Mozambique, coupled with intensified struggles in Zimbabwe, Namibia, and South Africa, provided the impetus for a rejuvenated campaign to impose sanctions. Several other factors played a role.

The threat came to be taken more seriously in 1977 because of a number of changes: Carter's new policy; a greater willingness by Britain and the rest of the EEC to contemplate the use of selective sanctions; the Nigerian policy of forcing a choice on Western firms between operating in their country or in South Africa; and, perhaps most important of all, the growing tendency of Western governments to disengage themselves from South Africa more effectively to counteract Soviet policies in the continent.[178]

These developments, combined with the slaying of Steve Biko and the accompanying crackdown, presented a unique political opportunity for antiapartheid forces. As recently as March 1977 Ambassador Young had convinced antiapartheid nations in the Security Council to shelve four resolutions designed to isolate Pretoria. But when he made similar efforts in October the African representatives were not persuaded. Young explained why: "for good reason the Africa group does not trust the West--any of us, not even me--because they sense a long heritage of betrayal.[179] Security Council members Libya, Mauritius, and Benin submitted draft resolutions along lines similar to those dropped in March. They called for a comprehensive ban on all military aid to South Africa, an end to all nuclear cooperation, and economic sanctions limiting foreign investment and trade with Pretoria.[180] When the three resolutions came up for a vote, along with a fourth resolution condemning apartheid but containing no punitive measures, the United States, Britain, and France approved the non-substantive resolution but exercised a triple veto to block the other three. This marked the fourth time in U.N. history that the western permanent members of the Security Council had exercised a triple veto, and each time it was over the issue of South Africa. The October resolutions were a crucial test of the Carter administration's stand on South Africa and

many observers saw the western vetoes as revealing the
hyprocrisy of U.S. policy.

       The UN action constituted a major setback for
Carter administration policy in southern Africa. The
photographic   image   flashed   worldwide   of   UN
Ambassador   Andrew   Young   raising   his   hand   in
opposition to stiff antiapartheid sanctions did much
to unravel Washington's painstaking effort to put a
new face on U.S. Africa policy.[181]

       Western officials knew in advance that the vetoes
would make them look bad so they attempted to compensate
for this intransigence by proposing a mandatory arms
embargo. A voluntary arms embargo had been in effect
since 1963 (Security Council Resolution 181) but Israel
and the major capitalist countries (particularly France)
had been negligent in their compliance.[182] This new
resolution was weak, calling for only a six-month embargo
that did not invoke Chapter 7 of the U.N. Charter.[183]
African   nations   attacked   the   "loopholes"   in   the
resolution and denounced it as "totally unacceptable".[184]
       On 1 November 1977 a compromise resolution was
worked out that only called for "review" of licensing
arrangements through which South Africa produces heavy
weapons (e.g., the French Mirage fighter-bomber), but
invoked Chapter 7 and therefore marked a certain victory
for antiapartheid forces.[185] The western countries were
careful to insert language in the resolution asserting
that apartheid per se was not a threat to peace and it
was only "acquisition...of arms or related materials in
the current situation" that posed the danger.[186]
       In all their statements, the Carter people were
careful to describe their support for the arms embargo as
a reaction to the specific events of October 1977 and not
to the general structure of apartheid. In a 28 October
interview Carter stated that "we are supporting sanctions
against South Africa" because of the "almost complete
abolition of any voice of dissent in South Africa last
week among groups representing black citizens."[187] One
State Department official privately confessed that
"nothing short of a South African invasion of the United
States" would get the U.S. government to support real
sanctions.[188]
       The mandatory arms embargo was largely symbolic. The
Americans were giving away little because there was
already a voluntary embargo and the new resolution would
not significantly alter U.S. policy. Pointing out that
"the South African government has been planning for this
day for years," the Washington Post noted that Pretoria's
self-sufficiency in arms production blunted the impact of
the embargo.[189]

The western arms embargo on South Africa now in
the making comes far too late to have any
significant effect on that country's ability to wage
war against other African countries or its own black
population in the foreseeable future.[190]

THE RETREAT TO A SOFTER LINE ON APARTHEID

The events of 1977 constituted a resounding defeat
for the regionalists in the Carter administration. In
response to the tough talk coming from Washington, Prime
Minister Vorster resisted U.S. efforts for a negotiated
settlement in Rhodesia, and cracked down on his internal
opposition. Then, running a campaign based on opposition
to Washington's policy, the Nationalists won their
largest mandate in thirty years.

When the majority of U.N. member states attempted to
punish Pretoria for its recalcitrance, the Carter
administration vetoed measures such as economic
sanctions. The United States, like its major allies such
as Britain, blocked sanctions because of the potential
damage these could do to powerful transnational
corporations. When antiapartheid members of Congress
proposed more than a dozen separate pieces of legislation
aimed at exerting economic pressure on South Africa, the
Carter administration actively lobbied against these
measures.[191] The image of a tough antiapartheid position
the White House had carefully nurtured during its first
year now lay shattered. It was clear to friend and foe
alike that Washington, even with Carter's regionalists in
control of policy, would not exercise the potential
leverage it had on Pretoria.

This inability of the administration to back up its
earlier threats against the white minority regime was not
the only factor that weakened the position of the
regionalists. As early as the summer of 1977 Congress was
witnessing a right-wing resurgence on southern African
issues, with votes favoring the white minority regime in
Rhodesia and banning aid to Mozambique and Angola.[192] The
Cuban/Soviet intervention in Ethiopia beginning in late
1977 further undermined the regionalists and caused
Brzezinski to get more directly involved in shaping
Africa policy.[193]

In spring 1978 the second invasion of Zaire's
mineral-rich Shaba province by guerrillas operating from
Angola brought a harsh anticommunist reaction from
Washington. The same Jimmy Carter who in 1976 had said
that "the Russian and Cuban presence in Angola...need not
constitute a threat to United States interests," was now
emphasizing the East-West component of conflict in
Africa.[194]

By mid-1978 the regionalists in the administration
and Congress were fighting a defensive battle over policy
toward Rhodesia. Ian Smith had brought black moderates
into an "internal settlement" government and it was
gaining conservative support in Congress. This created an
uphill battle for liberals to maintain U.S. compliance
with international sanctions and hold out for all-party
elections.[195] In addition, the regionalists suffered a
serious loss of allies in the 1978 congressional
elections. Senator Dick Clark (D-IA), who as chair of the
Africa Subcommittee had played a precedent-setting role
in liberalizing U.S. Africa policy, and four other
supporters of a relaxation of the cold war were defeated
by right wing Republicans.[196]
    The resurgence of a cold war perspective on Africa
from 1978 onward was part of a more general trend in
Washington. Analysts of various political persuasions
agree that by Carter's second year in office the
globalists led by Brzezinski, Huntington, and allies in
the Pentagon were rapidly gaining control of the
administration's foreign policy.[197] This process was
underway well before events in Iran and Afghanistan
pushed the discourse on foreign policy further to the
right. These later events, as well as the dismissal of
Andrew Young and the resignation of Cyrus Vance, sealed
the fate of the regionalist perspective that tentatively
held sway during 1977.
    This general swing to the right in Washington,
combined with Pretoria's refusal to cooperate, caused the
regionalists to acquiesce to a retreat on policy toward
South Africa. During 1978 the regionalists confronted the
fact that they could not force Pretoria to reform
apartheid and at the same time gain cooperation on the
Rhodesia conflict. By the fall of 1978 administration
officials had reverted to a Kissingerian policy that
regionalists such as Young and Lake had attacked early in
the administration. The new policy was a simple
trade-off: Washington would restrain its opposition to
apartheid in return for South Africa's cooperation in
ending the war in Rhodesia.[198] In October Carter sent a
confidential letter to South Africa's new Prime Minister,
P.W. Botha, outlining the new, more conciliatory
approach.

    South Africa responded enthusiastically. Mr.
    Botha, eager to play down the hawkish image he
    brought to office, spoke of his gratification with
    the President's letter. . . . Halted virtually
    overnight were attacks by officials on the "double
    standards" of American diplomacy.[199]

CONCLUSION

From 1978 onward, the Carter administration's
position on South Africa slid steadily to the right. It
eventually dovetailed into the position of Ronald Reagan:
a position more conciliatory toward the white minority
than even that of the Nixon administration. Substantive
pressure on Pretoria had never made it past the policy
memo stage, but now even verbal pressure was held in
abeyance. The major economic links binding the two
nations grew stronger.[200] The Carter administration left
office without having facilitated any reforms in the
system of apartheid.
During the period 1975 through 1978 U.S. policy in
southern Africa shifted to the left and then back to the
right. As we have seen, these shifts were limited to a
narrow tactical realm, but they were significant in
comparison to the neglect and indifference that
characterized U.S. policy in the pre-1975 period.
Although Washington paid greater attention to southern
Africa during this period, official goals remained the
same and the objective effects of U.S. policy were as
contradictory as ever.

NOTES

1. Africa News, 13 October 1980, p. 2.
2. Southern Africa, September 1976, p. 32.
3. Ibid.
4. For the full text of the Democratic Party
platform on Africa see Colin Legum , ed., Africa
Contemporary Record, 1976-77 (London: Rex Collings,
1977), p. C163.
5. Africa Report, May/June 1976, p. 20.
6. Ibid.
7. Anthony Lake, Caution and Concern: The Making of
American Policy Toward South Africa, 1946-1971 (Ph.D.
dissertation, Princeton University, 1974), p. 435.
8. Africa Report, January/February 1977, pp. 3-4.
9. Ibid.
10. Richard Falk, "Brzezinski Looking Out for #1,"
The Nation, 27 September 1980, p. 283.
11. "Carter Eyes US Investments, Race Experience in
Africa Policy," Washington Post, 30 July 1976.
12. Philip V. White, "The Black American
Constituency for Southern Africa, 1940-1980," in Alfred
O. Hero, Jr. and John Barratt, The American People and
South Africa (Lexington, MA: D.C. Heath and Company,
1981), p. 94.

    13. Ibid.
    14. Ibid., pp. 94-95. Also see back issues of
TransAfrica's newsletter, available from TransAfrica, 545
8th St. SE, Washington, DC, 20003.
    15. White, The Black American Constituency...,
p. 95.
    16. For the most detailed analysis of how
containment (the "Riga axioms") gained predominance in
the U.S. policy establishment see Daniel Yergin,
Shattered Peace: The Origins of the Cold War and the
National Security State, (Boston: Houghton Mifflin
Company, 1977).
    17. See Richard J. Barnet, Intervention and
Revolution (New York: Meridian Books, 1968).
    18. James Petras, "U.S. Foreign Policy: The Revival
of Interventionism," Monthly Review, February 1980, p.
17.
    19. Tom J. Farer, "Searching for Defeat," Foreign
Policy, #40, Fall 1980, p. 157.
    20. Patricia Fagen, "The United States and
International Human Rights, 1946-1977," Universal Human
Rights, 2, 3, July-September 1980, p. 31.
    21. See Howard Warshawasky, "The Department of State
and Human Rights Policy: A Case Study of the Human Rights
Bureau," World Affairs, 142, 3, Winter 1980; David P.
Forsythe, "American Foreign Policy and Human Rights:
Rhetoric and Reality," Universal Human Rights, 2, 3,
July/September 1980; Natalie Kaufman Hevener, ed., The
Dynamics of Human Rights in U.S. Foreign Policy (New
Brunswick, NJ: Transaction Books, 1981); Tom J. Farer,
"Defending Human Rights: Two Impediments for the West,"
Trialogue, #19, Fall 1978; "Human Rights: In the Soul of
Our Foreign Policy," NACLA Report on the Americas,
March/April 1979; and Patricia Weiss Fagen, "U.S. Foreign
Policy and Human Rights: The Role of Congress," in
Antonio Cassesse, ed., Parliamentary Control Over Foreign
Policy (Netherlands: Sijthoff and Noordhoof, 1980).
    22. Fagen, "The U.S. and Human Rights, 1946-1977,"
p. 33.
    23. For an insightful overview of Brzezinski's
gradual transition from being critical of the dominant
cold war paradigm to a hard-line position well within
that paradigm, see Simon Serfaty, "Brzezinski: Play It
Again Zbig," Foreign Policy, #32, Fall 1978.
    24. Farer, "Searching for Defeat," p.157.
    25. Robert M. Price, U.S. Foreign Policy in
Sub-Saharan Africa: National Interest and Global Stratey
(Berkeley: Institute of International Studies, University
of California, 1978), p. 4.
    26. Ibid.

27. Bruce Cummings, "Chinatown: Foreign Policy and Elite Realignment," in Thomas Ferguson and Joel Rogers, eds., The Hidden Election (New York: Pantheon Books, 1981), p. 206.

28. See ibid.; and Chapter 3 "The Carter Surrender" in Richard J. Barnet, Real Security: Restoring American Power in a Dangerous Decade (New York: Simon and Schuster, 1981).

29. Interview with former high-level State Department official under the Carter administration, May 1980.

30. "Carter Eyes U.S. Investments...."

31. Financial Mail, 5 November 1976, p. 501.

32. Ibid.

33. Sevendays, 20 June 1977, p. 10.

34. Quoted in George Houser, "US Policy in Southern Africa," The Africa Fund, #4/77, p. 4.

35. "Young Assails US Ties With White-Ruled Africa," The Afro-American (Washington) 24-28 August 1976.

36. See Holly Sklar, ed., Trilateralism (Boston: South End Press, 1980); Alan Wolfe, "The Two Faces of Carter," The Nation, 18 December 1976; Jeff Friedan, "The Trilateral Commission: Economics and Politics in the 1970s," Monthly Review, December 1976; "A Well-Connected Peanut Farmer," Sevendays, 26 June 1976; "Jimmy Carter: Trilateralism in Action," The Guardian (New York), 16 February 1977; and Samuel Bowles, "Have Capitalism and Democracy Come to a Parting of the Ways?," The Progressive, June 1977.

37. Much of this section is based on Laurence H. Shoup, The Carter Presidency and Beyond (Palo Alto: Ramparts Press, 1980).

38. Ibid., p. 24.

39. Ibid., p. 29.

40. For more details on the foreign policy prescriptions of these and other elite groups see Laurence H. Shoup and William Minter, Imperial Brain Trust: The Council on Foreign Relations & United States Foreign Policy (New York: Monthly Review Press, 1977); G. William Domhoff, The Higher Circles (New York: Vintage, 1970); and The Powers That Be: Processes of Ruling Class Domination in America (New York: Vintage, 1978).

41. Shoup details how important Donovan was to the Carter candidacy. Donovan was later repaid by Carter in a way that angered many Democrats. Carter appointed Donovan to head the Commission on the Agenda for the 80s, and in that position Donovan appointed all the staff. This group subsequently issued a report that among other things advised letting the "Frost Belt" section of the United States continue its decline while subsidizing the general shift of U.S. industry and workers to the "Sun Belt".

42. Laurence   H.   Shoup,   "Jimmy   Carter   and   the
Trilateralists: Presidential   Roots,"   in   Sklar,
Trilateralism, p. 202.

43. Although Jimmy Carter was sold to the American
people as a "farmer," with all the populist sentiment
that   conveys,   the   Carter   family   holdings   were   quite
extensive   and   not   limited   to   the   peanut   business.   The
overall family wealth, of which Jimmy was the principal
owner, was estimated in the mid-1970s to be $5 million.
This personal wealth helped in launching and sustaining
Carter's political career.

44. Jimmy   Carter,   Why   Not   the   Best?   (Nashville:
Broadman, 1975) p. 127.

45. Richard Falk, "A New Paradigm for International
Legal Studies," The Yale Law Review, 84, 5, April 1975.

46. For a list of Trilateral Commission members who
were appointed to posts in the Carter administration see
Sklar, Trilaterlism, pp. 91-92.

47. Philip   H.   Burch,   Jr.,   Elites   in   American
History: The New Deal to the Carter Administration (New
York: Holmes and Meier Publishers, 1980), p. 319.

48. Shoup in Sklar, Trilateralism, p. 203.

49. Burch, Elites in American History..., p. 316.

50. Ibid.

51. Ibid.

52. Ibid. Vance and Christopher, occupying the two
highest positions in the State Department, and Secretary
of Defense Harold Brown had all worked for IBM, a major
supplier of computers to South Africa.

53. Ibid., p. 319.

54. Ibid.

55. Ibid., p. 321.

56. Not   only   did   Carter's   top   policy   people   have
corporate   allegiances   before   their   government   service,
many followed their stints as policymakers by taking jobs
with   major   corporations.   A   good   example   of   this   other
side   of   the   "revolving   door"   is   Carter's   Assistant
Secretary of State for African Affairs, Richard Moose.
Within weeks of Ronald Reagan's inauguration Moose was
working for the prominent New York investment firm Lehman
Brothers, Kuhn Loeb. Also, the top Africa specialist on
Carter's National Security Council, Jerry Funk, went to
work for Bankers Trust.

57. "UN   Assembly   Blasts   S.   Africa,"   Christian
Science   Monitor,   11   November   1976;   "U.N.   Blasts   South
Africa in 10 Votes," Washington Star, 10 November 1976.
In an 11 November editorial the Washington Post berated
the General Assembly action as an "annual freakout, an
orgy   of   irresponsibility--directed   this   time   against
South Africa."

58. Stephen Talbot, "What Will Carter Do in Southern Africa?," International Bulletin, 3, 24, 17 December 1976, p. 1.

59. Ibid.

60. Ibid.

61. Although most African states and a substantial majority in the United Nations would continue to recommend the imposition of sanctions, even the most progressive Americans attending the conference (Senator Dick Clark and Congressman Charles Diggs) rejected the idea of a total economic boycott of South Africa.

62. Africa Confidential, 19 August 1977, pp. 1-2; and Africa News, 11 July 1977, pp. 2-3.

63. "State Disputes Young's Angola Remark," Washington Post, 3 February 1977.

64. "Tanzania Called Rebel Training Site," Baltimore Sun, 2 February 1977.

65. "Kaunda Asks U.S. Role in Africa," Baltimore Sun, 6 February 1977.

66. John Burns, "7 White Missionaries in Rhodesia Slain in Raid by Black Guerrillas," New York Times, 8 February 1979.

67. "Nigerian Sees Young, Urges U.S. Africa Role," New York Times, 11 February 1977; "U.S., Nigeria Reconcile Differences," Washington Post, 11 February 1977; "Young Meets with Angolan Leader; Scores Hit in Nigeria," Washington Post, 10 February 1977; "Different Style Pays Off For Young in Africa," New York Times, 10 February 1977.

68. "Nigerian Sees Young, Urges U.S. Africa Role," New York Times, 11 February 1977.

69. "Nigeria Threatens Economic Action Against Countries Supplying Arms and Investments to White-Ruled South Africa", Baltimore Sun, 29 March 1977.

70. John Darnton, "Nigeria: Africa's West Coast Giant," New York Times, 13 February 1977.

71. Washington Notes on Africa, Summer 1977, p. 1.

72. Stephen Talbot, "Carter Courts Nigeria," International Bulletin, 24 October 1977, p. 1.

73. "Nigeria Warns US of Embargo on Oil," Washington Post, 7 January 1981.

74. The timing of Western initiatives for negotiated settlements is not accidental. In Angola, Mozambique, Rhodesia, Namibia and South Africa, decades of dictatorial repression rolled by without any serious attempt at negotiations by the West. But in each case, when guerrilla movements with populist/socialist ideologies began to show strength, the West jumped in to "put an end to violence" and "reach a peaceful solution." It is hardly surprising that many Africans looked at these Western peace initiatives with a skeptical eye.

75. "SWAPO to Win," Windhoek Observer, 23 August 1980; The New Statesman, 21 August 1980; Johannesburg Star, 21 August 1980. The detailed study, conducted by South African military intelligence, was brought out be defecting Bureau of State Security and Foreign Affairs official, Ivan Himmelhoch.
76. Legum, The Western Crisis Over Southern Africa, p. 15.
77. Established by the General Assembly in 1967, the 25- member Council for Namibia was designated "the only legal authority to administer the Territory of South West Africa until independence and, in the meantime, to prepare it for independence." (United Nations Council for Namibia: What It Is, What It Does, How It Works, U.N. Office on Public Information, March 1978, p. 1) "The Council also gives continued support to SWAPO as the sole and authentic liberation movement of Namibia." (ibid., p. 4).
78. For details on the history of the legal status of Namibia see the following: "Namibia: A Unique UN Responsibility," Objective Justice, 11, 3/4, Autumn/Winter 1979; "Namibia Independence Proposals: Background and Chronology," Africa Today (special issue on Namibia), 26, 2, 1979; C.J.R. Dugard, The South West Africa/Namibia Dispute (Berkeley, CA: University of California Press, 1973); Elizabeth S. Landis and Michael L. Davis, "Namibia, Impending Independence?," in Carter and O'Meara, eds., Southern Africa: The Continuing Crisis.
79. On 13 December 1974 the General Assembly passed U.N. Decree No. 1, which outlawed the extraction of minerals and other resources from Namibia without express consent of the United Nations.
80. Legum, Western Crisis..., p. 47.
81. Ibid., pp. 46-47.
82. For a different slant on Pretoria's two-track strategy see Robert Manning, "Namibia: Pretoria's Double Strategy," New African, September 1980.
83. "We shot this young girl. She must have been about five...," Guardian (UK), 29 January 1981. This was not the only occasion when Angola was penetrated by South African forces. Document S/13473 of the U.N. Security Council, dated 27 July 1979, lists almost 200 separate violations of Angolan territory. These ranged from reconnaissance flights over Angolan air space to bombing, strafing and napalming of Angolan civilians. The South African army also had special platoons whose sole purpose was to operate for extended periods on the ground in southern Angola, harassing Angolans and Namibians alike. The commander of such a special unit defected to England and gave the following description of how these units function. "Our main job is to take an area and clear it. We sweep through it and we kill everything in front of us, cattle, goats, people, everything. We are out to stop

SWAPO." He confessed that this strategy was not very effective: "Half the time the locals don't know what's going on. We're just fucking them up and it gets out of hand. Some of the guys get a bit carried away. And SWAPO still get by us and cross the cut-line between Angola and Namibia. It's not as if we are stopping them." The disgruntled ex-South African trooper also had some revealing comments about Jonas Savimbi's UNITA movement, an organization touted by the American right-wing and which supposedly controled half of Angola according to Presidential candidate Ronald Reagan. "The point is that UNITA are a lot of crap. They hang around in the South-East where their tribe is and they can probably defend themselves, but they can't go out and take somewhere like Savate. We do it for them because it improves their bargaining position, gives them more talking power." "We shot this young girl...."

84. For backgound see The Cassinga File (Geneva: International University Exchange Fund, 1978); "South African Force Crosses Into Angola," New York Times, 5 May 1978; "The Cassinga Raid," Baltimore Sun, 9 May 1978; "South Africa's Adventure in Angola," New York Times, 7 May 1978. For a uniquely South African view of the raid see "The Angola File," Paratus (official organ of the South African military) 29, 6, June 1978.

85. "SWAPO Cancels New Talks, Citing South African Raids in Angola," Baltimore Sun, 9 May 1978.

86. "Namibia: A Unique UN Responsibility," p. 43.

87. "Angola: The Longest War," New African, September 1980.

88. "Heavy Casualties in Angola Raids," The Guardian (UK), 27 May 1980; "South Africa Reports 216 Killed in Raids on Namibians in Angola," Washington Post, 14 June 1980; "South Africa Says it Killed 220 in Angola," Baltimore Sun, 14 June 1980; "South African Troops Said to Occupy Angolan Towns," New York Times, 27 June 1980.

89. "The U.S. and Angola: The Recognition Factor," The Nation, 20 September 1980, p. 246.

90. Andrew Young, "An End to 'Carte Blanche' in South Africa," Washington Post, 30 June 1980.

91. Africa News, 24 November 1980. For a semi-official South African view on this see Marietjie Meiring, "SWA/Namibia: Playing for Time is SA's Best Strategy," To the Point, 31 October 1980. For the official U.S. view see Donald McHenry, Namibia: Review of Negotiations (Washinton, D.C.: Bureau of Public Affairs, Department of State, 1980).

92. Africa News, 24 November 1980.

93. Karis in Carter and O'Meara, Southern Africa: The Continuing Crisis, p. 342.

94. Legum, Western Crisis..., p. 251.
95. "What U.S. Is Up To In Africa," U.S. News and World Report, 30 May 1977, p. 31.
96. Legum, Western Crisis..., p. 251.
97. Ibid., p. 252.
98. Ibid., p. 253.
99. South African Digest, 1 July 1977, p. 21.
100. Southern Africa, June/July 1977, p. 14.
101. Ibid.
102. "Relations to Worsen, Vorster Says," Baltimore Sun, 22 May 1977; "Botha: 'No Way' South Africa Will Accept One-Man One-Vote," Washington Post, 6 June 1977.
103. "Vorster Briefs His Ambassadors," New York Times, 22 May 1977. For additional details on Vorster's reaction to the Vienna summit see Ronald T. Libby, Toward An Africanized U.S. Policy for Southern Africa: A Strategy for Increasing Political Leverage (Berkeley: Institute of International Studies, 1980), pp. 110-111.
104. "Vorster Briefs..."
105. In order to comprehend this moderate position of the Frontline States we need to remember that these countries (particularly Zambia, Mozambique, and Angola) were suffering severe hardships because of their support for the guerrilla movements. See "Raids Take Toll," New African, December 1979; and "South Africa, Rhodesia Step Up Attacks," Southern Africa, November/December 1979.
106. "U.S., Black Africans Collaborate at Meeting," Washington Post, 21 May 1977.
107. Washington Notes on Africa, Summer 1977, p. 5.
108. "Carter Asks End to White Rule in South-West Africa," New York Times, 18 May 1977.
109. Washington Notes On Africa, Summer 1977, p. 6.
110. The term "domestic imperialism" was in reference to the corporate control exercised over American politics. Young argued that after the Watergate scandal big corporations were no longer able to "buy the American government" with campaign funding. Some of the Africans present at the conference were later to remark that Young seriously underestimated their knowledge of the United States. Washington Notes on Africa, Summer 1977, p. 6.
111. "Maputo Conference-No U.S. Triumph," Southern Africa, June/July 1977, p. 9.
112. Ibid.
113. Washington Notes On Africa, Summer 1977, p. 6.
114. Ibid.
115. Ibid.
116. "U.S., Black Africans Collaborate at Meeting," Washington Post, 21 May 1977.
117. "Young, in Johannesburg, Urges Boycott by Blacks," New York Times, 23 May 1977.

118. Washington Notes on Africa, Summer 1977, p. 2.
119. "Young, in Johannesburg, Urges Boycott...."
120. For interesting details on the CIA's support for Buthelezi see former South African spy Gordon Winter's account (Chapter 31: "Gatsha Buthelezi and the CIA") in Inside BOSS: South Africa's Secret Police (Harmondsworth, England: Penguin, 1981).
121. "Young Opens Heart to South Africans," Washington Post, 23 May 1977.
122. "Carter Meets S. African Tribal Leader," Washington Post, 23 May 1977.
123. Southern Africa, June/July 1977, p. 14.
124. For a useful look at the American version of this phenomenon see Morton G. Wenger, "State Responses to Afro-American Rebellion: Internal Neo-Colonialism and the Rise of a New Black Petit Bourgeoisie," Insurgent Sociologist, 10, 2, Fall 1980.
125. Bruce Oudes, "The United States' Year in Africa: Reinventing the Wheel" in Colin Legum, ed., Africa Contemporary Record (New York: Africana Publishing Co., 1979), p. A68.
126. Kevin Danaher, "Mixing Business with Politics: Andrew Young's Africa Trip," Africa News, 12 October 1979.
127. Cyrus Vance, "US Policy Toward Africa," 1 July 1977, Department of State, Bureau of Public Affairs, p. 2.
128. Ibid.
129. Ibid., p. 4.
130. "U.S. Again Links South Africa Ties to Full Black Role," New York Times, 2 July 1977.
131. "Mondale Warns South Africa that Bias Will Hurt Relations," Washington Post, 21 May 1977.
132. A useful though somewhat dated overview of Pretoria's foreign policy, from a sympathetic perspective, is Seiler, "South African Perspectives and Responses to External Pressures," Journal of Modern African Studies, 13, 3, 1975. A more up-to-date summary is Colin Legum, "South Africa in the Contemporary World," in Robert M. Price and Carl G. Rosberg, eds., The Apartheid Regime (Berkeley, CA: Institute of International Studies, 1980).
133. South African Digest, 12 August 1977, p. 1. South Africa Digest is published by the South African government.
134. "Carter Africa Policy Assailed by Vorster as Payoff for Blacks," New York Times, 7 August 1977.
135. South African Digest, 12 August 1977, p. 1.
136. South African Digest, 3 June 1977, p. 1.
137. South African Digest, 10 June 1977, p. 1.

138. South African Digest, 27 May 1977, p. 2.
139. The most comprehensive account of the
Information Department scandal is an extensive interview
with former Minister of Information Eschel Rhoodie that
was published in the August 1979 edition of the Dutch
magazine Elseviers. Other sources on the scandal and its
connections to South African covert operations in the US
include: Winter, Inside BOSS...; "Smoldering Muldergate,"
International Bulletin, 20 November 1978; "Ruling Party
Apartheid Split Underlies 'Infogate' Scandal," In These
Times, 10-16 January 1979; "Scandal Changes the Political
Climate in Pretoria," Business Week, 9 April 1979; "Mr.
Botha Tries to Close Door on Muldergate," Manchester
Guardian, 17 December 1978; "Rhoodie Tells of
'Collaborators' in West," Washington Post, 29 August
1979; Karen Rothmyer, "The McGoff Grab," Columbia
Journalism Review, November/December 1979; Peter H.
Stone, "Muldergate on Madison Avenue," The Nation, 14
April 1979; "More Dirty Tricks," New Internationalist,
May 1980. A comprehensive source on South African
propaganda operations in the United States is Galen Hull,
"South African Propaganda in the U.S.: A Bibliographic
Essay," African Studies Review, XXII, 3, December 1979.
140. South African Digest, 27 May 1977, p. 2.
141. "Rhodesia Guerrilla Vise Tightens," Christian
Science Monitor, 4 August 1977.
142. "South Africa's Botha Backs Smith in quest for
Rhodesia Settlement," Washington Post, 5 August 1977.
143. South African Digest, 19 August 1977, p. 1. See
also "U.S., Britain and South Africa Discuss Rhodesia
Plan," New York Times, 13 August 1977.
144. "Pretoria Talks Close in Silence," Baltimore
Sun, 30 August 1977; "British-U.S. Rhodesia Plan
Resisted," Christian Science Monitor, 29 August 1977.
Later, in an interview with the New York Times, Vorster
swore that his government would resist America's "blatent
meddling" in South Africa's affairs. ("Vorster Warns US
Against Meddling," New York Times, 17 September 1977.
145. "South Africa Says It Is Not Planning Atomic
Bomb Tests," New York Times, 22 August 1977; "No Plans to
Test Bomb, Says Vorster," Washington Post, 25 August
1977.
146. South African Digest, 26 August 1977, p. 1.
147. Efforts to concentrate state power into the
hands of the chief executive and his top advisors
continued under Vorster's successor P. W. Botha. See
"South Africa: Day of the Generals," Now, 5-11 October
1979; and chapter 8, "Afrikaner Politics: How the System
Works," in Heribert Adam and Hermann Giliomee, Ethnic
Power Mobilized (New Haven and London: Yale University
Press, 1979).

148. "South Africa Plans Wider Minority Role," New York Times, 20 August 1977.
149. "South Africa Power-Sharing Plan Meets With a Mixed Reaction," New York Times, 23 August 1977.
150. Ibid.
151. "South African Whites' Confidence at Low Ebb," Christian Science Monitor, 12 September 1977.
152. "Mr. Vorster Rides a Wave of White Chauvinism," Financial Times, 28 September 1977.
153. "Carter 'Meddling' Is Issue in Pretoria Elections," Baltimore Sun, 14 November 1977; "South Africa - Rejected Suitor: Vorster Jabs at U.S.," Christian Science Monitor, 15 September 1977.
154. South African Digest, 9 December 1977, p. 3.
155. "Autopsy by Red Cross Asked," New York Times, 24 September 1977; "South Africa on Trial Again: Death of Black Brings Outrage and Questions," New York Times, 20 September 1977; "A South African Martyrdom," Baltimore Sun, 16 September 1977.
156. "Rites for Black South African Turn Into Protest by 10,000," New York Times, 26 September 1977; "100 Jailed After Protest On Biko Funeral Travel Ban," Washington Post, 25 September 1977. For background on Biko and the Black Consciousness Movement, see Gail M. Gerhart, Black Power in South Africa (Berkeley, CA: University of California Press, 1978); and Steve Biko: I Write What I Like (San Francisco, CA: Harper and Row, 1978).
157. "White Protest Over Black's Death Increasing in South Africa," Washington Post, 20 September 1977; "South Africa on Trial Again," New York Times, 20 September 1977.
158. Among the groups made illegal were The Black People's Convention, The Black Parent's Association, the South African Students' Association, the Soweto Students' Representative Council, the South African Students' Movement, the National Youth Organization, the Association for the Educational and Cultural Advancement of Africans, the Black Women's Federation, Black Community Programmes, the Zimele Trust Fund, the Medupe Black Writers' Union, the Union of Black Journalists, and the Christian Institute. See p. 40 of Legum, The Western Crisis..., for details.
159. "Banning" is a peculiar form of political punishment which the South African regime has relied on over the years. A banned person may not write for publication or address public gatherings. The stipulation that a banned person may speak to only one person at a time not only hampers political activity, it also has a devastating impact on one's social life. It is also illegal for a banned person to travel without express consent of the government. Many of those banned by the government are forced to quit their jobs and move to specially designated areas. Personal interviews verify,

however, that people frequently violate their banning
orders.
160. Legum, The Western Crisis..., p. 41.
161. Ibid, p. 43. Also see "Protests, Boycott
Continue," Baltimore Sun, 26 October 1977; "'Children's
Revolution' in South Africa," Washington Post, 24 October
1977.
162. Quoted in Legum, ibid., p. 42.
163. "South African Leader Eulogized at U.N. as
Symbol of Black Hope," New York Times, 24 September 1977.
164. Ibid.
165. Ibid.
166. "Autopsy by Red Cross Asked," New York Times,
24 September 1977.
167. "House Censures 'Repressive' South African
Tactics," Washington Post, 1 November 1977.
168. "U.S. Deplores Moves," Washington Post, 20
October 1977.
169. Karis in Carter and O'Meara, Southern Africa:
The Continuing Crisis, p. 350.
170. L.A. Jinadu, Human Rights and US-African Policy
Under the Carter Administration (Lagos: Nigerian
Institute of International Affairs, 1980), p. 74.
171. "Confrontation With U.S. Expected in South
Africa," Washington Post, 25 October 1977.
172. "Young Urges Sanctions on South Africa,"
Baltimore Sun, 25 October 1977.
173. "U.S. Is Said to Agree To Arms Sanctions
Against South Africa," New York Times, 26 October 1977.
174. For useful historical background on U.S. policy
toward South Africa in the United Nations see Anthony
Lake, Caution and Concern: The Making of American Policy
Toward South Africa, 1954-1971 (Ph.D. dissertation,
Princeton University, 1974), pp. 56-69, 70-79, 90-97,
100-104, and 121-25. Referring to a particular issue
dealing with South Africa, Lake summarizes the U.S.
tradition of speaking out against apartheid but
withholding support from substantive measures: "The U.S.
fudged its position on that issue, as it has ever since.
While attacking apartheid in its statements during
debates in the Assembly, . . . U.S. representative voted
with the minority . . . against placing the issue on the
agenda" (p. 66). For background see C.A. Bratton, "A
Matter of Record: The History of the United States Voting
Pattern in the United Nations Regarding Racism,
Colonialism and Apartheid, 1946-1976," Freedomways, 17,
3, 1977; C. Clyde Ferguson, "The United States, the
United Nations and the Struggle Against Racial Apartheid"
in Nathalie Kaufman Hevener, ed., The Dynamics of Human
Rights in U.S. Foreign Policy (New Brunswick, NJ:
Transaction Books, 1981). The Africa Fund of New York and
the U.N. Centre Against Apartheid have published numerous
compilations of the U.S. voting record on apartheid at
the United Nations.

175. Department of State Bulletin, 13 June 1977, p. 627.

176. "Carter Emphasizes Keeping Door Open to South Africans," Washington Post, 28 October 1977.

177. South African Institute for International Relations and South African Institute for Race Relations, South Africa and Sanctions: Genesis and Prospects, (Johannesburg: SAIIR/SAIRR, 1979), p. 32.

178. Legum, Western Crisis..., p. 48.

179. Department of State Bulletin, 5 December 1977, p. 792, transcript of 30 October 1977 ABC Television broadcast "Issues and Answers."

180. "Arms Ban on S. Africa Remains Stalled in U.N.," Washington Post, 2 November 1977. For the texts of the resolutions that were vetoed see United Nations documents S/12310/Rev. 1, S/12311/Rev.1, and S.12312/Rev. 1. For the resolution that passed see Department of State Bulletin, 12 December 1977, p. 865.

181. "U.S. Vetoes South Africa Sanctions," Guardian (N.Y.), 9 November 1977.

182. Although much of the research on this subject is from a left-of-center perspective, one can also find conservative voices who verify the ineffectiveness of the voluntary arms embargo. General Sir Walter Walker, NATO commander-in-chief until his retirement in 1972, reports in his book The Bear at the Back Door: "Despite the 15-year-old UN arms embargo, South Africa has been able to build up an impressive military capability. It is far greater than the estimates made by military watchdogs such as the London-based International Institute for Strategic Studies (IISS)." For other sources on western arms transfers to South Africa despite the previous arms embargo see Chapter One, footnote eight.

183. Chapter Seven of the U.N. Charter is the section that delineates the authority by which the Security Council can declare a nation "a threat to the maintenance of international peace and security" and accordingly apply comprehensive sanctions to isolate such a regime. The western version of the mandatory arms embargo was carefully worded to say that "the acquisition by South Africa of arms or related materials in the current situation" constituted a threat to peace. As pointed out by African diplomats, this wording refers to then current events in South Africa and not general conditions of apartheid, French and British officials conceded this point in private interviews. ("Arms Ban 'Loopholes' Criticized," Washington Post, 29 October 1977).

184. Ibid.

185. "Year in Review: The United Nations," Southern Africa, December 1977.

186. Karis in Carter and O'Meara, Southern Africa: The Continuing Crisis, p. 351.
187. Department of State Bulletin, 5 December 1977, p. 798.
188. Author's interview with State Department official, March 1980.
189. "Arms Embargo Comes Too Late to Affect South Africa," Washington Post, 29 October 1977.
190. Ibid.
191. For details on these pieces of legislation and Carter administration efforts to defeat them see: William Raiford, "South Africa: Foreign Investment and Separate Development," Issue, IX, 1/2, Spring/Summer 1979; "Crusade of Tokenism," Financial Mail, 20 October 1978; and U.S. Congress, House, Subcommittees on Africa and International Economic Policy and Trade, United States Private Investment in South Africa (Washington, D.C.: Government Printing Office, 1978).
192. "Thunder on the Right," Africa News, 11 July 1977.
193. "An Africa Policy Who's Who," Africa News, 10 April 1978.
194. "Jimmy Carter on Africa," Africa Report, May-June 1976, p. 19. Also see David Ottaway, "Africa: U.S. Policy Eclipse," Foreign Affairs (special year-end issue: "America and the World-1979), p. 657.
195. Richard Deutsch, "African Issues and Presidential Politics," Africa Report, January/February 1980.
196. Kevin Danaher, "South Africa, U.S. Policy and the Antiapartheid Movement," Review of Radical Political Economics, 11, 3, Fall 1979, p. 46, fn.
197. See William Stivers, "Doves, Hawks, and Detente," Foreign Policy, Winter 1981-82; Richard J. Barnet, Real Security: Restoring American Power in a Dangerous Decade (New York: Simon and Schuster, 1981); "Cold War Cripples Africa Policy," Washington Notes on Africa, Summer 1978; "U.S. Africa Policy: Hardening the Line," International Bulletin, 5 June 1978; and Bruce Cummings, "Chinatown: Foreign Policy and Elite Realignment," in Thomas Ferguson and Joel Rogers, eds., The Hidden Election (New York: Pantheon, 1981).
198. "U.S. Testing Policy on South Africa," New York Times, 3 December 1978.
199. Ibid.
200. "U.S./South Africa: Two Years After Vienna," Africa News, 25 May 1979.

6
The Reagan Administration, 1981–

Of all U.S. presidencies, the Reagan administration is the easiest to analyze on the question of South Africa. This is because early in the administration someone in the State Department leaked a set of confidential documents outlining the administration's strategy for southern Africa. Throughout its first four years, and even into its second term, the Reagan team did not waver significantly from the course charted in these early plans.

One set of policy papers was leaked to TransAfrica, an Afro-American lobbying group focusing on U.S. policy toward Africa and the Caribbean.[1] Another secret document was leaked to the New York Times and excerpted in a 1 June 1981 front-page story.[2]

The secret memoranda stress the linked themes of movement toward an "internationally acceptable settlement in Namibia," preferably excluding SWAPO; efforts "to foreclose opportunities for growth of Soviet influence in southern Africa; and greater acceptance of South Africa within the global framework of western security."[3]

The documents make a settlement in Namibia conditional on the removal of Cuban troops from Angola and the inclusion of South African-backed rebel leader Jonas Savimbi in the Angolan government. In a frank assesment of the likely African outrage at these demands, the document's authors suggest U.S. officials should lie about the linkage between a Namibian settlement and the demands on Angola: "We would insist that these are unrelated, but in fact they would be mutually reinforcing, parallel tracks of an overall strategy."[4]

The tone of the documents is arrogant: "African leaders would have no basis for resisting the Namibia-Angola linkage once they are made to realize that they can only get a Namibia settlement through us."[5] It is also threatening: U.S. recognition of Angola "is out unless the Cubans leave and they [the Angolans] cut a deal with Savimbi . . . if they won't play we have other options."[6] The documents do not go on to state what "other options" the administration was contemplating. But in light of President Reagan's stated willingness to rearm Savimbi's guerrillas, it is likely the administration was considering, and perhaps implementing, covert operations against Angola.[7]

A detailed memo on Assistant Secretary of State for Africa Chester Crocker's April 1981 visit to South Africa provides insights into official South African thinking. Regarding Washington's efforts to improve U.S.-South African relations, Crocker found the South Africans "suspicious of way US dropped SAG [South African Government] in Angola in 1975." Foreign Minister Botha "argued that SAG went into Angola with USG support, then US voted to condemn in UN." Botha and Defense Minister Malan "doubted whether, given domestic pressure and views of such African states as Nigeria, US could continue any policy favorable to South Africa which would not provoke constant criticism."[8]

Botha confidently predicted that within South Africa "developed moderate Blacks . . . will engage with us in common effort against communism. When whites see Blacks as allies, whites will move away from discrimination. With more distribution of economic goods, more Blacks will join us." Nevertheless, the South African leaders "cautioned against making success of P.W. Botha's [reform] program a condition of US/South Africa relations."[9]

On the question of a Namibia settlement the South Africans took a tough stand. Malan "flatly declared that the SAG can't accept prospects of a SWAPO victory which brings Soviet/Cuban forces to Walvis Bay. This would result from any election which left SWAPO in a dominant position."[10] Since it is widely accepted that a free election in Namibia would result in an overwhelming SWAPO victory, Malan's statement amounts to a rejection of an internationally acceptable settlement.[11]

The South Africans also told Crocker they would prefer prolonged warfare in Namibia to any political settlement leading to a SWAPO government. According to the South African leaders: "The longer it takes to solve the Namibia question, the less South African presence will be required there. We will reach a stage where internal forces in Namibia can militarily defeat SWAPO."[12]

Botha repeated South Africa's familiar claim to be a victim of an international communist onslaught, and threatened to engulf the region in bloodshed if SWAPO came to power.

> "We're convinced Moscow controls present government in Angola. We're convinced SWAPO is Marxist. Nujoma will nationalize the whole place and cause upheaval and civil war, involving South Africa. We will have to invade Namibia and other

countries as well . . . SAG's bottom line is no
Moscow flag in Windhoek. If US disagrees, let
sanctions go. South Africa can survive sanctions."[13]

The South Africans were also worried about Savimbi,
whom they consider a buffer for Namibia. "Having
supported him so far, it would damage SAG honor if
Savimbi is harmed."[14] Crocker responded to this position
by arguing that he saw "no prospect" for military victory
for UNITA, but that Savimbi's inclusion in the Angolan
government could be achieved "by playing on divisions in
MPLA."[15]

The "Soviet threat" is a major theme of the leaked
documents. In his Pretoria meeting with Botha and Malan,
Crocker "stressed that top US priority is to stop Soviet
encroachment in Africa."[16] A memo from Crocker to
Secretary of State Alexander Haig advises the Secretary
to assure South African officials that "a Russian flag in
Windhoek is as unacceptable to us as it is to you." In
the same memo, Crocker describes Pretoria's tough talk as
"partly bluster, partly an opening bargaining position
with us."[17]

As Crocker's memo to Haig reveals, the Reagan
administration was trying to make a deal with the South
Africans, exchanging a Namibia settlement for an "end to
South Africa's polecat status in the world . . . and
small but concrete steps such as the normalization of our
military attache relationship."[18]

Crocker urged Haig to tell Foreign Minister Botha
that the United States is "willing with them to open a
new chapter in our relationship," based on the shared
perception that "the chief threat to the realization
. . . of stability and cooperation in the region . . . is
the presence and influence in the region of the Soviet
Union and its allies."[19] The Reagan team's only
opposition to South African aggression against regional
neighbors was based on strategic concerns. "We cannot
afford to give them [the South African government] a
blank check regionally . . . SAG intransigence and
violent adventures will expand Soviet opportunities and
reduce Western leverage in Africa."[20]

Central to the Reagan administration's "constructive
engagement" strategy was the ability to claim that Prime
Minister Botha's government was seriously committed to
reforming apartheid. The secret documents reveal that
during Crocker's meetings in Pretoria, he told the South
African foreign minister: "US ability to develop full
relations with SAG depends on success of Prime Minister
Botha's [reform] program and extent to which it is seen
as broadening SAG's domestic support."[21] At another point
Crocker instructs Haig to tell the South Africans: "We
can cooperate with a society undergoing constructive
change. Your government's explicit commitment in this
direction will help us to work with you. You must help

make this approach credible." But Crocker assured Foreign
Minister Botha that "this is not a condition, but
reflects US desire to support positive trends."[22]
        For Crocker, a "credible" appearance of internal
change was enough. As the memo notes, "it is only the
problem of Namibia which . . . is a primary obstacle to
the development of a new relationship with South Africa."
Once the white minority regime agrees to an acceptable
settlement, they will be returned "to a place within the
regional framework of Western security interests."[23]
        The secret documents reveal in explicit detail that
Reagan's policy planners had a perspective on southern
Africa quite similar to leaders in Pretoria, and wanted
to get South Africa back into the western alliance. The
documents also reveal, however, that South African
leaders were aware they could not fully trust Washington.
They knew from experience that U.S. leaders had their own
distinct interests in southern Africa and would be
willing to betray the white minority if it became
politically expedient to do so. A close reading of the
documents shows that the quid pro quo on which
constructive engagement rested--friendlier treatment from
the United States in return for reform in South Africa
and Namibia--was explicitly rejected by the South African
leadership. But this did not stop Crocker and his
associates from plunging ahead with the policy anyway.

IMPLEMENTING CONSTRUCTIVE ENGAGEMENT

        The underlying rationale of the constructive
engagement policy was that by improving relations with
Pretoria, Washington could expect cooperation in two key
areas: a settlement in Namibia, and internal reform in
South Africa. The architect of constructive engagement,
Chester Crocker, argued that there was a key group of
reform-minded officials in the South African government,
and that P.W. Botha's administration represented a unique
opportunity for change.[25] As we will show later, there
are serious flaws in the assumption that South African
leaders are committed to either a withdrawal from Namibia
or significant reform of apartheid.
        In seeking to persuade South African rulers that the
U.S. government could be a trusted ally, the Reagan
administration began expanding U.S. military, economic,
and diplomatic ties, and portrayed South Africa in a
positive light to the American people.
        In a 3 March 1981 CBS television interview with
Walter Cronkite, President Reagan asserted that South
Africa was reforming away from apartheid and the United
States should be "helpful" in this process. Apparently
unaware of the National Party's support for the Nazi
cause in World War II, the president asked: "Can we
abandon a country that has stood beside us in every war

we've ever fought, a country that is essential to the free world, that has minerals?"[26]

The following week five high-ranking South African military intelligence officers secured visas to the United States and met with officials at the Pentagon, the National Security Council, and Congress. The White House originally claimed that no high-level members of the administration had contact with the South Africans, but it was later revealed that U.N. Ambassador Jeane Kirkpatrick had met with them. Despite Kirkpatrick's efforts to deny she knew who these people were, the incident marked a clear break with traditional U.S. policy of no visits by South African military officers, and was a violation of the spirit, if not the letter, of the U.N. arms embargo.

This visit by high-ranking military officials was to be the first in a long series of exchanges that would mark a new level of U.S.-South African collaboration. On 10-11 June 1981 Deputy Secretary of State William Clark held meetings in Pretoria with South Africa Defense Minister Magnus Malan. In late July one of America's most sophisticated military airplanes, the EC 135 Advanced Range Instrumentation Aircraft, arrived in South Africa for a three-day visit. In August South African military officers began training at the U.S. Coast Guard station at Governor's Island, New York. Also in August a group of South African nuclear experts visited Goodyear's Portsmouth Gaseous Diffusion Plant in Piketon, Ohio, where uranium isotopes are purified. In October the State Department granted visas to a 13-member delegation of South African police and military officers making a working visit to the United States. In early December it was reported that as part of the plan to upgrade official military ties, President Reagan had assigned U.S. Navy Commander Royce Caplinger as a naval attache to the U.S. Embassy in Pretoria. Increased contact between military planners of the two countries was to continue throughout Reagan's term of office.[27]

On 19 March 1981 the White House submitted to Congress a proposal to repeal the Clark Amendment, which since 1976 had outlawed U.S. military aid to UNITA rebels fighting the MPLA government in Angola. If successful, the proposal would have given South Africa a considerable boost in its efforts to destabilize the Angolan government, thus preventing Angola from aiding SWAPO's independence war in Namibia. Although the House Foreign Affairs Committee rejected the White House proposal and retained the Clark Amendment, the attempt at repeal signaled that the Administration would seek to aid South Africa in putting pressure on Angola.

In April the State Department announced that South African Foreign Minister Roelof "Pik" Botha had been invited to Washington for talks. The mid-May meetings with Reagan, Haig, and other U.S. officials, were the first for any African diplomat, and showed that the Administration was giving high priority to improving relations with South Africa.

In the diplomatic arena, the Reagan administration began establishing a record for protecting South Africa from international pressure. On 30 April 1981 the United States, along with France and Britain, vetoed five U.N. Security Council resolutions aimed at pressuring South Africa to allow implementation of a U.N.-sponsored transition to independence in Namibia. On 31 August 1981, following a massive South African invasion of Angola, the Reagan administration broke with major western allies to veto a U.N. Security Council resolution that would have condemned the invasion. Despite the hostility engendered among liberal congressmen and African diplomats by this complicity with Pretoria's aggression, the Reagan administration would continue to protect South Africa from international retaliation.

The White House initiated a series of measures to expand the sale of U.S. goods to South Africa's police, military, and nuclear agencies. On 30 June 1981 the Administration issued new trade guidelines rescinding the ban on the sale of medical equipment and supplies to the South African military. The new rules also permitted the sale of crime-control devices such as metal detectors used in combating hijacking. In October the Commerce Department granted a license for the export of a Sperry Univac 1100 series computer to the Atlas Aircraft Corporation, a subsidiary of the state-controlled South African Armaments Development and Manufacturing Corporation (ARMSCOR). The administration defended the sale by arguing that U.S. law only prohibited such sales to South African government corporations, not their subsidiaries.

In late February 1982 the Administration further loosened export restrictions, lifting the ban on sales of certain "nonmilitary" items to the South African police and military. These goods included computers, helicopters, and airplanes. Commerce Secretary Malcolm Baldrige said the Administration would adopt a "more flexible policy with respect to approvals of exports to South Africa of dual use [civilian and military] commodities, and other materials and other equipment which have nuclear-related end uses in areas such as health and safety uses."[28]

The new, looser restrictions allowed a wave of exports to South Africa that previously would have been prohibited. Among the items approved for sale: vibration test equipment used to test warheads and ballistic reentry vehicles; computers and multichannel analyzers capable of synthesizing data from hundreds of cables at nuclear bomb test sites; the heavy isotope helium-3 which can be used to make tritium for nuclear bombs; computers with nuclear and cryptographic applications; and hot isostatic presses, used in the production of nuclear weapons.

The most controversial sale of U.S. goods to South Africa came on 26 April 1982 when the Commerce Department approved the sale of 2,500 shock batons, used by police in crowd control operations. It would not be until September that critics would discover the sale and point out that it violated Section 502(b) of the Foreign Assistance Act, which prohibits exports to police and military agencies in countries with consistent human rights violations. Commerce Department officials claimed the issuing of this export license was "an honest mistake," a "simple, unfortunate screw-up."[29]

In its first three years the Reagan administration approved a greater value of Munitions List sales to South Africa than had been approved in the previous 30 years.[30]

These measures benefiting the white minority's repressive apparatus were part of a larger effort to increase U.S. corporate involvement in South Africa. The weakening of restrictions on U.S. business dealings with South Africa was justified with Reagan's free market ideology: getting the government out of the way and allowing more freedom to U.S. corporations would supposedly benefit Americans and South Africans alike.

The Reagan administration provided important support to South Africa's 1982 request for $1.1 billion in credit from the International Monetary Fund. Although thirty-five members of Congress and some members of the IMF executive board opposed the loan, U.S. representative Richard Erb argued strongly for approval, and on 3 November 1982 the money was granted. The amount of the credit was roughly equal to the cost of South Africa's war in Namibia and Angola over the previous two years.[31]

The Reagan administration's economic policies toward Pretoria probably helped offset negative economic conditions caused by the slump in the world economy. The price of gold declined from over $800 per ounce in 1980 to only $300 per ounce in early 1985. Because gold sales account for nearly half the country's export earnings, this decline seriously damaged the balance of payments position and eroded government tax revenues.[32]

The Reagan administration, with allies in Congress, fended off efforts by congressional liberals to pass legislation that would have: restricted U.S. investments, exports, and bank loans to South Africa; prohibited the sale of South Africa's gold coin, the Krugerrand, in the United States; and mandated fair employment codes for U.S. companies doing business in South Africa.[33]

Measures of this sort could damage South Africa's
cash flow: in 1982 Krugerrand sales in the United States
amounted to $363 million, and American bank loans
totalled $623 million.[34] A secret State Department study
leaked in mid-1983 showed that U.S. economic support to
South Africa was much greater than the standard figure
for U.S. direct investment (then $2.6 billion) given by
the Commerce Department. The study, entitled U.S.
Investment in South Africa: The Hidden Pieces, showed
total U.S. investments to be $14.6 billion, over five
times the figure for direct investment.[35] The traditional
calculation of direct investment does not include
investments by U.S. subsidiaries based in third
countries. In addition, the study pointed to the
importance of short-term loans from U.S. banks ($3.6
billion) and South African stocks owned by Americans
(over $8 billion). "The study suggests that a withdrawal
of American investors from South Africa would be much
more damaging to the apartheid economy than the business
community and the State Department had been previously
willing to admit."[36]

During its first four years in office the Reagan
administration gave more economic, military, and
diplomatic support to Pretoria than any previous U.S.
administration. The Reagan team was willing to withstand
domestic and international criticism for its friendly
relations with the apartheid regime. The policymakers
justified their strategy by claiming it was the best way
to bring peace and development to southern Africa.

PRETORIA'S RESPONSE TO CONSTRUCTIVE ENGAGEMENT

According to the logic of Crocker's constructive
engagement policy, the U.S. carrots would enduce the
South African government to relinquish control over
Namibia and its own black population. Yet from the Reagan
administration's earliest days in office, Pretoria
displayed rigid opposition to progress in these areas,
and stepped up its attacks against neighboring states.

In mid-March 1981 South African jets penetrated
nearly 200 miles into Angola to bomb Namibian refugee
camps. As in the many cases of South African aggression
that would occur over the next few years, the U.S. State
Department expressed concern over the events but refused
to condemn Pretoria for the aggression.

In what would be the first of several large
invasions, South African troops on 23 August 1981
launched an assault ("Operation Protea") into southern
Angola. Jet bomber sorties preceded a column of some
10,000 troops. The advancing forces, headed by 32 tanks
and 82 armored vehicles, penetrated nearly 100 miles
before being stopped by the Angolan army at Cahama.
Though able to hold their ground, the Angolan forces

could not push the South Africans back to their bases in northern Namibia. From this point onward, South African troops would permanently occupy large sections of southern Angola.[37]

Beginning on 1 November 1981 South African forces launched an 18-day assault on SWAPO bases some 150 miles into Angola, deeper than South African ground forces had penetrated since the invasion of 1975. News of this additional invasion did not circulate in the western press until early December.[38]

On the weekend of 2 January 1982 South African helicopters and jet fighters attacked Cuban troops stationed 190 miles north of the Angola/Namibia border in the area between Uia and Mujombe. The Angolan press agency, ANGOP, reported that three Angolan soldiers and one Cuban were killed, three Cubans were wounded, and one Cuban was taken prisoner.[39]

In early March 1982 South African commandos struck deep into southwestern Angola, reportedly killing 201 members of SWAPO and capturing tons of supplies.[40] In mid-May "South African air raids killed seven civilians and six Angolan soldiers during attacks on a power station and military targets in southern Angola."[41]

Then in August, just as negotiations on Namibia seemed to be making progress, South Africa launched another invasion, sending thousands of heavily armed troops some 175 miles into southern Angola. The timing of the assault, coming as it did while four of South Africa's top military officers were in the United States meeting with American officials, caused even conservatives to question Pretoria's motivations. As The Economist of London noted:

> For the umpteenth time South Africa has launched a major military operation into southern Angola just when the Namibia negotiations have reached a sensitive stage. It raises again the old question: does the South African government really want a settlement in Namibia, or is it just pretending to, with the intention of scuttling the talks whenever an agreement looks imminent?[42]

On 6 December 1983 South African forces began another major incursion into Angola. In the month-long operation, several thousand heavily armed South African troops encountered stiff resistance from Angolan, Cuban, and SWAPO forces. While inflicting heavy damage on Angola, the South Africans suffered greater casualties (21 dead, 1 captured) than in previous invasions. As with previous South African aggression, when the U.N. Security Council censured Pretoria for its attack, the Reagan administration abstained on the measure of condemnation.

Judging from the conduct of South African forces in
Angola, the goals of the recurring attacks were broader
than the obvious objective of retarding SWAPO's ability
to conduct guerrilla war in Namibia. South African troops
hit SWAPO camps, but also regularly attacked Angolan
civilian targets such as villages, power stations,
bridges, factories, mines, and food storage facilities. A
former South African commando leader gave the following
description of Pretoria's scorched earth policy in
Angola: "Our main job is to take an area and clear it. We
sweep through it and kill everything in front of us,
cattle, goats, people, everything."[43]
      In addition to keeping thousands of troops
permanently stationed inside Angola, the South Africans
continued regular bombing runs, commando raids, and
reconnaissance flights in a broad area of southern
Angola. As of 1982 South African attacks had cost Angola
an estimated 10,000 deaths, 160,000 homeless, and $10
billion in property damage.[44]
      While all these attacks on Angola were taking place,
making progress on a Namibia settlement impossible,
Pretoria was actively destabilizing other neighbors as
well. On 30 January 1981, within weeks of Ronald Reagan's
inauguration as president, South African commandos
launched a raid into Mozambique, attacking African
National Congress houses in a suburb of Maputo. The
commandos lost two of their own but killed twelve ANC
members and a Portuguese technician before retreating.
South Africa followed the attack with menacing troop
movements along the Mozambican border, and violations of
Mozambican airspace by South African fighter aircraft.[45]
      In addition to these sporadic cross-border raids
into Mozambique, the South Africans stepped up their aid
to the Mozambique National Resistance (MNR), an
antiFRELIMO guerrilla group carrying out acts of sabotage
and terrorism. Originally sponsored by Ian Smith's
Rhodesian Central Intelligence Organization, the MNR
switched to South African sponsorship when Zimbabwe
achieved independence in 1980. Since that time, Pretoria
has provided the MNR with bases and a radio station in
the Transvaal, and has given them abundant supplies and
training. This aid has included shipping and flying
provisions to MNR units inside Mozambique, and providing
technical assistance on some sabotage operations. During
the first four years of the Reagan administration the
MNR's terrorist attacks created havoc in rural areas, and
proved to be an important stumbling block to FRELIMO's
plans for economic development.
      By early 1984 FRELIMO was so desperate for a
cessation of South African aggression, it agreed to sign
a peace accord with Pretoria. Signed on 16 March 1984,
the Nkomati accord--named for the border river where it
was signed--ostensibly aimed to promote mutual security
and economic cooperation. A key aspect of the accord

required FRELIMO to refrain from supporting ANC guerrillas, and South Africa to stop supplying and training the MNR.

Although Mozambique had never provided bases for the ANC, soon after signing the Nkomati accord FRELIMO raided the homes of ANC members, forcing many into Swaziland and other countries. ANC was allowed to retain only a small diplomatic staff in Mozambique. On the other hand, prior to signing the accord "the South Africans pushed hundreds of heavily armed men across the border, and set up supply caches for them in Mozambique."[46] In the year following the signing of the accord, MNR destabilization continued unabated and Mozambique's economic and security conditions approached total breakdown. It was under these conditions that Mozambique sought improved relations with the United States.[47]

While Angola and Mozambique were being bludgeoned by South African aggression, other countries in the region were also suffering the effects of Pretoria's destabilization policy. On 9 December 1982 the South African military launched a commando raid on Maseru, the capital of Lesotho, killing 42 people, many of them members of the ANC. Pretoria also increased support to rebels seeking to topple the government of Lesotho prime minister Leabua Jonathan. Then South Africa began blocking the shipment of goods in and out of this landlocked state and threatened to block the transit of Lesotho migrant workers travelling to their jobs in South Africa. With the majority of Lesotho's workers and 40 percent of gross national product dependent on jobs in South Africa, the latter move alone would bring the Lesotho economy to its knees.[48]

The apparent goals of Pretoria's destabilization policy were summed up by an associate editor of Foreign Affairs: "Pretoria aims, first of all, to terrorize its neighbors into cutting all ties with South Africa's own broadly backed insurgent movement--the African National Congress" and "to weaken and perhaps even topple left-leaning and uncooperative governments in neighboring countries."[49]

It can only be assumed that the Reagan adminstration was in agreement with these goals. Washington was willing to engender the enmity of African states by failing to protest Pretoria's belligerence and continuing to meet regularly with top South African military and intelligence officials. In every forum of African and third world opinion the Reagan administration was denounced for its seeming complicity in Pretoria's regional destabilization.

But what of the two issues--Namibia and reform in South Africa--on which the Reagan administration asked that its policy be judged? Was progress made on these issues, thus justifying Washington's tolerant response to Pretoria's belligerence?

THE NAMIBIA QUESTION

At the time of Reagan's second inauguration in 1985,
a settlement of the Namibia dispute was no closer than
when the Reagan administration initiated its constructive
engagement policy in 1981.

During the closing days of the Carter administration
a conference had been convened in Geneva, for the first
time involving all the parties in the struggle for
Namibia. The January 1981 U.N.-sponsored summit raised
hopes that finally South Africa was ready to cut its
losses and allow the U.N. transition plan to be put into
effect. SWAPO was willing to make concessions in order to
bring about a ceasefire and U.N.-monitored elections. Six
of the eight "internal" parties signed a statement saying
they were willing to cooperate.

The conference collapsed within days, however, when
Pretoria declared that conditions were still "premature"
to set a date for a ceasefire and independence. What the
South Africans meant by premature was revealed by the
leader of the Democratic Turnhalle Alliance (DTA), a
Namibian party lacking in popular support but favored by
Pretoria to run the territory. Dirk Mudge, the white
agribusinessman heading DTA, made the bizarre admission
that his party would not agree to elections until it was
certain that DTA had at least a 50-50 chance of beating
SWAPO.[50] Given SWAPO's overwhelming popular support, this
was tantamount to rejecting a democratic transition to
independence. Pretoria and DTA knew that with the
electoral defeat of Jimmy Carter in November 1980, it was
in their interest to delay negotiations until the more
sympathetic Reagan administration took over.

Early on, the Reagan team let it be known that they
would be lenient toward South Africa's illegal occupation
of Namibia. On 6 March 1981, when the U.N. General
Assembly adopted by large majorities ten resolutions
opposing South Africa's presence in Namibia, the United
States abstained on every vote. In late April the
Security Council considered five resolutions critical of
South Africa's policies in Namibia. The United States,
along with France and Britain, blocked the measures.

Administration officials announced they were seeking
modifications in the U.N. plan for Namibian independence,
as outlined in Security Council Resolution 435. Under 435
the party winning a majority of seats in the legislature
would have a relatively free hand in writing Namibia's
constitution. The Reagan administration sought
constitutional agreements prior to elections in order to
restrict the power of what was likely to be a SWAPO
government.

Pretoria welcomed the proposals but western members of the Contact Group were harder to convince. On 26 October 1981 the five western nations submitted their plan to the parties in Windhoek. The proposal would require the legislature to ratify a new constitution by a two-thirds majority, and all significant groupings would have to be represented in the legislature. In addition, the plan called for "an independent judiciary and a bill of rights that would contain guarantees of a multiparty system as well as the protection of private property against seizure without just compensation."[51]

Although it initially raised hopes, the new plan would eventually come to grief on the same obstacle that had blocked all previous attempts at settlement: Pretoria's unwillingness to allow elections. In the past, South Africa had raised numerous objections to the U.N. plan: everything from an alleged U.N. bias in favor of SWAPO, to the color of uniforms to be worn by the U.N. observation team. But now Pretoria had an objection that would prove deadly for hopes of a negotiated settlement, and the obstacle had been created in Washington.

During talks between South African and U.S. officials in mid-1981, it was agreed, along the lines laid out in the leaked State Department documents, that Pretoria's cooperation on a settlement in Namibia would be linked to a withdrawal of Cuban troops from Angola. A Cuban troop pullout would give Pretoria and Washington an attractive sop to their right-wing critics at home. It was hoped this would dull the pain of Namibian elections that would probably bring SWAPO to power.

However neat the idea of linkage may have been on paper, it proved unworkable in reality. African states overwhelmingly rejected the demand, and Pretoria refused to back down now that it found strong support from Washington. Not only SWAPO and the Angolan government found the idea of linkage distasteful. The Frontline States, the Organization of African Unity, the Commmonwealth Nations, the U.N. General Assembly, the Namibian Council of Churches (representing over 80 percent of Namibian Christians), and a broad coalition of U.S. groups, all rejected linkage and criticized the Reagan administration for contributing to the delay of a Namibian settlement.[52]

The Reagan administration claimed that Pretoria had originated the demand for linking a Cuban pullout from Angola with South African withdrawal from Namibia. State Department officials such as Chester Crocker asserted that linkage was a reasonable demand from the security-conscious South Africans. Despite these denials of U.S. authorship of the linkage idea, there was the evidence of the leaked State Department documents. Based on these, and off-the-record interviews with Reagan policymakers, the New York Times had reported in mid-1981: "Reagan Administration officials say they have

decided on a strategy of tying final agreement on
independence for South-West Africa to a withdrawal of
Cuban forces from Angola and a commitment by the Marxist
leaders in Angola to share power with Western-backed
guerrillas."[53] Finally, on 15 February 1983 in testimony
to the House Subcommittee on Africa, Crocker admitted
that the linkage issue "was our effort. I am not denying
that."[54]

As U.S. officials conducted round after round of
shuttle diplomacy, the situation in Namibia steadily
deteriorated. A combination of drought, recession in the
world economy, faulty policies by Pretoria's surrogate
rulers, and the continuing war, produced a serious
economic crisis. The two big agricultural earners, beef
and karakul, were suffering. The cattle population
declined from 2.9 million in 1978 to 1.3 million in
1984.[55] Karakul dropped from five million head in 1978 to
roughly two million in 1984, at the same time that world
prices for karakul pelts were steadily declining.[56] With
world industrial activity in a slump, mineral exports
were depressed.[57] Namibian fishing grounds had been so
overfished that fishing and canning operations once
providing work for roughly 10,000, by 1982 employed only
a few hundred.[58] A major Windhoek newspaper reported in
January 1985 that "unemployment has escalated
tremendously in the past few years" and related to this
unemployment "social degeneration is rearing its head
. . . in the form of crime, hunger, child prostitution,
an increasing number of shebeens and child negligence."[59]

To compensate for declining revenues, the
administrator-general's office in Windhoek piled up bank
loans, mainly from South African banks. The foreign debt
was $580 million and still growing in 1984, causing the
business press to forecast a bleak future: "Even if
Namibia's exports were to recover from today's depressed
levels . . . debt service would be in the region of
15-20% by 1986/87, putting the country well into the top
half of the league of major African debtors."[60]

The depressed economic conditions and government
mismanagement did little to enhance the popularity of DTA
and other parties collaborating with South Africa's
colonial administration. The ongoing war against SWAPO
drained funds from the state's budget. Widespread
atrocities by the military against Namibian civilians,
coupled with reports of sexual scandals and corruption in
the colonial government, further undermined the
legitimacy of the collaborator politicians.[61]

With Pretoria's political position in Namibia
deteriorating and its military position still strong,
there was little incentive to withdraw from the territory
and allow free elections. In late 1984 the Angolan
government gave the U.N. Secretary General a set of
proposals showing consideration for South African
security concerns, and proposing a detailed timetable for

withdrawal of Cuban troops from Angola in return for South African withdrawal from Namibia. Angolan President Jose Eduardo dos Santos emphasized that his platform "was a categorical rejection of linkage" because it required the South Africans to begin a transition to U.N. rule in Namibia before Cuban forces would be removed from Angola.[62]

Pretoria's response virtually ruled out the possibility of a settlement.

The South African Foreign Minister, 'Pik' Botha, said the Cubans would have to leave Angola before Pretoria would grant Namibian independence. This reply clearly turned the platform round and was an insistence on "prior or parallel" linkage, which has been consistently rejected by Luanda.[63]

With South Africa refusing to budge from Namibia without a withdrawal of Cubans from Angola, and the Angolans rejecting this demand on their sovereignty, a Namibia settlement seemed more distant in 1985 than it had in 1981. Chester Crocker's endless shuttle diplomacy had brought no tangible results. South Africa, rather than becoming more flexible in response to the friendly gestures of constructive engagement, hardened its resistance to a Namibia settlement. Pretoria had simply gobbled up the American carrots with no sign of a quid pro quo.

INTERNAL REFORM IN SOUTH AFRICA

The other major component of constructive engagement asserted that in response to American friendliness, Pretoria would be encouraged to reform apartheid and move toward full political participation for its black population. In an article on South Africa published at the outset of the Reagan administration, Crocker asserted that "white politics are demonstrating a degree of fluidity and pragmatism that is without precedent in the past generation."[64] He went on to argue that because "the balance of coercive power remains overwhelmingly in favor of the whites," and the United States has very little leverage in South Africa, it would be necessary to work through the status quo and hope for incremental movement away from minority rule.[65]

We recognize that a measure of change is already underway in South Africa. At such a time, when many South Africans of all races, in and out of government are seeking to move away from apartheid, it is our task to be supportive of this process so that proponents of reform and nonviolent change can gain and hold the initiative.[66]

A key flaw in Crocker's reasoning, as detailed by
liberal critic John de St. Jorre, is the assumption "that
P.W. Botha's government represents a unique opportunity
for change in the Republic."[67] Constructive engagement
assumes that there are genuine reformers in power, and
that they see it in their interest to move away from
white minority rule.

A detailed examination of the reforms of the Botha
government is available elsewhere.[68] But it is important
to briefly review these changes to see if they augur the
demise of apartheid or its preservation in a modified
form.

The Botha government lifted many of the restrictions
on black businessmen. Prior to 1978 African entrepreneurs
were limited to owning one enterprise apiece; were
required to live in the area of their business; could not
own operations larger than 350 square meters; and could
only hire employees of their own race.[69] These
restrictions and others have been dropped. Dr. Simon
Brand, Economic Advisor to the Prime Minister, gave the
rationale for these moves. "Blacks must be allowed to
take part fully in the free enterprise system if we want
them to accept it and make it their own. They must have a
vested interest in it."[70]

Based on the 1979 recommendations of the
government-appointed Wiehahn Commission, the Botha regime
implemented measures aimed at promoting a skilled section
of the black working class.[71] Training and employment
opportunities for Blacks were expanded; the government's
industrial relations apparatus for settling labor
disputes was streamlined; segregation in workplace
cafeterias and restrooms was relaxed; and most
importantly, the laws providing trade union rights to
white workers were expanded to include African workers as
well.

Although Africans were previously allowed to form
unions, these were not officially recognized before the
1979 changes, and employers could simply refuse to
bargain collectively with African workers. Prior to 1979
it was illegal for Africans to go on strike. Hence
African workers were in a very weak position, and very
few employers even bothered to arbitrate with them.

The government did not simply bestow union
privileges without expecting anything in return. The
legislation that bestowed the expanded union rights also
hemmed the African unions in with requirements to
register with the government. In becoming officially
registered, an African trade union: must provide the
government with details of its membership, officers, and
activities; can have its registered status revoked at any
time by the government; and comes under the Fund Raising
Act (1976) which can restrict international funding. The
new trade union legislation also prohibits a registered

African union from engaging in "political activity," as
defined by the government.
   While expanding trade union rights for Africans, the
government also stepped up its use of police repression
to limit the activity of radical trade unionists.
Hundreds of union activists were jailed, tortured, and
otherwise harrassed. Strikes were broken up by police,
with thousands of striking workers deported to the
bantustans. Some union leaders, such as Dr. Neil Aggett
of the Food and Canning Workers Union, died under
questionable circumstances while in police custody.[72] In
sum, the government attempted to give with one hand while
taking away with the other: in response to business
leaders calling for more orderly industrial relations,
the government allowed more trade union organizing by
Blacks, but the regime also tried to limit the politics
of the black unions via strict regulations and selective
repression.
   Another set of reforms was based on the 1979
recommendations of the Riekert Commission.[73] The
proposals stayed within the limits of Pretoria's
bantustan strategy of dividing Africans into ten ethnic
categories and making them citizens of the homelands. But
it provided greater freedom of movement and looser
housing restrictions for the roughly one-fourth of
Africans qualifying to reside legally in "white" South
Africa. The system of labor bureaus that shunt rural
Africans to urban jobs was streamlined to gain greater
control over migrant workers. By linking urban housing
privileges more closely with job status, the government
hoped to restrict "squatting," i.e., Africans migrating
illegally from rural areas hoping to hang on long enough
in the townships to find jobs. The government began
enforcing more strictly the laws limiting black freedom
of movement: In June 1983 The Economist reported that
"arrests for pass law offences have almost doubled in the
past three years, and the government plans to tighten
influx controls, imposing much heavier fines on employers
of 'illegal' blacks."[74]
   Another Riekert proposal involved a limited form of
urban government for Africans. The Black Local
Authorities Act (1982) provided for the election of
community councils in African townships. These councils
would be responsible for matters such as collecting
state-housing rents from fellow Blacks and would not be
able to affect broad policy. Understandably,
participation in community council elections was
extremely low: In Soweto, for example, voter turnout in
thirty wards ranged from 1.6 percent to a high of 13
percent.[75]

The goal of the Riekert reforms was to provide some social and economic rewards to the minority of Africans with legal urban residential status, while cracking down on the majority who are either migrant workers or permanent residents of the bantustans. These changes are part of a larger strategy of divide-and-rule. Africans are already divided into ten ethnic categories, now the attempt is to divide them along class lines as well.

The reforms gaining most attention in the West were those involving a new constitution providing for Coloured and Indian chambers of a tricameral parliament but completely excluding the African majority. The Coloured and Indian parliamentarians were hemmed in with constitutional restrictions on their power, and the vast majority of Coloured and Indian citizens refused to participate in elections for the new parliament.[76]

The most disturbing aspect of the new constitution, other than its total exclusion of the African majority, is its concentration of power in the hands of the state president, P.W. Botha. Under the new system the president can veto legislation, can pass laws by plebiscite, and has the power to dissolve parliament. Rather than being directly elected by the people , he is chosen by an electoral college composed of fifty whites, twenty-five Coloureds, and thirteen Indians. The president also holds the crucial power to decide whether any particular issue should be handled by an ethnic chamber or the parliament as a whole.

The government sought to portray the new constitution simply as a move away from the British model of parliamentary democracy toward an executive president model similar to the United States. But as the <u>Washington Post</u> pointed out, the new plan

> has none of the checks and balances of the U.S. system. There is no judicial role limiting executive power, and the legislature is given no constraining authority.
>
> There is no suggested mechanism for impeachment of the president, who would be elected for a seven year term and be eligible for reelection.
>
> The South African constitution contains no bill of rights or clauses protecting individual freedoms. It is a simple act of parliament, changeable at any time by a majority of one.[77]

Understandably, the constitutional reforms were opposed by a wide array of forces in South Africa and internationally. Parties to the right of Botha's NP, and far-right elements within the ruling party, denounced the reforms as the thin end of a wedge that would eventually split the white power bloc.[78] Within the black community, Coloureds, Indians and Africans came out in large numbers to protest the constitutional reforms. The United

Democratic Front, described by The Economist as "the
broadest alliance of anti-government groups since the
Congress movement of the 1950s," brought together
hundreds of church, labor, student, and civic groups to
actively oppose the plan.[79] Even voices of the
international business community such as The Financial
Times and The Wall Street Journal rejected Botha's
reforms.[80]

The various reforms, portrayed by the South African
government and its allies as representing a change of
heart by white rulers, can only be understood by looking
at the historical background of the reform period. In the
mid-1970s, South Africa's rulers were confronted with
mounting internal unrest and crumbling white minority
regimes in neighboring states. They decided it would take
more than military power to keep the black majority under
control. By the late 1970s an alliance was hammered out
between reform-minded military leaders and political
groups representing large corporate interests.[81] P.W.
Botha, as head of the Cape branch of the National Party
(dominated by financiers and agribusinessmen) and for
fourteen years Minister of Defence, was a logical choice
to oversee the partnership.

The businessmen wanted looser restrictions on the
mobility and training of African workers. They also saw a
need for greater labor discipline, and hoped that limited
trade union rights would increase productivity in the
long term. Military planners saw the need for a "total
strategy" that would expand security planning into
non-military areas.[82] Part of the plan was to cultivate
an urban elite within the black population: a class that
would enjoy more freedom of movement, better living
conditions, and more upward mobility than the majority.
It was hoped that such a "black middle class" would act
as a buffer against mass revolution.

To ensure that they would be able to implement their
changes, the reform alliance devised a strategy for
taking state power away from the parliament and
concentrating it in a militarized president's office.
Much of this shift to authoritarian rule is embodied in
the State Security Council (SSC).[83] Since P.W. Botha came
to power in 1978 the SSC "has emerged as perhaps the most
influential decision-taking political institution in the
country and is the main forum for formulating and
planning the implementation of the much-trumpeted total
strategy."[84] Dominated by military personnel and chaired
by the president, the SSC's fifteen interdepartmental
committees extend security planning into every facet of
South African life.

The government's central goal is the same as before:
to denationalize and retribalize the African majority.
The bantustan program continues, with over 3.5 million
Africans forceably removed to these desolate rural
areas.[85] As of early 1985 four bantustans (Transkei,

Bophuthatswana, Venda, and Ciskei) had been granted
"independence," but no government in the world other than
Pretoria recognizes these quisling fiefdoms as real
nations. The central government continues to dump
Africans in these rural labor reserves despite the fact
that its own figures show "only 13 percent of the total
income of blacks in the national states is
self-generated."[86]
    All of the significant opposition groups in South
Africa have called for an end to the bantustan system.
The international community has echoed this demand. The
African National Congress has vowed to continue its armed
struggle until the bantustans and other basic aspects of
apartheid are halted. Yet the government shows no sign of
acceding to these demands. The Economist reported that
even the liberal wing of the white political
establishment ruled out such changes as

> one-man-one-vote in a unitary state; the
> surrender of "the white power-base", meaning white,
> and ultimately Afrikaner, political control; the
> same laws and institutions for all South Africans,
> rather than separate ones for different ethnic
> groups; and a fourth chamber for Africans in the
> new tri-cameral parliament."[87]

    The government has no intention of changing basic
aspects of white minority rule. What have changed are the
methods of control. The government seeks black middle
class allies in its struggle against democratic demands
from the masses. The system of labor control has been
updated and tightened. The military has greatly expanded
its manpower, its technical power, and most importantly,
its political power.
    The Reagan administration's constructive engagement
policy did not lead to a softening of apartheid. Rather,
it gave Pretoria valuable time, free from international
pressure, to consolidate white minority rule.
    In late 1984 South Africa experienced a significant
upsurge in popular protest against the apartheid system.
Coinciding with implementation of the new constitution
and elections for the Indian and Coloured parliaments,
mass protests swept the country. Students boycotted
classes, workers went out on strike, church and civic
groups warned the government to begin dismantling
apartheid. In early November 1984 the largest general
strike in South African history shut down industrial
operations in the Vaal Triangle.[88] The government
responded as it had in the past, sending in police and
military units to suppress the dissent. Homes were
searched in the middle of the night, opposition leaders
were rounded up and jailed, and hundreds of protestors
were shot down in the streets.[89]

Responding to increased conflict in South Africa, antiapartheid forces in the United States stepped up their activity. Years of patient educational work had paid off: many Americans now had an understanding of the barbaric injustices of apartheid. The divestment movement was forcing colleges, churches, and government bodies to remove money from companies doing business in South Africa.[90] In late November 1984, antiapartheid forces in Washington began daily protests at the South African embassy. These caught the imagination of the mass media and the public, and the protests spread to other cities.[91] Members of Congress petitioned the Reagan administration to end its failed constructive engagement policy and begin applying pressure to Pretoria. The White House responded with some token criticism of apartheid but made no substantive policy changes.[92]

CONCLUSION

During the late 19th and early 20th centuries U.S. policy toward South Africa was essentially "accumulationist," i.e., concerned with facilitating access of American capital to South African labor and resources. But as capitalist development produced proletarian classes in South Africa and the United States, it created the objective basis for sustained, mass opposition to apartheid and its foreign backers.

The significance of U.S. involvement in South Africa's development as a capitalist economy goes deeper than this general contradiction of capital creating its own opposition. The fact that U.S. penetration of the South African economy is concentrated in the most advanced industrial sectors has direct implications for the counterrevolutionary potential of U.S. policy. As James Petras points out, "the principal contradiction between the periphery and metropolis is located in the technologically and economically advanced productive units of the periphery."[93]

In twentieth century revolutions, the original impetus, organization, leadership, and ideology of the revolutionary struggle began precisely in the more advanced sectors of the peripheral economy: in Russia, the Petrograd proletariat led by the Bolshevik Party; in China and in Vietnam, in the coastal cities; in Cuba, in Havana.[94]

In South Africa, as in many other countries, Washington is burdened with the conflicting responsibilities of protecting the regime facilitating capital accumulation by U.S. transnational corporations, while at the same time trying to legitimate the coercive measures used to guard that accumulation. It is these

contradictory functions of the U.S. state that reveal why
U.S. policy toward the white minority regime has seemed
hypocritical, i.e., denouncing the repressive measures
used by Pretoria but at the same time reaping material
rewards from that repression. As the white regime becomes
more threatened by an insurgency possessing widespread
international   support,   these   accumulation   and
legitimation functions grow more contradictory.
     The initial phase of the activist period of U.S.
policy (1975-78) saw Kissinger's intervention in Angola
fail on both counts. He could not prevent the replacement
of a pro-West regime with a leftist one, and in the
process of intervening he reduced U.S. credibility in
Africa to its lowest point ever.
     In attempting to prevent a similar outcome in
Rhodesia, U.S. policymakers, beginning in the last year
of the Ford administration, enunciated a tougher stand
against white supremacy. Speaking out in favor of
majority rule in Rhodesia was deemed necessary to
strengthen U.S. credibility and gain the cooperation of
the Frontline Presidents. This would provide indirect
leverage over the insurgents and hopefully lead to a
political rather than military solution to the conflict.
It was hoped this would limit Soviet/Cuban influence and
keep the insurgents from gaining complete control of the
society, while at the same time allowing Washington to
posture in favor of majority rule and peace. The problem
with this formula was that the most popular Zimbabwean
parties were also the most radical, and those parties
deemed most desirable by western rulers had the least
popular support. Western rulers confront a similar
dilemma in Namibia and South Africa.
     The Carter administration, less burdened than its
predecessor by political debts to the American right
wing, attempted to distance itself from traditional U.S.
Africa policy and establish credibility in Black Africa
by denouncing white minority rule in the harshest terms
ever used by the White House. This posture, and the
appointment of Andrew Young as U.N. Ambassador, opened
doors in Black Africa. But it simultaneously closed doors
to the white-ruled states. During 1977 Pretoria
demonstrated that it could successfully resist the
pressure for reform coming from Carter's regionalists.
     From the very start, Carter had ruled out use of the
economic weapons that stood some chance of coercing
Pretoria into changing its ways. As it became clear in
Washington that Pretoria's cooperation was necessary to
end the conflict in Rhodesia, the advocates of a less
critical line on apartheid gained the upper hand in
Carter's foreign-policy apparatus. After its initial year
of mostly symbolic attacks on apartheid, the Carter
administration retreated to a status quo ante policy that
failed to pressure South Africa for change.

The conservative regression of the late Carter administration dovetailed into the Reagan administration: the most openly proapartheid presidency in U.S. history. The many friendly gestures of constructive engagement--intended to foster reform in South Africa and Namibia--were accepted by Pretoria with little offered in return. Instead of promoting liberalization and movement toward majority rule, constructive engagement gave Pretoria time to streamline its methods of control, consolidate the power of conservative Afrikaners, and intimidate neighboring countries. After more than four years in office, the Reagan administration was no closer to solving the contradictions that have plagued U.S. policy toward South Africa.

* American trade with and investment in South Africa continued to grow, thus ensuring a powerful constraint on U.S. politicians wanting to use punitive measures against Pretoria.
* The South African government continued its repression of regional neighbors and its own population.
* The United States, along with a few allies, remained isolated internationally by its willingness to protect South Africa from punitive action such as economic sanctions.
* Leftist forces in South Africa, estranged from the United States government, continued gaining strength in South Africa and internationally.

There can be little doubt that a showdown will come in South Africa: the only question is when. The crisis will be determined by a combination of labor strife, escalating guerrilla war, popular protest by church, student and civic organizations, factional struggles within the white community, and increasing international isolation of the apartheid regime, all within the context of a world economic crisis putting additional pressure on South Africa.

As the situation in South Africa polarizes and becomes more violent, thus jeopardizing various U.S. interests, the policy options for Washington will become more contradictory. A key regional ally, deemed important for both economic and strategic reasons, will be battling a mass-based, left insurgency that is backed by the overwhelming majority of nations, including the Soviet Union. Decisive U.S. intervention on the side of the white minority is ruled out by all but the most right-wing analysts.

The most likely outcome is that U.S. policy will be hamstrung and ineffective as it has been in many other revolutionary situations. Foreign and domestic opposition to U.S. intervention will prevent Washington from rescuing a pro-capitalist regime. Yet the domination of

U.S. policy by bourgeois and national security interests will prevent Washington from pressuring the white minority into making the substantial reforms necessary to avert civil war.

The one policy option Washington has not yet tested—forthright support for antiapartheid forces—is the one course that would best ensure the long-term interests of most Americans and South Africans alike. But such a policy could be created only by a mass movement of truly historic proportions, and that will be a product of political organizing, not academic research.

NOTES

1. TransAfrica News Report, Special Edition, August 1981. The documents leaked to TransAfrica included: a briefing paper on U.S.-South Africa relations written by Assistant Secretary of State for Africa Chester Crocker to prepare Secretary of State Alexander Haig for a 14 May 1981 meeting with South African Foreign Minister Roelof Botha; a summary of an April meeting in Pretoria between Crocker, Botha, and South African Defense Minister Magnus Malan; and a short paper detailing South Africa's request for resumption of enriched uranium deliveries from the United States (the Carter administration halted uranium shipments in 1977).

2. Leslie Gelb, "U.S. Seeks Angola Compromise As Price for Accord on Namibia," New York Times, 1 June 1981; p. 1.

3. TransAfrica News...

4. "U.S. Seeks Angola Compromise..."

5. Ibid.

6. Ibid.

7. See Jack Anderson, "CIA Said to Plan New Links With Anticommunists," Washington Post, 26 August 1981; and "CIA Gearing Up for Operations with Foreigners," Washington Post, 27 August 1981.

8. TransAfrica News...

9. Ibid.

10. Ibid.

11. Even a study by South Africa's military intelligence found that SWAPO would win over 80 percent of the vote in a fair election. The report was leaked to the press by a defecting official who had served with the Bureau of State Security (BOSS) and the Ministry of Foreign Affairs. See "SWAPO to Win," Windhoek Observer, 23 August 1980; and New Statesman, 21 August 1980.

12. TransAfrica News...

13. Ibid.

14. Ibid.
15. Ibid.
16. Ibid.
17. Ibid.
18. Ibid.
19. Ibid.
20. Ibid.
21. Ibid.
22. Ibid.
23. Ibid.
24. Ibid.
25. Chester A. Crocker, "South Africa: Strategy for Change," Foreign Affairs, Winter 1980/81.
26. Quoted in William Raspberry, "Why Cozy Up to South Africa," Washington Post, 20 March 1981.
27. For a detailed chronology of these and other events see Kevin Danaher, In Whose Interest?: A Guide to U.S.-South African Relations (Washington, D.C.: Institute for Policy Studies, 1984).
28. Quoted in Anna DeCormis, "Trading with Enslavers," The Guardian (NY), 26 December 1984, p. 1.
29. Quoted in "South Africa gets U.S. shock batons," The Guardian(NY), 6 October 1982.
30. Thomas Conrad, "Legal Arms for South Africa," The Nation, 21 January 1984. Also see NARMIC/American Friends Service Committee, Automating Apartheid: U.S. Computer Exports to South Africa and the Arms Embargo (Philadelphia: AFSC, 1982); U.S. Congress, House, Committee on Foreign Affairs, Enforcement of the United States Arms Embargo Against South Africa (Washington, D.C.: Government Printing Office, 1982).
31. Jim Morrell, "A Billion Dollars For South Africa," Center for International Policy, 1983, p. 1. Also see Jonathan Kwitny, "An IMF Happening," CSIS Africa Notes, #15, 6 June 1983; Martin Bailey, "Behind the SA cash row," South, December 1982; and Raymond Bonner, "Loans for South Africa Assailed in U.N. Report," New York Times, 21 October 1982.
32. "South Africa strains as the gold price fades," The Economist, 28 July 1984, pp. 55-56.
33. "Summary of Anti-Apartheid Legislation Authored by Members of the Congressional Black Caucus in the 98th Congress," The Congressional Black Caucus, 1983; Lexie Verdon, "South Africa Becomes Target of Hill Debate," Washington Post, 5 June 1983; "Congress Considers South Africa Bills," Washington Notes on Africa, Summer/Autumn 1983; and William Raspberry, "No New Money for South Africa," Washington Post, 17 October 1983, p. A13.
34. South African Institute of Race Relations, Survey of Race Relations in South Africa, 1983 (Johannesburg: SAIRR, 1984), p. 110.

35. James Cason and Michael Fleshman, "Dollars for Apartheid," Multinational Monitor, November 1983.

36. Ibid., p. 19.

37. "The invasion that split the West," Africa Now, October 1981; Geoffrey Godsell, "What Pretoria hopes to gain from attack," Christian Science Monitor, 31 August 1981, p. 6; Marga Holness, Apartheid's War Against Angola (New York: United Nations Centre Against Apartheid, 1983).

38. Joseph Lelyveld, "Raid Kept Secret by South Africans," New York Times, 8 December 1981.

39. Steven Vegh, "Pretoria moves deep into Angola," The Guardian(NY), 20 January 1982, p. 1.

40. "South Africans Kill 201 in Angola Raid," New York Times, 17 March 1982, p. A3.

41. "Angola Reports South African Raids," Washington Post, 18 May 1982.

42. "South Africa and Angola: A spoiling raid?," The Economist, 14 August 1982, p. 29.

43. "We shot this girl, she must have been about five...," The Guardian(UK), 29 January 1981.

44. "Angola: South Africa's devastating war," Intercontinental Press, 26 December 1983.

45. Tony Gifford, South Africa's Record of International Terrorism, (London: Anti-Apartheid Movement, 1981); Allen Isaacman and Barbara Isaacman, "South Africa's Hidden War," Africa Report, November/December 1982.

46. Joseph Hanlon, Mozambique: The Revolution Under Fire (London: Zed Press, 1984), p. 263.

47. Howard Wolpe, "Don't Praise Pretoria," New York Times, 4 April 1984, p. A27; "Angola and Mozambique pressed into talks with South Africa," Africa Report, March/April 1984.

48. Survey of Race Relations..., p. 118; Michael T. Kaufman, "Tiny Lesotho Turns to World to Parry Pretoria," New York Times, 30 September 1983; Allister Sparks, "South Africa, in Retaliatory Move, To Choke Traffic Flow Into Lesotho," Washington Post, 17 July 1983, p. A20.

49. Jennifer S. Whitaker, "Pretoria's Wars," New York Times, 21 January 1983.

50. "Namibia Talks Collapse as S. Africa Says It Is Premature to Set Elections," Washington Post, 14 January 1981.

51. "West Delivers Its Plan on Namibia Autonomy," New York Times, 27 October 1981, p. A15.

52. Namibia: The Crisis in United States Policy Toward Southern Africa, published by a coalition of 24 organizations, led by TransAfrica, 1983; "Reagan's Namibia Charade," Washington Notes on Africa, Summer 1981; Brenda M. Branaman, "U.S. Relations with Black Africa: The Impact of a Close U.S.-South African Relationship," Congressional Research Service, 1 June 1982; "U.S., Nigeria Divided On Namibian Issues,"

Washington Post, 14 November 1982; Jay Ross, "Zambian Leader Kaunda Assails Reagan," Washington Post, 31 October 1982; James Khatami, "Africans Rebuff Bush on Namibia," The Guardian(NY), 8 December 1982; William Claiborne, "Commonwealth to press New Drive on Namibia," Washington Post, 29 November 1983, p. A13.
   53. "U.S. Seeks Angola Compromise As Price for Accord on Namibia," New York Times, 1 June 1981, p. 1.
   54. Washington Notes on Africa, Winter 1983, p. 2. Also see Joseph Lelyveld, "Namibia and the Cubans in Angola: U.S. Linkage Pleases South Africa," New York Times, 15 July 1982, p. A10.
   55. "Agriculture...," International Herald Tribune, 1 November 1984, reprinted in Facts and Reports, 14, X, 23 November 1984, p. 4.
   56. Ibid.
   57. "Mining chief reviews 1983," Windhoek Observer, 7 April 1984.
   58. Richard Moorsom, "The Namibian Fishing Industry," paper presented to the International Seminar on the Role of Transnational Corporations in Namibia, Washington, D.C., 29 November - 2 December 1982.
   59. "Unemployment...," Windhoek Advertiser, 4 January 1985, reprinted in Facts and Reports, 15, B, 18 January 1985, p. 7.
   60. "Namibia's Financial Legacy," African Business, October 1984.
   61. "Mudge is named in slush fund claim," Rand Daily Mail, 19 September 1984; "Dr. Ben Africa loses election," Rand Daily Mail, 25 September 1984; "Namibians live in fear of police," The Guardian(UK), 28 May 1984; "On the Namibia Front, Everybody Seems to Lose," New York Times, 23 March 1984, p. A2; "Atrocity claims against SA force," The Guardian(UK), 29 August 1984. Also see the results of the South African-appointed Thirion Commission of Inquiry, which found widespread misuse of government funds in Namibia.
   62. "The dos Santos 'platform'," West Africa, 3 December 1984, reprinted in Facts and Reports, 21 December 1984, p. 11.
   63. Ibid.
   64. Chester A. Crocker, "South Africa: Strategy for Change," Foreign Affairs, Winter 1980/81, p. 324.
   65. Ibid., p. 344.
   66. Assistant Secretary of State for African Affairs Chester Crocker addressing the American Legion, 29 August 1981, Current Policy Paper #308, U.S. Department of State, Bureau of African Affairs.
   67. John de St. Jorre, "South Africa: Is Change Coming?," Foreign Affairs, Fall 1981, p. 107.

68. Kevin Danaher, "Government-Initiated Reform in South Africa and Its Implications for U.S. Foreign Policy," Politics and Society, 13, 2, 1984.
69. Judy Seidman, Facelift Apartheid: South Africa After Soweto (London: International Defense and Aid Fund, 1980), p. 36.
70. Quoted in ibid., p. 37.
71. For background on the Wiehahn Commission, see D. Michael Shafer, The Wiehahn Report and the Industrial Conciliation Amendment Act: A New Attack on the Trade Union Movement in South Africa (New York: United Nations Centre Against Apartheid, 1979); David Hauck, Black Trade Unions in South Africa (Washington, D.C.: Investor Responsibility Research Center, 1982); Jud Cornell and Alide Kooy, "Wiehahn Part 5 and the White Paper," South African Labour Bulletin, 7, 3, November 1981.
72. Lawyers' Committee for Civil Rights Under Law, Deaths in Detention and South Africa's Security Laws (Washington, D.C.: Lawyers' Committee, 1983).
73. For background on the Riekert reforms, see Doug Hinson, "The New Black Labour Regulations: Limited Reform, Intensified Control," South African Labour Bulletin, 6, 1, July 1980; Ken Luckhardt and Brenda Wall, Working for Freedom: Black Trade Union Development in South Africa Throughout the 1970s (Geneva: World Council of Churches, 1981); and Hauck, Black Trade Unions....
74. The Economist, 4 June 1983, p. 54.
75. "Few Turn Out in Soweto to Elect a Council with Increased Power," New York Times, 4 December 1983, p. 18.
76. "Only 5 pc of Coloureds voted," The Observer(UK), 26 August 1984; "Indians low poll," The Times(UK), 30 August 1984; "SA poll protesters whipped," The Guardian(UK), 29 August 1984.
77. "S. African Panel Unveils New Plan for Charter Reform," Washington Post, 13 May 1982.
78. See "South Africa's Ruling Party Split by Conservatives' Revolt," Washington Post, 25 February 1982; "South Africa: Crack in the White Monolith," Time, 26 April 1982; "South Africa: Towards English Realignment," Africa Confidential, 24, 8, 13 April 1983.
79. "South Africa: A New Opposition," The Economist, 27 August 1983.
80. "South Africa Catalyst...," The Financial Times, 15 May 1982, reprinted in Facts and Reports, 12, K, 28 May 1982, p. 9; "South Africa's Move to Relax Race Laws Stymied by Botha's Conservative Critics," The Wall Street Journal, 4 January 1982.
81. Danaher, "Government-Initiated Reform..."; Dan O'Meara, "Muldergate and the Politics of Afrikaner Nationalism," supplement to Work In Progress, #22, April 1982; Kenneth W. Grundy, "South Africa's Domestic Strategy," Current History, March 1983.

82. International Defense and Aid Fund, The Apartheid War Machine (London: IDAF, 1980); and Kenneth W. Grundy, "The Rise of the South African Security Establishment (Braamfontein: South African Institute of International Affairs, 1983).

83. O'Meara, "Muldergate..."; "South African Military Exerts Greater Influence on Policy," Washington Post, 30 May 1980; "South Africa: Entrenchment of White Domination," Focus, November 1981; "South Africa's Generals in the Corridors of Power," The Times(UK), 1 September 1980.

84. O'Meara, Muldergate..." p. 17.

85. South African Council of Churches/Southern African Catholic Bishops' Conference, Relocations: The Churches' Report on Forced Removals in South Africa (London: Catholic Institute for International Relations, 1984).

86. "South Africa's Political Options" (backgrounder by the Information Minister of the South African Embassy, Washington, D.C., April 1982, p. 3.

87. "South Africa: As far as they can go," The Economist, 26 January 1985, p. 33.

88. "The stayaway--a new phase," The Star(SA), 26 November 1984; "Strike toll reaches 16 as Transvaal blacks flex industrial muscle," The Times(UK), 7 November 1984.

89. "S. African Police Round Up 2,300," International Herald Tribune, 15 November 1984; "Botha endorses police repression but concern grows amid white minority," The Guardian(UK), 19 November 1984; "1,093 people detained in 11 months," South Africa Report(SA), 14 December 1984; Focus (bulletin of the International Defense and Aid Fund) #56, January/February 1985.

90. Michael Isikoff, "South Africa Divestment Drive Has U.S. Firms Worried." Washington Post, 2 December 1984, p.F1; "Divestment Information Packet," American Committee on Africa, 1983; "Church and University Action Against Apartheid: A Summary of Withdrawals and Divestment," The Africa Fund, 1983.

91. John Matisonn, "South African awareness erupts following protests," National Catholic Reporter, 14 December 1984; "Protests Spreading in U.S. Against South Africa Policy," New York Times, 5 December 1984, p. 10; Christine Keyser, "No welcome mat in Oakland for goods from South Africa," San Francisco Examiner, 19 December 1984, p. B15; "Apartheid attack grows in S.F.," San Francisco Examiner, 7 December 1984, p. A3; David E. Sanger, "Anti-Apartheid Rallies Reviving Rights Coalition, Organizers Say," New York Times, 6 December 1984, p. 20.

    92. "U.S.   Denies   Policy   Aids   South   Africa's
Segregation System," Washington Post, 4 December 1984, p.
Al; "Reagan aide says 'rubbish' to critics of tolerance
of S. African policy," San Francisco Examiner, 4 December
1984, p. A8
    93. James   Petras,   Critical   Perspectives   on
Imperialism and Social Class in the Third World(New York:
Monthly Review Press, 1978), p. 275. 94. Ibid.

Index

DATE DUE

DEC. 31 1988			

HIGHSMITH 45-220